# Passport
# to
# Danger

## _Diary of an Adventurer_

Nick Mangieri

Valor Press Ltd.
Williamsburg, Virginia

VALOR
PRESS LTD.

Library of Congress Cataloging-in-Publication Data
Mangieri, Nick
Passport to Danger, Diary of an Adventurer / by Nick Mangieri
p.312          cm
Included index.

ISBN 0-9665364-3-6

I. Title.
2002

02-107013 CIP

Printed in Canada

Published by
Valor Press Ltd.
Williamsburg, Virginia

Book editing and design by Karen T. Morgan, Hampton, Va.
Printed by Transcontinental Printing

For my sister, Diane, who knew me *when*,
and my wife, Jill, who knows me *now*.

*This is a true story.*
*All of the events depicted in this book*
*are a matter of factual record,*
*and the people are real.*

# Other books by Nick Mangieri

**"Broken Badge**, The Silencing of a Federal Agent," 1998
**"Frozen Shield**, Alaska Cover-up," 2000

# Introduction

This is a true adventure story. There is, of course, some "literary license" taken to enhance some of the various episodes in the retelling of this portion of my life and to dramatize certain events. However, the necessity to do so is minimal. The recollections of these episodes are based upon newspaper accounts, magazine articles, letters and diary excerpts, and although it is many years later, they still remain very vivid.

To the reader, some of these events may seem exciting. To others, they may seem stressful. At the time, no thought was given to either of these emotions because I always was totally immersed in the action or activity at hand. All were deemed challenging before they were attempted, and any successes were always extremely gratifying. There were never any thoughts of failure. Even my ongoing quests for additional adventures never wavered because of the possible risky consequences. Perhaps it was this egotistical drive that wouldn't permit hesitation or allow failure.

The book encompasses the period after World War II, specifically during the fifties, when the world was a different place. Americans were liked and respected, and overseas travel to foreign or exotic locales was considered normal. Explorations and discoveries of unknown peoples and places were commonplace. Shooting and hunting were acceptable — and desirable — pastimes to the average male since most had handled firearms while in uniform. Even the "men's magazines" of the day were *men's* magazines. They catered to hunting lions, tigers, rhino, water buffalo and elephants — and any other big game that considered a human fair prey. There were stories about living among cannibals and headhunters and still others of uncovering a lost city in the jungles, or of discovering an unknown tribe. It was an exciting time. It was my time.


This is my story


Nick Mangieri
*(Formerly Marty Roland)*

"A frame of adamant,
a soul of fire,
No dangers fright him,
and no labors tire"

Samuel Johnson
*From "An Imitation of the
Third Satire of Juvenal"*

# 1

I grabbed the duffel bag, heavy with the weight of a 30/30 rifle, .45 caliber automatic and ample ammunition for both weapons, and prepared to disembark from the silver DC-3 that had just landed at the Managua, Nicaragua, airport. It was 1954, and although it was only early summer, a stifling burst of hot air hit me in the face as I trudged up the narrow aisle toward the plane's exit. I half-expected to see armed soldiers board the plane before we were allowed to leave, but none appeared.

The nonstop flight from Tegucigalpa, Honduras, was uneventful, not unlike my initial flight from Miami to that Central American country's capital. The similarities ended there, however. I was more aware of open hostilities between Nicaragua and the countries that bordered it: Guatemala to the west and Costa Rica to the south. Although communist-backed rebels in Guatemala engaged in sporadic border clashes on Nicaraguan soil, it was Costa Rica against whom Nicaragua virtually declared a state of war. President Somoza, in response to an unsuccessful April assassination attempt, had imposed a modified military law in the country and announced a state of siege. Costa Rica was blamed for hatching the plot and military actions escalated on both sides of the border.

It was into this turmoil that I knowingly flew. I didn't know who initiated the fighting, and I didn't particularly care. All I wanted to do was to continue hunting wild boar.

I knew that Honduras wasn't involved in any of the armed conflicts. Although I had no specific information regarding the superiority or even the availability of such wild game in Nicaragua, I was convinced it had to be better than the Honduran countryside. On the spur of the moment, I decided to change locales.

Long drawn-out decisions were never one of my strong suits, and I considered this time to be no different. I neither thought about the existence of a strained military atmosphere in the area, nor considered the possibility of dire consequences arising because I brought guns into the region. I knew that as a legitimate tourist, I played no part in any of the politics. I was even more fully convinced that, as an American citizen, I would be untouched so long as I only pursued my avowed goal of hunting. I had gone through all the necessary levels of authorization to accomplish that desired objective. The only problem was my sudden decision to change countries in midstream.

Whatever prompted me in early 1954 to hunt wild boar in Honduras has long since been forgotten. What I do recall, however, is that my foreign solo vacations became increasingly boring and unappealing. I needed a change of pace from the exotic bar scene that was usually the extent of my sightseeing. Fortunately, Florida's proximity to the Caribbean countries always made those trips convenient and reasonable.

To alleviate the dulling sameness of the past few years, I selected Honduras as that year's unique vacation spot and proceeded with plans in spite of recent mounting tumultuous events in that section of the continent. I felt those hostilities were always occurring in the banana republics and would be short-lived.

I visited a local travel agency I had used for previous journeys into the Caribbean area. When I announced to the agency's personnel the intentions of my proposed trip, they shook their heads solemnly.

"I'm sorry, " they said in unison, "you can't possibly take guns into a Central American country at this time."

"Why not?" I asked. "Honduras is not involved."
They remained adamant in their objections.
"Who do I have to contact to get that permission?" I
asked impatiently.
They looked up at me in amazement, smirked and
glanced at each other.
"You'll have to contact the local consulate in Miami,
of course, " the agency owner responded, quickly adding,
"if you're serious, that is."
I saw I was being humored, but her comment didn't
discourage me.
As I turned to leave, they both smiled broadly and too
cheerfully, too loudly wished me, "Good luck!"
I did exactly as they suggested and met with the
Honduran officials at the consulate. I calmly and tactfully
explained my specific offbeat reason for wanting to visit
their country. I reiterated my purpose for taking guns into
Honduras. I only wanted to hunt. I was a tourist. I was a
neutral party to any hostilities in the region. I had no interest in the politics of any country, and I certainly had no
intention of harming anyone. I was a hunter, nothing more.
Both of the consulate officials to whom I addressed
my fervent appeal, however, looked at me incredulously.
Apparently my type of request was one they rarely, if ever,
heard. I saw their looks of strained disbelief change to that
of firm denial, but I persisted in my request. I added that I
was a federal employee (although I didn't cite the fact that
I merely worked for the U.S. Post Office), and stressed that
as such, I was a responsible individual.
Whether that final comment convinced them of my
intentions or my repetitive and insistent harangue wore
them down, I didn't know. The junior official turned the
palms of his hands upward in a gesture I interpreted as
futility and indecision as he looked over at his superior.
In an exasperated tone, the senior official hesitantly
said, "The only one who can grant you that permission is
the Minister of War in Tegucigalpa."
He said it with a grand flourish of finality, undoubt-

edly intending to discourage and dismiss me right away. I listened with respect, but when he finished, I asked in a low but firm tone, "Can I have that address?" The two officials sat motionless for a moment and appeared simultaneously to take a breath. Finally, the senior official glanced quizzically up at me, scribbled an address on a piece of paper and handed it over.

I looked at it, nodded slightly, thanked him quietly and left.

That night I composed a concise but comprehensive letter to the Minister of War, setting forth my intentions and repeating what I had told the consulate officials. I gave a full description of both guns with their identification numbers. As an afterthought I added that, as a federal employee, I should be considered honorable and that my intentions should be seen exactly as I had represented them to be. As I mailed the letter, I was characteristically confident as to its results. I felt my request would be taken seriously and permission would be granted.

Two weeks later, I received an official-looking envelope with foreign postage bearing a return address from the Minister of War in Tegucigalpa, Honduras. I opened the thin envelope quickly and extracted two sheets of paper stapled together. The top copy was entirely in Spanish. As I scanned down the page trying to recall what meager knowledge I had retained from my own high school Spanish lessons, I noticed references to the two guns that I had cited in my query letter. I flipped over the page and found its English translation on the bottom copy.

I was granted permission to take guns into Honduras for the sole purpose of hunting. Both weapons were listed with their descriptions and identification numbers. The signed authorization was as impressive as the official heading at the top of the letter.

Armed with the letter, I returned to the travel agency and waved it triumphantly in the faces of the same two agents who mockingly wished me "good luck" two weeks earlier.

"I'll be damned," the owner said in complete surprise. "I wouldn't have believed it."

The employee was equally shocked but seemed pleased for me.

She then added, "I guess we'll have to get you started."

All the necessary landing papers were arranged and the tickets prepared for LACSA Airlines, a Latin American subsidiary of Pan American Airways that flew into Central America.

By late June, I was en route to my initial destination in Tegucigalpa. However, my expectations of good hunting never materialized. In fact, I neither saw a wild boar nor any other type of wild game worth pursuing. Frustrated and discouraged at what seemed to be a waste of time and an empty vacation, I decided to move south into Nicaragua.

The decision, at the time, seemed logical. Putting it into practice also presented no problems. I merely purchased another ticket for Managua, its capital. No one at the LACSA airline counter questioned me about my landing papers or prevented me from boarding a plane with guns to take into a neighboring country.

As my feet hit the ground at the Managua airport, the other passengers and I were directed to Immigration and Customs. My passport was examined, and the immigration officer nodded approval and waved me on to the customs section. All went smoothly. However, as I approached the table with the uniformed customs officer behind it, he asked me what I had to declare. I hoisted my bulky duffel bag onto the rack in front of me and casually mentioned *"escopetas,"* the Spanish word for guns.

His eyes tightened into two narrow slits as he loudly repeated the word.

*"Si, escopetas,"* I said again, *"por caza."*

I tried to sound as casual as I could the second time I

mentioned the guns by referring to their use in hunting. From his agitated tone, however, my response apparently didn't satisfy him. He swiftly opened the bag sprawled in front of him and looked inside. His eyes grew wider as he viewed its contents. He started to gingerly touch the .45 caliber automatic that sat on the top of the bag, but immediately jerked his hand from it and excitedly called for assistance. A supervisor and a dark khaki-clad soldier, with a rifle slung loosely over his shoulder, quickly joined him. In a staccato Spanish that I couldn't understand, except for the word *"escopetas,"* he pointed emphatically at the duffel bag and gestured wildly at me. The supervisor questioned me in equally rapid Spanish as the soldier unslung his rifle. He didn't point it at me, as yet, but I was beginning to get a little uncomfortable.

*"No entiendo mucho español,"* I said slowly. *"Habla ingles, por favor."*

The supervisor was exasperated as he tried to rephrase his questions in broken English.

"Why do you have guns? Why are you bringing them into Nicaragua? Where did you arrive from?"

His questions came hard and fast, but I answered them as best I could in my own broken Spanish, interjected with simple English words.

He was clearly disturbed and totally dissatisfied with my responses.

*"Por caza, solamente,"* I reassured him, as I extracted the Honduran letter of permission from the Minister of War to explain my motives.

He studied the wording of the letter slowly, looked at the signature at the bottom of the page and stared at the official seal before thrusting it back into my hands.

*"No, señor!"* he exclaimed loudly, violently shaking his head from side to side. In an exaggerated gesture he motioned me out of line and into a small office behind him. Simultaneously, he directed the soldier to stand guard at the door and called to another soldier to join the first.

I saw him through a glass partition in an adjoining

room speak breathlessly into a phone as he jabbed a stiff-ened finger at the contents of the bag emptied on his desk: the gun belt with the .45, the 30/30 rifle and the boxes of ammunition.

Events moved so rapidly from the moment I reached the customs section up to the forced relocation that I had no time to think, much less plan what to do or say next. I didn't expect the overreaction I received, because I knew I had done nothing explicitly wrong and had no underlying ulterior motives I tried to hide. However, it became increasingly obvious these officials thought otherwise.

Within a short time, two other officers arrived. One, I later learned, was a captain in the Managua police force. The other was a major in the Nicaraguan army. Both spoke stilted English, and both interrogated me at the same time, each barely waiting for the other to finish. I again gave my reason for being there. Yes, I was sorry I did not possess the required landing papers, but no, I was not smuggling any guns into their country, nor was I a spy as the major believed. Had I realized, I tried to say calmly, that I would cause so much trouble, I would certainly have made the proper arrangements before I arrived in Managua. I sensed my explanations were not acceptable to either of them because they constantly interrupted my responses.

As a last resort, I stated that LACSA Airlines was well-aware of the contents of my duffel bag because I men-tioned them at the airport when I first arrived in Honduras and again before I departed. I also told the interrogating officers that I showed the airline employees my letter from the Minister of War.

For some reason, that innocuous remark momentarily seemed to appease them. They looked at each other and stepped out of the room to have what sounded like a heat-ed discussion. Their voices were muffled, and because my Spanish was limited, I couldn't discern the scope of their brief exchange. They approached the customs official, who had initiated the call to them, spoke to him briefly and dis-appeared. The official then entered the small office with the two soldiers who had been stationed outside the room and indicated brusquely that I should accompany them. I briefly objected but saw that it was useless.

Flanked by the two soldiers, I was escorted through the small terminal to a shack on the outskirts of the airfield. One of them opened the door, motioned me inside, and bolted it shut from the outside. It was a windowless structure, apparently used for some type of sparse storage. It had a low table in one corner with a couple of crude chairs near it. Before they shut the door, I noticed a single light in the ceiling with a string dangling from it. I pulled on it and a bulb dully illuminated the room.

I sank heavily onto one of the crude chairs, pulled it over to the wooden table and tried to figure my way out of the situation. Nothing specific came to mind. I could think of no solution other than to maintain my innocence to whatever charges they might dream up. Up to that point I hadn't even thought of asking to see someone from the American Embassy. As soon as someone arrived, I'd request a representative right away, as an American citizen. With that reassuring thought, I waited.

The time dragged by, and finally after an hour or so, there was movement outside the shack. The door opened. A swarthy heavy-set Latin, dressed in civilian clothes, quickly stepped inside. He spoke fluent English and identified himself as a representative of LACSA Airlines. I repeated my story again while he listened intently.

When I finished, he smiled weakly. "I understand, *Señor* Roland," he offered, "but we have a small problem."

"What's that?" I demanded.

"The police think that you are trying to smuggle guns into their country and want to take you into the city and put you into their jail."

He looked at me, waiting for the words to sink in before he continued.

"The army thinks that you are a spy and want to treat you accordingly."

I looked at him in amazement.

"You've got to be kidding. They must be crazy." I insisted.

"I'm afraid not, *señor*," he said seriously. "I'm sure that you are aware of the trouble with the Guatemalan rebels and the Costa Rican military."

I nodded.

"What's that got to do with me?" I stressed.

"Well," he answered, "bringing guns into a country that is surrounded by its enemies does raise certain questions."

"I came from Honduras," I responded, "and as far as I know they are not one of your enemies."

He smiled slightly at the comparison.

"Besides," I added quickly, "the Hondurans knew of my intent to hunt in their country and gave me written permission."

I started to extract my authorization from the Minister of War again, but he held up his hand.

"I've been told, *señor*," he said sympathetically.

"Then what's the problem?" I asked impatiently. "They know my intent was only to hunt. Maybe I should've gotten permission form the Minister of War here, but I didn't."

He nodded briefly but didn't smile at my statement.

"Besides all that," I said again, "your people at the Tegucigalan airport *knew*," and I stressed the word, "that I was carrying guns on the plane and that I was heading for Managua."

He looked at me quizzically for a moment and slowly nodded his head in agreement.

When I saw his glimmer of understanding, I continued more firmly, "On top of all that, I'm an American citizen, and," I added more confidently, "the U.S. is helping your military."

"I'm aware of that, *Señor* Roland," he said evenly, and in a lower voice added, "both officials are aware, as well."

"Then why am I here?" I asked, waving my arm at the inside of the dimly lit shack.

"They sent me in here to talk to you ... to get the full story, as you Americans say."

His tone was low and appeared to be supportive. I couldn't help but smile at the way he said it.

Still, my mood had not changed.

"I want to see someone from the American Embassy, now," I demanded.

"I've been trying to reach someone since I first heard." His voice sounded sincere as he said it.

"And?"

"I'm afraid," he said quickly, "that I'm unable to do so."

I looked at him.

"It's a weekend," he continued, "and there is no one readily available."

"Great, now what?"

He hesitated slightly before he spoke, but when he did, his initial morose expression appeared to brighten somewhat.

"I have an idea that might benefit you," he said, then slowly added, "and might also eliminate an embarrassing situation for all concerned."

"What is it?"

"I don't want to get your hopes up, *señor*, before I speak to them, but I'll do my best."

He suddenly rose from his chair, shook my hand firmly and walked to the door.

He knocked, and as it was opened by one of the soldiers, he turned toward me again. "Please don't worry, *señor*; I'll do my best." He tried to sound reassuring.

I heard shuffling outside the door, muffled voices and then quiet.

I waited and wondered.

Finally, after what seemed like an eternity, although barely an hour had passed, the door was unbolted again. I didn't know what to expect.

The heavy-set Latin stepped briskly inside with the door left open behind him.

He smiled.

"You're free to go, *Señor* Roland."

I looked outside. There was no one there.

"Go where?" I wanted to know.

"Out of the country," he said in a matter-of-fact tone as if I should have known all along.

"Out of the country," I repeated dumbly. "To where?"

"Costa Rica," he answered quickly.

"Costa Rica," I said in a loud voice, disbelieving what I had heard. "Why there? Aren't your countries at war?"

"Not yet, *señor*," he said, "although there have been a few border clashes."

"That's not what I heard," I said. "The situation sounds worse than that."

"You don't have a lot of choice, *Señor* Roland," he said in a low serious tone. "If you stay here, well..." He shrugged his shoulders. "If you accept, your chances are very good and the embarrassing situations can be eliminated for all concerned. Besides," he added, "I hear the hunting is very good in Costa Rica at this time of year."

I thought about it a moment and realized what he said made sense.

"How can I argue with that," I said resignedly. "When does all this happen?"

"A flight to San José leaves shortly," he said. "Your luggage is being loaded at this moment with your guns, and I am personally to escort you to the aircraft now."

# 2

The LACSA flight was not crowded, and my new-found benefactor directed me to an empty window seat near the front of the twin engine aircraft. He handed me a ticket to San José and gave me my claim tickets for my luggage.

"Your bags are on the plane, and your guns are safely secured," he said. "I want to wish you luck with your hunting," he said, holding out his hand in friendship. "I don't expect you'll be visiting us again, will you, *señor*?"

"I doubt it," I said.

"Good," he answered. "Now, have a safe and comfortable flight, compliments of LACSA."

Before I could thank him, he abruptly turned on his heel and exited the aircraft.

An elderly, distinguished-looking man seated across the aisle from me observed the brief exchange and glanced at me inquisitively for a moment.

I gave him a half smile, then turned to look out the window, still trying to understand all the events of the past few hours.

The airplane door shut, the engines kicked over and the slim dark-haired stewardesses checked the interior of the cabin and the passengers before they, too, buckled themselves in their seats.

Once airborne, the distinguished-looking gentleman tried to make small talk with me.

"Are you on vacation?" he asked in English. His accent was slight but obviously Spanish.

I acknowledged that I was.

His curiosity obviously couldn't be contained.

"These are not good times to be a tourist here," he noted.

I agreed with him again.

"Then..." he paused, apparently trying to phrase a question that did not seem too personal.

I saw discomfort in his hesitation.

*Oh, what the hell,* I thought. *I'll give him the full story.*

I told him in detail all that had transpired since my plane touched down in Managua earlier that day.

He voiced sincere concern, as the elderly are apt to do.

"You are a very lucky young man," he said.

The realization of how lucky I actually was set in, and I nodded in agreement.

He observed my response and quickly added, "Perhaps a little foolish, too, if you don't mind my saying so."

"Perhaps."

He changed the subject when he noticed that I was not in full agreement.

"Where will you be staying in San José?" he asked.

For the first time, it dawned on me that I had no clue where to stay or where to go once I landed.

I shook my head slowly, showing my indecision.

He suggested a few good hotels in downtown San José that catered to Americans, and added, "This is a good country here. We are a democracy, unlike some of our neighbors."

I assumed he referred to Nicaragua, or perhaps to Guatemala, or even Honduras, but he didn't elaborate. Although I hadn't particularly followed Central American politics on a day-to-day basis, in the months prior to my departure I was generally aware of conditions. My understanding, however, had increased with the hectic events of that day.

I asked what he did, and he replied that he was a professor at the university in San José.

"What field?" I asked, trying to make conversation.

"History."

I was interested.

"What can you tell me about relations between the countries?" I asked.

"Which ones?" he wanted to know, as he fingered his small graying goatee.

"Well," I answered, "since I've just been forced to leave Nicaragua, that would be a good start."

He smiled. "I presume you want to know more about current events, rather than past history."

I nodded.

He continued.

"I'm sure you've heard of the Somoza assassination attempt."

I nodded again.

"Are you aware that a representative of my country was sent to Honduras immediately afterward to personally deny that charge?"

"No."

"Or that the same representative was also dispatched to El Salvador to explain the situation to them as well?"

"No," I answered again, "but it looks like this whole thing is escalating."

"What do you know of President Somoza?" he continued.

"Not much, only what I occasionally see in the papers."

"I'm sure you are aware he is a military dictator."

"So I heard."

"Or," he continued, "that he has amassed a fortune by stealing from his country's Treasury."

"No," I admitted, trying to steer the conversation toward Costa Rican involvement.

"Why is there a conflict between Nicaragua and your country?" I wanted to know.

"There are Costa Rican rebels involved," he answered, "who follow our ex-President and want to see him back in power."

"Where does Nicaragua fit into the picture?" I asked, trying to make sense of Central American politics.

"They flee into Nicaragua for sanctuary," he offered simply.

I was beginning to understand the situation and the fact that the border clashes were more that just sporadic fighting over some isolated territories.

"These military actions are just starting then," I noted.

"That's why these are not good times to be a tourist here," he repeated.

I grunted acknowledgment and turned to look out the window again.

He was momentarily quiet. But when I briefly turned my gaze toward the front of the cabin, he continued.

"What is it that you intend to hunt in Costa Rica?" he asked.

"Wild boar, I imagine."

"I don't know about the boar," he said, "but I know there are many snakes in the mountains."

"Snakes," I repeated. "What kind of snakes?"

"All kinds, I hear," he noted. "Especially the boa constrictor."

"Boa constrictors," I said, conjuring up a mental picture of one, its tightening coils entwined around some hapless animal.

"How big?"

"Not as big as those you would find in the Amazon," he continued, "but I'm sure big enough to interest you."

He frowned as he said it.

"I gather you don't like snakes," I said.

"No," he stressed, and proceeded to tell me things that he had heard about boas, their awesome power and the size of the water boa constrictor, the anaconda.

The more he spoke, the more interested I became.

"Are there anacondas in your country?"

"Perhaps," he answered.

"It would make a good hunt," I mused aloud.

"Undoubtedly, *señor.*"

Suddenly, the scope of my hunting changed. I decided I had to get a boa, especially an anaconda, if I could find one.

"Any ideas where I could locate one?" I asked hopefully.

"Not really," he answered, "since that is not my interest."

"I understand," I said.

Before I started to say I would inquire further, he raised his hand.

"A friend of mine has been in Cartago," he continued, "and did mention that he had seen a dead one stretched across a road once."

"Where is this Cartago?" I wanted to know.

"It's south to southeast of San José," he answered. "Perhaps 20 some-odd miles from there."

I thanked him and wrote down the name of the section.

"It's in the mountains," he said. "It's wild and isolated, and the area has much rain and dense forest."

"It's not like Tegucigalpa then," I said referring to the Honduran countryside.

He shook his head.

The balance of the hour or so flight into Costa Rica went quickly with sporadic comments between us and with my thoughts centered on the challenge of a boa hunt.

The plane banked over green lush mountains. In the distance, I could see a city.

"San José," he called out, gesturing through the window at the ground below us.

I smiled.

The landing was smooth, and the aircraft taxied toward the terminal and stopped. The few passengers disembarked, with the professor and I trailing the slow procession out the door.

"I wish you luck, my young friend," he said sincerely, extending his hand to me.

"*Muchas graçias,* professor," I said, exercising my Spanish.

He stepped ahead of me and headed toward Immigration and Customs, where he was quickly waved through.

As I walked toward the immigration section, I noticed that the inside of the terminal was not busy. I didn't see any soldiers milling about with rifles slung over their shoulders. The scene was passive, the atmosphere more relaxed than at my previous stop.

*Good,* I thought, *not like Managua. I should be out of here in no time.*

I was wrong.

As I approached the Immigration Officer, I held out my passport and expected to be waved through also. Instead, the official who looked at it, stopped and glanced up at me inquiringly.

*Now what?* I wondered.

"You don't have permission to visit our country, *señor,*" he said half-apologetically as he handed me back my passport.

"What?" I said in amazement.

He repeated himself again and flipped through the pages of my passport, indicating that Costa Rican authorities had not stamped it.

I shook my head in confusion and frustration as I tried to explain that my arrival had all been arranged by the LACSA airline official in Managua.

"I'm sorry, *señor,*" he said again, "but I cannot permit your entrance."

"Who do I have to see to get that permission?" I asked as politely as I could, but in agitated exasperation. I looked round the terminal.

He looked back at me blankly as if he hadn't understood the question.

"*Quien?*" I said. "Who?"

"*Quien?*" he repeated, as he raised his voice at the end of the word.

"*Si, quien?*" I said again. "*Donde está su superior?*" He brightened.

"*Entiendo, señor,*" he answered. "I understand now," he repeated in English.

"Please wait here," he said, motioning for me to remain in line while he left his post.

There was no one else behind me, and I had little choice but to do as he said. I was thankful that it was not like my last experience going through customs at the Managua airport. Still, I was growing impatient with the situation. I thought that my entry had been resolved.

Within a few minutes another Immigration official arrived, who appeared to be the first man's superior. I explained the situation again slowly, and this time, stressed the fact that it was LACSA airlines that was to blame, not me. He looked at me thoughtfully for a moment.

"Wait here, *señor, por favor,*" he said before walking away. The first official remained with me.

"What the hell is going on?" I said in a low voice, but loud enough for the first official to respond.

"*Señor?*"

"*Nada,*" I said quickly, trying not to upset the situation any more than it was.

The senior official came back with a young worried-looking civilian who introduced himself as a LACSA official.

"How can I help you, *Señor* Roland?" he asked with barely a trace of an accent.

I took a deep breath to calm myself before repeating my story. I made a point of citing the fact that it was the Nicaraguan LACSA official who should have made sure I would have no problems when I landed in Costa Rica, since it was his idea — not mine — to enter the country.

He looked concerned, and I continued.

"If I had known that I needed such authorization, I'd have gotten it," I insisted.

He thought about what I said and then held up his hand in an attempt to calm me down.

"Let me see what I can do," he said, motioning me into a nearby office to wait.

The senior immigration official left, and the first official continued with his duties. I looked around the small cubical and out into the terminal. This time, no soldiers stood outside the door, and no one seemed overly concerned by my presence.

Within a short time, the young bespectacled LACSA official reappeared. He had a quick nervous smile that twitched at the corners of his mouth.

"I have good news," he said breathlessly.

I was tempted to say, "I've heard that before," but I didn't.

"Well?"

"The authorities have agreed to let you enter our country..." and he hesitated briefly.

"Great," I said, before he had a chance to complete what he was saying.

I started to get up from my seat and head toward the entrance to the office when he gently touched me on the shoulder to indicate that he was not yet finished.

"Now what?" my tone was edged with impatience.

"Before you can be admitted to Costa Rica," he continued, "you must have proper authorization, however."

I looked at him curiously, not understanding what he meant.

"How do I get that?" I demanded.

"You will have to leave the country," he continued quickly, "and then be readmitted — officially."

I shook my head in exasperation.

"How am I going to do that?" I wanted to know. "Where am I supposed to go this time? Who's supposed to take care of all this?"

He interjected himself before I went any further.

"It's all been arranged," he said confidently. "We will fly you to Panama City at our expense, roundtrip back to here."

"Panama City," I repeated dumbly after him. "You mean Panama."

He nodded his head.

"Why Panama?" I wanted to know. "What's there?" He tilted his head as he spoke.

"The American Embassy, of course," he answered, as if I should have known all along the purpose of that destination.

I was completely taken by surprise with this sudden announcement. And the look must have registered on my face.

"Do you have any objection to our plans, *señor?*" he asked in a low voice.

I thought about it briefly, smirked and then shook my head

"No," I answered. "I've never been there either."

"Good," he responded. "I'll make final arrangements for your flight and your stay there."

"My stay there?" I asked, still not fully understanding exactly what was to happen.

"Yes, *señor*, your stay there," he said. "I am told that it could take up to three days, but we are prepared to accommodate you," and he stressed, "at our expense."

I couldn't believe my luck. Although I was being told to leave their country, too, because I didn't have the proper authorization to be there, I was permitted to return — and it was all at the airline's expense.

"If you don't mind my asking," I continued, "where will I be staying in Panama City?"

"At the Hotel International," he responded. "It's very nice."

"I'm sure it is," I said in continued amazement. "When do I...," and before I could finish the questions, he answered.

"There is a flight out late this afternoon," he said. "You should arrive there by early this evening.

"What about my guns?" I asked.

"We will hold them here for your return," he said. "I believe that it will be less complicated than if you take them into Panama and back out again.

I thought about it a moment.

"I agree with you."

"In the meantime, you are free to remain here in the area. However, please do not leave the terminal," he cautioned.

I nodded.

"I will return with your tickets shortly," he added, "and then see that you take the proper flight to Panama City when it is scheduled to leave."

I couldn't help but smile at the similarity of my forced evacuation of Managua, but the manner in which it was done was far different.

As promised, the young LACSA official returned with my tickets and a couple of American magazines.

"For your reading pleasure, *señor*," he commented. "It will allow you to pass the time."

It did, and when I grew tired of reading, I walked around the enclosed section. Pedestrian traffic picked up as incoming and outgoing passengers walked through the adjoining portions of the terminal. Finally, a voice announced in Spanish over the loudspeaker a departing flight.

As I heard the word, "Panama," I saw the LACSA official approaching me.

"Are you ready, *señor*?"

"Ready."

"Please follow me."

He led me through a throng of outgoing passengers and paused at a gate.

"This is your flight, *Señor* Roland. Are there any questions?"

His tone was pleasant and his mannerisms were not abrupt, unlike my Nicaraguan benefactor.

"Only about my arrival in Panama City," I said.

"You will be met at the airport by one of our representatives and taken to the hotel," he answered. "I am sure that they will assist you in all that must be accomplished at that end."

"OK, I have nothing else."

He smiled a relaxed smile for the first time.

"Have a safe flight, *señor*," he said as he indicated the departing aircraft I was to board.

It was the second time that day, I was given that information. However, this time, I was not being personally escorted across the tarmac and onto the airplane.

# 3

The 300-mile flight to Panama City was not a pleasant one. The plane flew low, skirting mountainous terrain pockmarked with sporadic rain squalls punctuated with sudden violent downdrafts. All the while, slashing sheets of rain, prevalent at that time of year in the tropics, continued to buffet our small airliner as we flew over the Caribbean to our grateful landing at the Panamanian airport.

As promised, a LACSA representative met me as I disembarked and entered the terminal. He was dark, neatly-dressed and young.

"How was your flight, *señor?*" he asked, noting the stormy conditions in the area.

"*Malo,*" I answered, using gestures to demonstrate the turbulent shaking we experienced in the air.

"We will try to make your stay here as pleasant and as productive as possible," he said, successfully guiding me through both Immigration and Customs.

His assessment was accurate. I was immediately impressed with the Hotel International and with my accommodations there and eagerly relayed that information to him.

The balance of my time was primarily occupied with being taken to the American Embassy in Panama City and receiving the proper authorization to return to San José. My sightseeing was confined to that of the city itself.

Although the Canal Zone was nearby, and I could have visited it, I was not in a touring mood because I was eager to return to Costa Rica to commence my boa constrictor hunt. I just hoped it would be an exciting experience. It wasn't too long before I would find out.

The morning of the flight back to San José was, thankfully, bright and clear. The plane's lift-off from Panama City airport into sunny skies was smooth, as was the majority of the flight back into Costa Rica. I had the necessary authorization to enter that country legally, and everything was done at the airline's expense. I felt elated at my recent change of luck. It was a good omen. I felt the hunt would be challenging and unique. I couldn't wait.

The DC-3 touched down at the airstrip and once more rolled toward the terminal. Again, as promised over the phone to the Panamanian LACSA representative, the Costa Rican agent met me at the airport.

"I hope your stay in Panama City was pleasant, *señor*," he said, "and your trip productive."

I acknowledged that it was.

"After you pass through Immigration and Customs, I will show you where your guns are kept, and you will be free to do as you please in our country."

I thanked him, and thanked him even more effusively after I retrieved my bag with the guns and the ammo.

"It is my pleasure," he said. "I hope that you have not been inconvenienced too much."

"Not at all because of your help," I answered truthfully.

I had already put the Nicaraguan experience behind me and was not even thinking about the minor inconvenience when I had first arrived in Costa Rica.

"Do you know where you'll be staying?" he asked.

I gave him the names of the hotels the professor had suggested on my initial flight into San José.

He recommended one that was in the downtown area.

"I'm sure that you will find it to your liking." he said assuredly. "If there is anything else I or LACSA airlines can do for you, please do not hesitate to ask."

"I appreciate all you have done," I said, as I grasped his hand firmly. He directed me to a local taxi where I gave the driver the name of the hotel.

It was not as grand as the Hotel International but nevertheless was one of the larger hotels in San José. The main entrance opened on a side street just off the main thoroughfare. It was neat and clean and the desk clerk spoke fairly good English. When he inquired of my reason for visiting Costa Rica, I told him. His eyes widened when I described what it was I wanted to hunt.

I gathered he, too, had an aversion to snakes and gently chided him on it.

"What do you know of Cartago?" I asked him, the section that the professor had mentioned on my first flight.

"Only that it is in the mountains, *señor.*"

"How do I get there?" I wanted to know.

"I can send one of the bellhops up to your room" he said. 'I believe he likes to hunt, also."

I thanked him and felt a tingle of excitement with the news that there was someone who could help me reach my goal.

There was a light knock on my door shortly after I checked into my room. A short youngish bellhop, clad in the uniform of the hotel, stood in the hallway.

"I have been told," he announced, "that you are interested in hunting in Cartago."

I invited him into my room, told him of my intentions and asked what he knew of the Cartago section.

He knew of the area and had been there before with other small hunting parties.

I was elated at the news.

"Would you or any of your friends be willing to take me into the mountains?" I asked in my broken Spanish.

He looked interested.

"*Si, señor,*" he answered quickly.

When I pressed him for how soon it could happen, he thought about it a moment.

"Perhaps," he said, "*en Sabado o Domingo,*" referring to the coming weekend.

"*Usted o quien?*" I asked, trying to pin him down as to whether it would be him or someone else.

"I have friends," he responded simply. "I will ask them."

He said that he would let me know before he left for the day.

The remainder of the morning and into the early afternoon I wandered around the downtown section taking in the unique sights of that foreign capital.

Shortly after I returned to my room, there was a louder rap on my door. It was the same bellhop, accompanied by another young Costa Rican, who appeared to be someone from the maintenance section. The bellhop announced that they would indeed be going hunting again on the upcoming weekend and asked if I would like to join their small party.

I jumped at the opportunity. "*Si, si,*" I answered quickly.

Both seemed amused at my eager response.

"*Quando?*" I asked.

"*En Sabado de la mañana,*" the young maintenance man joined in the conversation.

"*A qué hora?*" I wanted to know.

"At six o'clock, *mas o menos,*" the bellhop answered in both English and Spanish.

We all nodded in agreement.

"I will come for you," he said, "and we will eat out before we all leave."

I didn't know what he meant, "by eating out," but I readily agreed to his plans.

For the next two and a half days, I played the tourist. I covered the city by foot. I ogled the gorgeous *señoritas.* I sat at the local bars drinking *mucha cerveza* of their local brands: *Dos Echis* and *Carta Biancha,* I believe. Perhaps, I've confused those names with beers I've drunk in Mexico or in other Latin American countries. In any case, they were both good. *Carta Bianca* was the lighter color of the two and was milder while *Dos Echis* was darker and stronger in taste.

Late Friday night, I checked my guns over and oiled them again. Sleep didn't come easily that night. I was eager for the morning to arrive.

Even before the light knock on the door at six a.m., I was dressed and ready to go.

"*Buenos dias, señor,*" the young bellhop greeted me. He was alone. "Are you ready?"

Gone was the hotel uniform he had worn before. Instead, he wore loose-fitting khakis and looked more at ease.

"*Listo,*" I answered.

He led me down the stairway to an old battered four-door sedan that waited at the curb outside the hotel. Inside were four other young men, including the maintenance man who accompanied the bellhop to my room a few days earlier. Brief introductions were made, and all shook my hand warmly, especially after the bellhop mentioned that I was the *Americano.*

My rifle was put in the trunk of the car with the other guns. I was the only one wearing a gun belt and carrying a pistol. The others all had large hunting knives on their belts. When I made a brief comment to that effect, one of the men asked if I would like one to use. I naturally agreed and was handed a six-inch hunting knife in a worn leather case that was kept under the front seat. I thanked the individual for his generosity, and the old vehicle lumbered away from the curb with the weight of its occupants.

Although it was still dark, the city was rapidly coming to life. Small eating shops were open, and peddlers were parked at various intersections to hawk their food to passersby.

Within minutes of leaving the hotel side street, the driver pulled up in front of a small shop with food in its window. This stop was to be our "eating out." However, because I didn't know what to order or what to expect from such unfamiliar food, I didn't pick anything to eat. Instead, I chose to get only a cup of black coffee.

The others selected some type of hot food to take with them in the car. In all truth, as strange-looking as some of it appeared, the aroma in a closed car smelled pretty good at that hour of the morning. When the bellhop noticed that I was interested in what was being eaten by some of the others, he offered me some of his. I declined.

The bellhop then said something to the driver in Spanish, who after driving a couple of blocks guided the vehicle to the curb near a street vendor.

The sole proprietor of this stand sold fruit as well as tortillas with hot beef wrapped within its steamy folds. I had no qualms about picking up a couple of pieces of fruit. As to the tortillas, I hesitated. It looked and smelled good. A couple of the occupants saw me eyeing the tortillas.

"*Es delicioso, señor,*" they chimed in unison.

I thought about it a moment, and decided, *oh, what the hell, I'll try it.*

They all smiled and seemed pleased that I ate with them.

Although the ride from the city was cramped, I concentrated on the upcoming hunt. *What would I get? Would I even see a boa? How big would it be?*

Those thoughts kept me occupied. My companions also were silent as they looked out of the windows at the disappearing sights of the city.

Buildings and inhabitants became sparser as the countryside became more rural.

The further we drove, the more the narrow highway twisted upward into the wild thick vegetation of the mountains.

A light mist enveloped the area and obscured our visibility.

Everything glistened darkly around us.

Finally, after what seemed like an hour or more of climbing into the mountains, the driver yelled out "*aqui*," steered toward a slight clearing beside the road and stopped. They all grunted some form of approval and climbed out of the vehicle. They stood and stretched in the moist air while one of the guys opened the trunk and took out the guns. Each was handed his shotgun, and my 30/30 rifle was given to me. It was not a practical weapon in thick brush, but because my hunting experiences had been more or less in open country, it was the one I elected to take with me. On future Latin American hunts, I would choose more wisely.

Four of the group decided to walk up the road and fan out on both sides of it. The bellhop, who suddenly became my self-appointed guide, motioned that we would take the opposite direction. A fine drizzle came down as we slowly walked back in the direction from which we had come. My new guide carried an old weather-beaten shotgun as he trudged beside me. I never asked what they hunted but assumed it was rabbit or other small game they could eat. I heard one of the group mention *conejo*. However, rabbit was not what I came for.

"*Donde estan las culebras?*" I asked curtly.

It was not a well-phrased question as even I was aware that they could be anywhere and everywhere, but because my flawed Spanish was incapable of intelligently asking, "where are boa constrictors more likely to be found?" my question was stated very simplistically. Fortunately, my guide understood what I meant and pointed ahead.

"Perhaps near the river," he said quietly.

I nodded knowingly as we moved down the gently descending road. By now, we both were drenched by the light rainfall. My exposed hands began to tingle from the damp cold of the mountains, and my eyelids were partially closed from the fine rain. We silently searched the surrounding area for some type of movement. He for his small game and me for my more exotic quarry.

About a quarter of a mile from where we started, we came to a bend in the road. By now we were out of sight of our party. It was quiet. It was as if we were the only two people in those desolate mountains. The grayness of the low-lying clouds intensified the feeling of isolation. A short distance further, he motioned for me to stop.

"The river, *señor*," he announced, gesturing toward a long steep embankment beyond us to our left.

My feeling of elation returned.

When we reached the section he spoke of, he stopped again.

"I wait here, *señor*," he said abruptly.

I looked at him briefly and began my slippery descent on the wet undergrowth. I glanced back at him momentarily to make sure I was headed in the right direction. He indicated a large group of trees maybe a hundred yards ahead of me to my right. I adjusted my gun belt, which had shifted slightly on my downhill slide, and grasped my rifle in a tighter grip as I forged ahead.

Halfway toward the clump of trees, I looked to where I had left my guide. Tree limbs and thick brush nearly obscured him. I continued forward, squinting my eyes in the light rain as I searched low-lying limbs and the area directly ahead of me.

Suddenly, I was startled by a crackling sound in the brush between the river and me. I stopped briefly and raised the rifle to my shoulder. With that instinctive reaction to that distant sound, there also came a fleeting thought: *What good is a rifle here?*

I quickly dismissed the unsettling message as I listened intently and scanned the thick surroundings.

Nothing.

I moved ahead slowly.

The soft crackling sound repeated itself. It seemed to be directly in my path, perhaps a hundred feet or less in front of me. In order to get a better vantage point, I ran awkwardly on the still-sloping hill toward a nearby fallen log.

As I stepped up on its slippery surface, the front of my boot struck something soft that seemed to move. Before I had a chance to even look down at my feet, it suddenly sprang to life. A sinewy contorting brownish-colored coil lashed back at my legs and threw me off balance. I fell forward toward the writhing coils and attempted to get back on my feet. It was useless.One foot was enmeshed. I couldn't stand erect because of the ever-undulating mass beneath me. I couldn't tell its length as its lower section was still half-coiled and the upper section appeared to be moving away from me. All I could see was a mixture of brownish spots or designs that were about as thick as the calf of my leg. I still held the rifle in my right hand as I fell, and I tried to aim at the slowly-moving head. That, too, was futile because I was frantically concentrating on getting out of the encircling movement.

As I kicked violently at the lower end of its coils, its flattened head snapped back in my direction. I felt the coils tighten. I fired wildly into the mass below me and the coils relaxed momentarily. I tried to extract my boot from its grip but it constricted again. I fired another shot with the same result.

It was beginning to raise its coil higher on my leg. I struck at it with the butt of the rifle but that, too, was ineffective. I reached with my left hand for the hunting knife that I carried on that side and hastily drew it. I slashed repeatedly at the slowly moving coil still wrapped around the lower part of my leg. It was like slashing at a rubber tire with a wooden knife. I realized that it was just a matter of time before I would be completely helpless. Reluctantly, I hastily propped the rifle on the side of the log I half-straddled and grabbed my .45 that had swung slightly behind me. I pulled it from its holster and took careful aim at the small bobbing head that became larger as it weaved closer toward me.

I squeezed off a single round that caught it in the side of the head and seemed to lift it high in the air. It immediately relaxed its constrictions, and I yanked my foot from its loosening coil. It was still rolling over slowly and twitching. I brought the pistol into a firing position but I couldn't see its head any longer. It was obscured by its own coils and by the vegetation around it.

I waited, still poised, expecting some type of threatening movement, but there was none.

I kicked at the ever-decreasing contortions nearest me, but there was no indication of life. I cautiously moved closer to where the head lay partially buried and saw that the snake lay completely still. It was dead.

I was so completely preoccupied with all of my actions that I failed to hear or see my guide stumbling down the slippery slope toward me.

"*Señor,*" he said breathlessly when he approached me. "Are you OK?"

I pointed at the mass of lengthening brownish coil that lay on the ground beside me and slowly nodded my head.

# 4

The conversation among the occupants of the car was more animated on the ride back to San José than it had been during our initial foray into the mountains. All discussed in rapid-fire Spanish what they had seen and shot at or failed to shoot at because of some weather-related or terrain problem. My guide, the bellhop, was even more effusive in his description of the dead boa, although the scene and my actions had already been described once on our return to the car.

His retelling of the episode dwarfed what the others had to say about their own experiences, and they all seemed to relish the details, especially the size of the snake. He kept repeating the word *"grande"* and extending his arms in the cramped interior to show what he considered an awesome length. The others were duly impressed and nodded approvingly at me.

*"Bueno, señor!"*

*"Bueno!"*

"You are most fortunate!"

"When you return to *los Estados Unidos,* you can tell them of your great hunt."

Their comments, in Spanish and broken English, were animated and complimentary. I reveled in them.

*"Gracias, muchas gracias,"* I acknowledged. "It was *nada."*

They beamed at my responses and thanked me for

joining their hunting party.

Before I reached the hotel, I decided this was the life for me: exploring the unknown, the challenge of the hunt where I became the prey and especially the climactic survival aspects of it.

Although my remaining few days in San José were pleasant enough, playing tourist and doing the sightseeing scene were no longer what I wanted to do. The flight home, too, brought little respite to my daydreams since they were all free-floating thoughts with no concrete plans. I only knew I had to pick some exotic locale where I could combine excitement and challenge.

As I settled back further into my seat and gazed nonchalantly out the aircraft's window, I recalled the events of the two weeks since I had left the states — especially the boa hunt.

The more I dwelled on the episode, the more exhilarated I became. Gone was the thought of what could have been. Instead was the realization that I triumphed over a dangerous situation that could easily have had deadly results. Even the unsettling events of my arrival in Nicaragua earlier in my trip failed to dampen my ardor for future foreign vacations. Those recollections of my forced military confinement at the Managua airport, however vivid at the time, rapidly faded into dull memories.

I then concentrated on the past, both immediate and distant, to examine my motives as to what prompted me to pursue the path I was now on.

My friends and family considered my present solo junket into Central America somewhat extreme, but I did not share their concern. I recalled my first foreign vacation.

It was a solo trip to Mexico City and Acapulco in 1951. Then there was the solitary vacation to Havana, Cuba, and Kingston, Jamaica, in the summer of '52. Nobody thought those trips were abnormal, and I certainly didn't think so. I just enjoyed the bachelor life. Most of my friends envied me, so when one of my buddies at work wanted to accompany me to the Dominican Republic and Haiti in the summer of '53, I reluctantly agreed. I was used to traveling alone, coming and going as I pleased. I wasn't sure I wanted to conform to another person's plans and schedules, especially in a foreign country where life is completely different. I knew you always had to be careful about what you said or did. I trusted my own judgment but was wary about the actions of others.

The Dominican experience would soon support my original beliefs.

My very personable friend persuaded me that it would be fun with a companion. And it was until we hit the airport at Ciudad Trujillo, the newly named capital of the Dominican Republic, formerly called Santo Domingo.

As the two of us slowly wound our way through Customs, my perpetually comical friend noticed a very prominent picture of some general hanging on the wall. He asked the Customs official who it was. The proud reply was, "It is *Generalissimo Trujillo,* our *Presidente.*"

Without hesitation, my rotund jovial friend quickly raised his hand in my direction and jerked his thumb toward me.

"Oh, he's the *Generalissmo's* nephew."

I was taken by surprise by the remark, but since I didn't want to make a minor scene in front of the official, I disregarded it. I wasn't sure that he understood what was said since his exclamatory comment was, "*Oh, señor!*" However, he did wave us quickly through the line.

Out of range of the official, I questioned the wisdom of my friend's remark.

"It's OK," he joked. "He probably didn't understand me anyway."

I had reason to doubt that retort in the days that followed our arrival in the city.

Shortly after we checked into the Hotel Jaragua, a very plush new hotel on the beachfront, we headed for the bar and adjoining casino to try our luck. Just a few minutes after entering the casino, a tall, swarthy individual placed a bet at one of the tables near us. As he reached over to retrieve his immediate winnings, we noticed a blued six-inch revolver protruding conspicuously from his jacket. That sighting wasn't the last time we would see him. Everywhere we went for the next few days, he was always nearby. We never knew whether he was guarding us or monitoring our movements, but it seemed suspicious.

Although my friend's seemingly innocuous remark at the airport could have caused us some problems, fortunately, it did not. What it did do was support my aversion to having a travel companion on all future trips. It also enhanced my awareness of potential excitement on a foreign vacation.

At the end of our Dominican stay, I reminded my friend to watch what he said and where he said it since our next stop was in Port au Prince, Haiti, on the other side of the island. That country, too, possessed unknown qualities. He seemed somewhat chastened by our recent experience and agreed to dampen his usual exuberance. I wasn't overly concerned, but then it wasn't he who was carried away by our Haitian trip, it was me.

I had always been intrigued by voodoo, and that was one of the primary reasons I chose Haiti as a vacation spot. Although my comical friend didn't share my enthusiasm for that possibility, he went along with me.

Shortly after we checked into the Riviera Hotel, another complex near the beach flanked by a native village, I started asking questions.

"Where could I see a voodoo ceremony?"

"Was anyone aware of any in the city or in the area?"

Everyone I asked was reticent to answer me or wanted to know why I had that particular interest. Finally, someone approached to tell me of a nocturnal ceremony scheduled for the mountains above Port au Prince. Although the sightseeing proved interesting, the trip was fruitless. I found nothing in the section to which I had been directed, and no one admitted knowing about anything going on that night.

When we returned to the hotel the next day, we learned there had been a voodoo ceremony the night we were gone — right behind us in the native village. We were deliberately misled so we would not be around when the ceremony was being conducted.

The balance of our vacation in Haiti, while not interesting from my point of view, could have been productive if I had followed up on some of the contacts I had made while roaming the Port au Prince streets. Two specific requests were:

*the owner of the Cabane Chacoun nightclub in Port au Prince wanted a feature story on the acts in his club, with pictures;

*a mahogany furniture manufacturer in the city needed additional outlets in the states for his products.

I was trying to remember the other requests I had encountered in Haiti when I was jolted out of my reverie and back to the small plane in which I was riding from Costa Rica. We had hit some unexpected turbulence and were buffeted about a bit.

The stewardess appeared as soon as the aircraft leveled off and asked what I'd like to drink. I asked for a beer.

*"Cerveza, por favor."*

She returned with the cold bottle, and as I nursed the beverage, my mind flicked to next year's vacation.

At the time of course, I had no idea what that would be.

It wasn't long before events would materialize and I would be on the trip of a lifetime.


In the meantime, however, I returned to work on a Monday morning and resumed my mundane job as a parcel post window clerk at the main Fort Lauderdale post office. Although I contracted parasites in my intestines as a result of the trip — a condition that caused me to lose weight rapidly — it was not an item to brag about. (My local doctor resolved the problem.)

Everyone warmly welcomed me back and joked about Central American conflicts and how I had personally contributed to the unrest in the countries that I visited. I waved their comments aside, not knowing what they referred to — but nevertheless relishing the mystique of my imagined association with Latin American rebels.

During lunch, I visited the local travel agency that initially scheduled my trip to Honduras. I not only wanted to relay my adventures but also wanted to prove that I had done what they said I could not do.

Their amazement at my exploits equaled my own when they told me that an article in the *Miami Herald* had just reported that a lone military aircraft strafed a hotel and its courtyard in downtown San José.

It was the same hotel where I stayed.

Coincidentally, the attack took place immediately after my departure, and everyone seemed to attach some relevant significance to it. My own joking protestations of the event, however, failed to fully convince them of my sincerity.

It was from this point onward that my reputation as an offbeat adventurer began to grow.

It was a reputation I took great pains to nurture.

# 5

I don't recall when it was that I first started to think about South America as my next venture, but I vividly remember the magazine article that cemented that new desire.

It appeared in the fall or winter of '54 in *Argosy Magazine,* one of the top two men's magazines of the day. That fascinating article (at least to me), was a first-person account of some Italian count's experiences in the Venezuelan jungles prospecting for diamonds. As a result of his adventure, he allegedly emerged with a half-million dollars of the precious gems. Although the story described the hardships he endured and the dangers he encountered, it was his outcome that intrigued me. He was successful in his venture, and he was virtually a millionaire, a major accomplishment in that era.

I had no reason to doubt the authenticity of the account and didn't really want to doubt the story itself. It was something that strongly appealed to me. I felt that if some European count could do it, I certainly could. Although I had never heard that diamonds were found in South America, believing they were only mined in Africa, I entertained the possibility.

I first contacted the editors of *Argosy,* who assured me that the story was indeed true. I then researched every book and article I could find on the subject at the local library. Everything I read not only confirmed the existence of South American diamonds but described how and when they were formed and in what geographical areas they were to be found. The more I read, the more fascinated I became. I learned that diamonds formed in crystallized carbon located primarily in alluvial soil deposits, which were common in certain South American countries. Those countries encompassed what was known as La Gran Sabana region, and included not only Venezuela, but also Brazil, and what was then known as British Guiana (now called Guyana).

I focused on Venezuela since that was where the count's exploits were and where he found his diamonds. I then contacted every source of information in that country that could assist me in my desire to diamond prospect. If I recall, the information received from those contacts, while helpful and supportive, revealed that I would have to pay a specific amount of customs duty on any raw diamonds leaving the country. That amount seemed exorbitant to me since I didn't want to give up any more than I had to for my own efforts.

Inasmuch as the adjoining countries of Brazil and British Guiana had the same alluvial soil, I decided to write the officials in those places for the same information. Within a short period, I had responses similar to the ones I received from Venezuela. Brazil also had customs duties, and they were almost as high as they were in Venezuela. British Guiana, on the other hand, had very reasonable duties. They were, I believe, in the neighborhood of $10 per carat (perhaps more). It didn't take much figuring to realize that it was in my best interest to go to a country that would take the least from me. Besides, the English language in British Guiana would obviously prove no impediment, while the Spanish and Portuguese in Venezuela and Brazil might hamper me in my travels.

I also noted from the *Argosy* article that the Italian narrator had an unpleasant experience with a military patrol in the interior. Because he was on one of the smaller river tributaries, he was unaware that he had inadvertently crossed over the Brazilian border. That mistake almost cost him his freedom. The possibility of a similar occurrence happening to me led me to change my mind about my destination.

British Guiana, I decided, would be my next target, and I concentrated all of my efforts in that direction.

Over the next few months, I zeroed in on everything I could learn about the country: its geography, its weather — especially the rainy season — the scope of its diamond prospecting, and specifically, where the best location might be to accomplish my goal. One excellent source of information was the newspaper from Georgetown, its capital. It described where the latest "*shouts*" were, episodes mentioning where diamonds were found, or in what direction the trend was headed.

Because I could only take a summer vacation from the post office, that being their slow period for tourists, I chose the end of the summer to go. I managed to wrangle six weeks off from my postmaster, with a good portion of the time on unpaid leave. Since I was single, it was not a problem, although I would have preferred to have some extra operating capital. All those who heard of my new plans fell into two categories. Either they "oohed" and "ahed," wishing they could emulate me — although I had no offers — or I was ridiculed or warned, especially by family members.

"Why are you going into the jungle alone?"

"Where do you get your ideas?"

"Why can't you go on a normal vacation like everyone else?"

"Are you crazy?"

"You'll never come out alive," or if that didn't convince me, then a contrary statement, "Even if you do make it out, you'll come back a broken man with all the diseases there."

The barbed comments far outweighed the favorable ones but my mind was made up, and I was not dissuaded. I did, however, receive unexpected support that contributed to my decision, and would continue to do so for the next few years.

That source, a prominent newspaper, caught wind of my plans and gave me extended full coverage.

# 6

In the Friday, August 19, 1955, edition of the *Miami Herald,* staff writer Duane Jones did a comprehensive job of publicizing my trip. Splashed across the front page of Section B of the paper was a serious-looking photo of me holding a shotgun that rested on a map of South America. Below the picture were several descriptive captions and a long article:

## "THAT'S WHERE
## THE GEMS SHINE BRIGHT

. . . Marty Roland points to British Guiana where he'll hunt

### A Sparkling Adventure
### Diamonds Will Be Guy's Best Friend

FORT LAUDERDALE — Still looking for a place to spend your vacation?

How about a diamond expedition deep in the jungles of an uncharted section of South America?

That's where Marty Roland is going and he's looking for a partner.

If you're the rugged type, adventurous and have $1,000 to $1,500, Roland would like to talk with you.

He's leaving for British Guiana the first week in September and hopes to return early in October with a handful of diamonds worth a fortune.

Roland, a 28-year-old Fort Lauderdale postal employee, recently read of an explorer who went to the South American country and found diamonds valued at close to $500,000.

"At first I thought the man and his story were phony but found out later they weren't," Roland said.

The diamonds he found were in riverbeds and that's where the postal employee hopes to find his wealth.

"If I do, fine, but if I don't I won't be too disappointed," explained Roland, a native of New York City who has traveled all over the world.

Last year he hunted wild game in Central America and as a crew member of a patrol bomber during World War II visited various sections of the world.

Fortune or no fortune, Roland says he intends to write a book on his return from the unexplored jungles of British Guiana.

He plans to leave Miami aboard an airline plane that goes to Georgetown, and from there will charter a private plane to take him back into the jungles.

All supplies, except for a couple of guns he has will be purchased in Georgetown. A native will accompany him as a guide.

Why did he choose British Guiana instead of areas in this country where uranium is being found or some other section where his chances of becoming a millionaire would be better?

"I want to do something different," Roland explains. "Everyone is looking for uranium. I want something adventurous, something everyone isn't doing."

Roland plans to be away six weeks. In the jungles he'll eat canned food mostly and will sleep in a hammock. "Too many snakes to sleep on the ground," he added.

And what's he going to do with the fortune he hopes to find?

"We'll talk about that later," Roland smiled. "I may buy out the post office department."

The follow-up article two weeks later, by the same staff writer showed a close-up of the same head shot of me. Below the unsmiling photo was the eye-catching brief wording:

## "MARTY ROLAND
. . .seeks gems"

captioned with further abbreviated descriptive terms to grab the reader's attention:

### "Three Guns, Too
### Diamond Hunter Arms With Pills

FORT LAUDERDALE — Armed with three guns, a box of malaria pills and a tobacco can he hopes to fill with diamonds, a Fort Lauderdale mail clerk, Marty Roland, will leave Sunday for South America in quest of adventure and a fortune.

Roland's six-week expedition will take him into the dark jungles of British Guiana where explorers before him have found valuable diamonds in riverbeds.

The 28-year-old clerk will fly from Miami to San Juan and then transfer to a flight to Georgetown. From there he'll charter a small plane that will take him back into the jungles.

In Georgetown, Roland will pick up food,

medical supplies and a guide. His weapons will include a pistol, rifle, double barrel shotgun and a machete.

Reared in New York City, Roland, a World War II bombardier, has traveled all over the world. Last year he spent several weeks hunting big game in Central America.

Roland decided on the diamond expedition after reading of an explorer who recently found stones valued at $500,000 in British Guiana.

Whether he finds any isn't too important to him.

"Primarily I'm interested in exploring the jungles and plan to write a book on what I see when I get back," Roland said.

Will he keep the post office job if he finds wealth?

"I probably will at least for a while." he grinned. "It's a pretty nice place to work and some of the fellows there have offered to act as financial consultants on a 60-40 basis. They're pretty generous that way."

The informative and interesting piece, especially to the armchair observer, needed a couple of minor editorial changes to be a hundred percent accurate. First, I only took two guns with me: a shotgun and a pistol (no rifle). Second, I regrettably did not travel all over the world as a bombardier, as the article stated. I was, instead, a Navy aviation ordnanceman/airman assigned to a squadron in the southwest Pacific, primarily on Saipan. Also, while it was really insignificant to the story, the article stated that a prior explorer found diamonds in British Guiana. The country was Venezuela. Other than that, it was good publicity, and those who had prior negative comments to make, changed their tune. I remained favorably in the limelight until my departure a few days later.

Once airborne, I did not dwell on any of the dangers
or hardships that awaited me — that would come later. I
thought only of the fortune in diamonds there for the taking and of overcoming any obstacles that I would certainly
face. My zeal for the undertaking never diminished even
though I had read and heard about the difficulties of a jungle exploration — especially a solitary one. I knew I could
handle it and looked forward to the excitement of the
unknown. I soon discovered how much those daily chal-
lenges would exceed my expectations.

The commercial flight to Georgetown was uneventful,
and as I disembarked, I was hit by the same blast of hot
humid air I had experienced a year earlier in Central
America. Since that tropical country was only four to five
degrees above the equator, the heat and humidity should
have come as no surprise to me, but it caught me a bit off
guard in spite of being accustomed to similar heat in
Florida.

The minor discomfort the heat caused me, however,
was lost in the myriad of red tape that accompanied my
landing in another foreign country — with guns. Although
it was an English colony, and I had paved the way before I
arrived, I still had to follow the rules.

There were the usual Customs and Immigration officers who queried me about my intentions and then duti-
fully stamped the necessary papers to facilitate my entry.
There were the typical slow-moving lines that frustrated
my movements. I should have remembered how drawn-
out the procedures always were in another country, but
being eager to get under way, I did not. Fortunately, my
mention of being a prospector was not met with the raised
eyebrows I half expected. The authorities were used to visiting prospectors. I was the only North American on that
flight, but I overheard the singsong dialect of East Indian
blacks who mentioned the *shouts,* a term I knew referred to
diamond sightings. They were traveling here for the same
purpose. I was tempted to ask them where they were headed, but decided against it. I had a good idea of my destina-

tion since I had been following the Georgetown newspaper coverage of the latest *shouts*.

Custom's officials, in turn, advised me that my guns would be held at police headquarters until my scheduled departure for the interior. I gratefully thanked them for the information and asked the name of a good hotel in the city for my brief stay.

The Tower Hotel seemed to be the unanimous decision of those who overheard my question. For my expectations, it appeared to be the only hotel that accommodated tourists, or in my case, foreign prospectors. The desk clerks, aware of my intentions in that British colony, commented that I was the only white prospector in the hotel. For that matter, I was the only one they had seen in quite a while. Black prospectors from the Indies, known as *pork-knockers*, were the most common diamond prospectors in that South American region. It was a name I would hear repeatedly in the next six weeks.

The next day dawned bright and hot. While I waited for the various government offices to open, I wandered around the downtown section near the hotel. Other than a nearby church, the only thing of note was the wide uncovered sewers that ran down the main street. Even Haiti, one of the poorest countries I had ever visited, did not have exposed sewers in the main part of the city. I was eager to leave the capital and begin the first leg of my expedition.

My first stop was at the police headquarters to inquire about my guns and pay the required fee. Then, I located the Bureau of Lands and Mines to purchase a detailed map of the Mazaruni District, the area I wanted to explore. I returned once more to obtain my license to prospect, since the hours were limited, and returned, again, for what was known as a mining privilege. Each time, there were lines, and each time I was the only white prospector in a mass of *pork-knockers*.

On one occasion, I raised the blood pressure and the ire of a fat, sweating official who didn't appreciate my impatience with what I considered unnecessary bureaucratic bumbling. Also, I twice visited a small shack near the Demarara River that housed the office of British Guiana Airways so I could schedule a charter flight into the interior. I then had to go back to the Customs Department to notify them of my plans. In the interim, I purchased the minimal supplies I thought I would need with which to prospect and to maintain myself. Contrary to what the first newspaper article reported, I did not buy food of any kind to take. I relied on whatever the natives ate and on what I could acquire by hunting or foraging. In retrospect, it was not a great plan. But I thought it was practical. I was not prepared to lug in more that I could carry.

My final trip was to the police headquarters, again, to retrieve my two guns.

The whole process took me several days, and when I climbed aboard the cramped space of the slowly rocking Grumman Amphib sitting low in the river, I was relieved and more than a little ready.

Two other passengers occupied the overcrowded cabin. One was a male Guianan, who I saw assist with the loading and unloading of all the supplies and small boxes being flown in. He sat near the front. The other passenger was a middle-aged native woman who sat mid cabin. I, being the last one to board, sat on a hard bucket seat at the rear of the plane. Space was limited so I was forced to half-straddle the narrow depressed aisle that ran the length of the rear compartment — about ten to twelve feet long and roughly twelve inches wide. Before long that narrow, shallow trench of an aisle would transfix me.

As the huge engine roared to life, the rocking movement of the plane ceased and we moved rapidly over the surface of the river. The sharp slapping sensations on the underbelly of the plane suddenly stopped as the pilot pulled back on the controls and the craft lifted off of the murky river. I looked out a small window near me and watched the houses and then the city itself disappear from view as we headed toward the interior.

My destination was the small native village of

Tumureng on the Mazaruni River. As the crow flies it was approximately 200 miles from Georgetown, and according to my detailed map, it was but a pinhead in the middle of nowhere. I chose that particular village because the latest newspaper indicated that's where the latest *shouts* were, and that was the only information that I had. Unfortunately, that information was three to four weeks old, and I had found no other sources in Georgetown from which to get updates.

The loud monotonous drone of the plane's engine hampered any conversation within the cabin. As near as I could tell, my fellow passengers weren't interested anyway. The male Guianan was busily arranging supplies in the front of the compartment and also trying to noisily ask questions of the pilot. The woman looked uncomfortable and began taking deep breaths. She began moving erratically, constantly moving her head from side to side as though she was searching for something. I grew nervous.

Suddenly, her head jerked over the aisle and she vomited heavily into its narrow confines. The Guianan looked at her disgustedly and raised his hand to cover his nose. The pilot, who had just been alerted by the baggage handler, raised his hand in frustration and motioned to have his cabin door shut. Sitting but a few feet from the native woman, I caught the full stench of whatever it was she had eaten — and then disgorged. The vomit ran and sloshed down the trench-like aisle, forcing me to raise my feet to keep my boots out of the muck. As the nose of the plane rose, the vomit slid down the aisle toward me. When the plane dipped, the vomit rolled toward the front. Its putrid aroma was intensified because of the heat, and I began to gag as well. I was close to repeating that same scenario, as was the baggage handler who was gulping noisily. For the next thirty to forty-five minutes my eyes were glued to the aisle as the foul-smelling concoction first rolled forward and then back toward me.

Finally, after what seemed like hours, the pilot began a sharp descent to the jungle below and a sparse settlement that hugged the river. The plane hit hard and the amphib bounced over the water toward a cleared riverbank. When it came to a complete stop, the Guianan rushed to the cabin door, opened it and exited the plane. The native woman quickly followed him and I after her. The pilot was the last to leave. He said something to the baggage handler, who found a rusted bucket nearly, filled it with river water and returned to the plane. While he attempted to clean the aisle, the pilot made a brief mumbled apology to me and started unloading some of the supplies himself.

It wasn't long before the baggage handler joined him and they swiftly completed unloading the plane. The pilot motioned me back aboard again with a curt "Tumureng next," and the three of us were once again airborne. The woman remained on the ground, but the foul-smelling odor did not. It was difficult to keep from retching, but periodically the pilot opened a window in the cockpit. I was grateful for whatever meager air forced its way to the rear of the compartment. The baggage handler also tried to make our flight more bearable by spreading newspapers in the aisle to mask the smell.

With some of the supplies unloaded at the last settlement, I moved closer to the window to gaze out. All I could see was thick impenetrable jungle below me. The solid mass of dense green foliage was so compacted that even the individual trees were indistinguishable from each other. I saw no houses, no shacks. I couldn't even see any of the small boats that often made their way down the winding river that snaked through the massive wall-like fortress below. As I stared at the endless green desolation of the jungle and realized that I would soon be on the ground engulfed in that same jungle — alone — a momentary chill swept over me. The sudden wave passed but not before a strange thought went through my mind.

*The die is cast.*

I shook my head to rid myself of that ancient Roman saying. There was a finality to that thought that I didn't want to dwell on.

# 7

The plane banked sharply to the left. Just off the wing tip, I caught a glimpse of some small structures nestled among the trees near the river ahead.

"Tumureng," the pilot yelled above the two engines as he gestured below.

The Guianan rose unsteadily from his seat as the aircraft leveled off and began its slow descent. He made sure there were no loose boxes or small supplies that would shift on landing then sat back down.

The Grumman hit the water and taxied effortlessly toward a low riverbank fringing the small settlement. The pilot cut its engines. A small group of natives approached the plane and watched in curiosity as I emerged from the hatch. They eyed me intently at first and then shifted their attention to what I had on and what I carried.

I wore GI olive fatigue pants, a green T-shirt, tight-fitting at the neck, and a fatigue cap. My gun belt with my revolver, a .357 Colt, was slung around my waist. In my right hand, I carried a double-barreled shotgun, and in my left, I had a small bag containing ammo for both weapons and other small items, including a large hunting knife. I must have looked bizarre to the onlookers. Here was a white man — the only one in the area — garbed in clothes that were clearly alien to them. Their loose fitting garments were all faded from the sun and tattered from use. It not only was the sight of the two guns that riveted their gaze but what I wore on my feet. Two highly laced combat boots completed my jungle outfit.

My appearance would be changed drastically by the end of my prospecting venture, six weeks down the road. Even the pilot who dropped me off — and would return six weeks later — would comment on the transformation from clean-shaven, neat explorer to weather-beaten prospector.

The Guianan handed me my laden duffel bag. Among other things, it contained a mesh hammock, a small shovel and a machete, which would become my most useful implement in the days to come. The pilot from the aircraft briefly assisted the baggage handler in transferring supplies from the plane's interior to the hardened riverbank. He then told me he would return and went up the short hill to what appeared to be a trading post.

As I waited, I glanced around the sparse settlement. It was too small to be labeled a village — even a jungle village. It had none of the outer appearances of what one would expect from inhabitants who participated in ongoing daily activities. Numerous small wooden shacks half-surrounded the river and the trading post. That was all there was to Tumureng. In front of the shacks were natives whom I assumed were *pork-knockers* because of the prospecting supplies they carried. No children were visible, and only a few women appeared. They stared, seemingly as interested in my arrival as the men.

When the pilot returned to where I stood at the top of the riverbank, some of the onlookers dispersed while a few others remained in our vicinity.

"Good luck," he said, firmly grasping my hand. "You'll need it here," he said, gesturing to the settlement.

"I'll return to pick you up six weeks from today," he continued. "Don't be late. I can't hang around long."

I thanked him for his concern and assured him that I would be there.

He turned and strode back down the hill toward the plane. The Guianan, who had been waiting for him at the river's edge, nodded in my direction, and they both reentered the aircraft.

I waited until the engines kicked over, then watched as it taxied down the river and, with a roar, lifted off.

A brief feeling of being completely alone descended on me as my last vestige of contact with the outside world disappeared from view. That alien sensation passed as quickly as it arose, however, because a stronger feeling of anticipation replaced it.

I turned to trudge up the hill toward the ramshackle trading post, gear in hand. The natives who remained in the area eyed me silently. I was surprised there were so few *pork-knockers* around since the last information I had was that the area around Tumureng was the last-known diamond *shout.*

A few natives stood at the entrance to the wooden shack. I didn't know if they were waiting for me to enter or standing around to purchase supplies. From the outside beams hung some sieves and small spades. The structure was off the ground and had openings for windows but no obvious shutters to cover those windows.

As I approached the entrance, the natives easily moved aside, allowing me to enter the small building. Inside, a wooden counter filled with prospecting implements lined one wall. Behind it were shelves with some meager food supplies.

The only other person in the store was the proprietor. He appeared to be an East Indian. I would learn that they were usually the merchants in the bush. His singsong dialect, apparently from the Caribbean Islands, supported my belief.

"What can I do for you, mon?"

When I told him of my plans and of what I had learned from the Georgetown papers, he half smiled.

"I know. Your pilot, mon, told me what it wuz you wuz here for," he said, then hesitated. "But de diamonds have moved upriver now."

Surprised by his statement, I took a deep breath and noisily exhaled my frustration.

"To where?" I demanded.

His demeanor softened slightly, seeing my obvious displeasure at his remark.

"To Kurupung, on da Kurupung River," he exclaimed as if I should know the location.

I had never heard of Kurupung, nor of the river, and quickly extracted my map from my gear for him to show me. He looked at the large map stretched out on the counter, squinted and thrust a thick finger at it.

"Here be Tumureng on da Mazaruni River," and he traced his finger on it toward a smaller tributary off the main river.

"This be the Kurupung River," and then moving further up its length, stopped at a dot beside the river, jabbed heavily at the speck and proudly announced, "Kurupung."

I took another deep breath.

"How far?"

He shrugged.

"Forty or fifty miles from here," he said, "maybe more."

I stopped a minute to regroup my thoughts.

"How do I get there?"

He stared back at me, obviously pleased at what he had to say next.

"You are a very lucky mon," he said. "A river boat will be here in Tumureng tomorrow with many supplies. It goes on to Kurupung."

I couldn't believe my good fortune. I half expected to be stranded there.

"What time?" I asked him.

I knew it was a dumb question as soon as the words left my mouth, but it hadn't quite sunk in that I had left civilization behind.

He shrugged again.

"Maybe in the morning, or maybe in the afternoon. It is hard to know."

I nodded in acknowledgment

"Where can I stay until then?"

"Here," he motioned around him. "You can sleep in the back, or..." and he gestured toward a nearby shack, "...you can sleep with the other *pork-knockers*."

I chose to take him up on his offer.

"If you need a hammock, I sell them," he said, pointing to a loose pile of them in the corner.

"I have my own," I answered, patting my duffel bag.

"I see you are well prepared for the bush," he said matter-of-factly, noting my guns.

"I am," I said firmly, as much for his benefit as for the small group of curious natives that formed outside the entrance.

"Do you need food?" he asked.

"What do you have?" I asked, glancing at the small supply of canned and dried food he carried.

He rattled off a small list of what was stocked on the shelves, and I selected a few cans of fish, meat and fruit. I figured that would last me two or three days, and I would replenish what I had in Kurupung.

My diet for the next six weeks would be a far cry from what I now stuffed into my duffel bag.

For the balance of the day, I was barraged by comments from the natives about diamond prospecting in general and more specifically about my equipment — especially my two guns. I also was questioned about where I was headed and whether I needed a guide. I briefly considered their offers, but then quickly dismissed them. I didn't feel comfortable around those who asked.

Dusk came and with it the grateful solitude that I sought, to think about and plan my next moves. Thankfully, the proprietor kept to himself much of the time, indicating only where the hooks on the inside posts were so that I could sling my hammock. The easy part was arranging the widely spaced soft mesh hammock. The more difficult part was figuring how to sleep in it without falling out. I had never slept in one. I hadn't even tried it out before I left the States. I had talked to people who had slept in them, and they instructed me to use a diagonal position, northwest by southeast — or the opposite side — to allow my body to be horizontal. After several unsuccessful tries, I managed it, but it was not a restful night. Before long, I would have no trouble mastering the horizontal position, nor would I have many restless nights.

My first full night in the jungle, thankfully, was without incident. Occasionally, I heard dogs barking for whatever reason, but by-and-large the settlement was quiet, and I grabbed whatever fitful sleep I could manage.

With the first illumination of dawn filtering in the open window, the settlement awoke. Natives noisily prepared themselves to go into the surrounding bush to begin their prospecting day. I was no exception. My preparations, however, involved very little. I clumsily rolled out of the hammock, unhooked it and folded it back up to be packed. I hadn't removed my boots, only my gun belt, and I had placed that directly beneath me. My cased hunting knife was tucked into the front of my pants since I was forced to sleep on my back. Its ready-to-use availability was what I considered to be paramount to my own security. I had no one to rely on but myself. The authorities in Georgetown had warned me that it was inadvisable to travel alone in the bush and supported their admonitions by citing the misfortunes and disappearances of various prospectors.

The trading post opened and the proprietor did a brief brisk business with the *pork-knockers* who came in for last-minute supplies. I fended for myself, opened a can of fruit for breakfast and propped myself outside his shack to watch the river. The proprietor indicated the spot where the riverboat would dock — whenever it came.

From early morning until late afternoon I searched the river for any signs of activity. The proprietor would periodically inquire about my welfare, scrutinize the river himself and then throw his hands up in exasperation.

Finally, when the sun was beginning to settle at the top of the towering trees, a chugging sound filled the sporadic stillness of the jungle, and a long low-slung boat came into view.

I watched in awe as it slowly approached the river-bank. It was a scene reminiscent of the classic movie, "African Queen". The dense green foliage that fringed the river seeming to engulf the solitary boat. The proprietor emerged from behind the counter and commented unfavorably about the lateness.

As the boat neared land, I got a good look at its occupants and its cargo. It was approximately forty feet in length and about fifteen feet or more at its greatest breadth. A canvas-type canopy extended from mid-ship to perhaps two-thirds to three-quarters of the boat's length. Beneath the canopy were boxes, crates and small bits of mechanical equipment. Wedged in and around these supplies were chickens and some goats. There may even have been a pig or two but from my vantage point I couldn't see the contents of the entire boat.

The proprietor motioned me forward after it docked, and spoke to the captain of the supply boat. He nodded his head, agreeing to allow me to hitch a ride on his craft. He indicated that I could find room near the bow.

I thanked the proprietor for his assistance and the captain for his accommodation and picked my way among the supplies and the chickens to a small area not beneath the canopy. At least eight to ten natives were crammed on the small vessel, and all eyed me as curiously as the others had the day before. The majority seemed to be *pork-knockers* trying their luck upstream, as I was now doing.

After some of the supplies were unloaded and before it got underway again, I asked the captain when we would arrive in Kurupung.

"Tonight," he answered mechanically. When he saw me still staring at him quizzically hoping for an approximate time, he held up five fingers on one hand and then slowly added, "maybe more."

The boat loudly lurched forward, belching smoke, as it pulled away from the riverbank and headed out into the wide Mazaruni River.

From my forward perch, I got a good look at what lay ahead — and at the murky water that lay beneath. On either side of the boat, an unbroken wall of vegetation grew down to the water's edge. Occasionally a ripple in the river indicted something below its surface. It was a beautiful unspoiled scene. Greenery shimmered in the water as the sun reflected off its brownish mirror-like surface. As the boat probed further upriver, I was lost in reverie, transfixed by the hypnotic scene around me. Out of the corner of my eye, I suddenly noticed some large floating tree limbs. As I briefly examined them, I saw something thick slither off the branches. One of the natives nearby saw me eyeing it intently and casually mentioned that it was an anaconda, a water boa constrictor.

Although his comment was casual enough and did not raise any concern in me at all, the anaconda's habits would one day soon be a cause for great caution for me.

Meanwhile, the riverboat continued its relentless journey, and I became more aware of the wildlife that surrounded us. Large crocodiles lazily resting on the shore quickly raised up and slid effortlessly into the water as the engine's reverberation grew closer to them. Other animals crashed into the nearby jungle at the sound of our boat. I couldn't see what they were, but in time I would find out.

Twilight came, and then blackness, but the boat never slowed its movement. The skipper of the craft shined his searchlight ahead, illuminating our watery path and I watched it reflect from eyes on the shore or in the water.

After hours of straining my eyes into the inkiness of the night, the boat suddenly slowed and began a sharp turn to the left.

"Kurupung River" one of the natives nearby called out to me.

I acknowledged him and tried to make out its width in the darkness as the searchlight combed the nearby shores. It was much narrower than the Mazaruni, which seemed about a quarter to about a half-mile wide at its greatest. This river that we were now on appeared to be no more than a hundred yards across. Because we were closer to the banks of both sides, movement in the jungle was more pronounced and more eyes reflected back to us from the water's edge.

After an hour or more of our long journey, I noticed some faint illumination ahead of us on the right bank.

I glanced back at the captain, whose figure would occasionally be illuminated by the glare of the powerful searchlight.

He was mute for the moment, but gestured ahead.

My pulse quickened with anticipation. I knew I was finally beginning the venture for which I had long planned. I also was well aware that the challenge of the unknown I sought was upon me. Yet, it was the immenseness of the surrounding blackened jungle that I didn't quite expect.

Then, as the boat rounded a bend in the river, the captain shouted "Kurupung," above the din of the engine. He steered toward the shore.

# 8

The boat slowed, and as it approached the riverbank, I saw numerous kerosene lanterns being held by small groups of natives crowding around the docking space. Behind them were wooden shacks with faint illumination coming from inside. It looked to be slightly larger in area than Tumureng, but at night it was hard to discern.

Once we pulled up to the muddy bank, all of the occupants scrambled off. I was one of the last to leave. I had no idea where I was headed. I hadn't made any specific plans as to what I would do next. I only knew that Kurupung was where the diamonds were — and that's where I wanted to be.

The area around the riverboat bustled with activity, as various supplies quickly were unloaded. I stood to one side in order to acclimate myself to my new surroundings and to the darkness around us.

One of those who seemed to be directing the movements of supplies to shore was a middle-aged East Indian who glanced in my direction once or twice. When the unloading was complete, he stopped and spoke briefly to the captain, who nodded at me while they talked. While I watched their discussion in interest, the East Indian thanked him and slowly walked toward me.

"I am Pena," he said in a soft voice, tinged with a slight Trinidad accent. "How can I help you?"

His offer was unexpected, but it sounded sincere. I

liked the look of the man.

I explained my reason for being there, although it might have been fairly obvious at that point. I also asked where I could stay while I prospected, and looked curiously around at the small village.

Without hesitation, he answered me.

"You may stay in my shop." He pointed to a small path that led away from the river.

I was uncertain about accepting his offer. I didn't know what sleeping arrangements that might entail, but I also realized that I had no other choice at that hour.

He noticed my brief hesitation and smiled.

"I have space behind my shop," he continued. "You may stay there until my woman returns."

I nodded thanks and followed him up the narrow dirt path to his trading post, similar to the one at Tumureng.

His lantern reflected the same type of shop interior that I had seen the day before, although his building was slightly larger. He led me to the back of the shack where his own hammock was slung.

"You may use those posts," he said, pointing at nearby hooks on which I could sling my hammock.

"I have to attend to the supplies," he said as he walked toward the door.

"I'll leave this lantern for you." He placed it on a small crude table that sat in front of a window opening. "For the bats," he added.

I didn't know what that meant, and didn't have time to ask him before he left. I just considered myself lucky to fall into this kind of arrangement.

As soon as he left, I checked his living area — and what would soon become mine. His hammock was stretched between two posts close to another window opening. I noticed that he had mosquito netting canopied over his hammock. Fortunately, I brought my own netting and removed it from my duffel bag. Regretfully, I foolishly had not used it the previous night in Tumureng. The only respite I had the entire night was placing my cap over my face to protect it from the unrelenting mosquitoes. I was determined not to have a repeat performance in Kurupung.

Pena's living space was Spartan. A few clothes hung on a railing of sorts over an old dresser. A large wooden chest sat on the floor nearby. The rough boards on the floor were even more remarkable. None of the boards meshed together. There was a half-inch or greater opening between each one. The floor itself was raised about one foot above the ground, something I had noticed about other buildings in the bush. Looking upward, I saw larger beams that ran the length of the structure and noticed that some type of tarpaper had been used to seal the inner surface of the roof. I was thankful for that, as there appeared to be no leaks from prior rains.

By the time I arranged my gear and mosquito netting, Pena reappeared with a second lantern. He made some small talk about directing his supplies to his trading post and asked if I was ready to retire.

"We'll talk tomorrow," he said, climbing easily into his hammock. He dimmed the flame on the lantern but kept it lit and placed it nearby.

I removed my gun belt and placed it in my boots directly below the hammock. I loosened my belt so my oversized buckle wouldn't dig into my stomach. Because I was still on my back, and would be forced to sleep that way as long as I was in a hammock, I slipped my hunting knife into the front of my pants. This was a habit I would follow for a few days and then disregard as I became more comfortable and grew to trust Pena.

Daylight streamed through the opened windows as I heard Pena moving around the adjoining shop. I slept longer than I had wanted but felt more rested than I thought I would. When he heard me moving around, Pena came to the back of the shack and placed some opened canned food on the table.

"After we eat, we'll talk," he said laconically.

In the weeks that would follow, I would learn that he

did not engage in meaningless conversation but in whatever was pertinent to the occasion.

After we ate, he asked about my plans and intentions. I answered him as simply and completely as I could. He then told me that he would be pleased for me to share his home while I was in the bush, and would even prepare food for me. Dumbfounded by his generous offer, I asked him, "Why?"

"I have diamonds," he stressed carefully, "that I buy from the *pork-knockers*. It is more secure to have two of us here instead of me only."

I was surprised by his admission to me, a complete stranger. I would learn, however, that his assessment of me was similar to my own of him at our first meeting. In our brief association, he came to regard me as a son he never had, and I was flattered.

I readily agreed to our mutual arrangement and would do everything in my power during the ensuing weeks to compensate him as best I could without paying him money, which he refused to accept.

After a firm handshake on the unusual bargain, he said, "You will need a guide to assist you. I know one you can trust."

"A *pork-knocker?*"

He shook his head.

"An Akawaio Indian, who does not live in the village," he replied.

Kurupung, I learned was inhabited by about 100 *pork-knockers*, who did not always get along well with the Indians who lived in the area.

Pena, who observed my questioning look as to the choice of a guide, added, "not all *pork-knockers* can be trusted."

I nodded in understanding, remembering the warnings I received from officials in Georgetown.

"I will send for him," was his terse comment.

While I waited, I wandered around the small village. There were only a half dozen, or more, dirt paths in the large clearing near the river. Beside the paths and on the outskirts of the settlement were numerous wooden shacks that housed the diamond-prospecting natives. It didn't take long for me to realize I was the only white man in the black encampment, and I drew countless silent stares from the onlookers as they readied themselves for their daily tasks. I noted several of them had already begun their trek into the surrounding jungle that engulfed the sparse clearing. All carried the implements of their trade: spades, axes, sieves and, of course, the ever present, highly-sharpened machetes. At the far end of Kurupung, I came across a much larger wooden structure that had a raised porch across its front with crudely cut railings. Above the entrance to the building was a hand-printed sign, *Police*.

I was surprised to see this incongruous sign posted in the middle of nowhere, but equally pleased to know that, even out here, there were traces of civilization.

Although the building was there, I didn't see anyone around. I learned that there were usually two constables on duty, but they were frequently away in the bush attending to their far-flung duties in the district.


Mid-afternoon, the Akawaio appeared, and Pena introduced him.

"This is Shanks," he said. "He has agreed to be your guide."

I quickly sized him up and felt at ease with what I saw. He was short, but muscular, with a shock of thick gray hair that came forward on his forehead. He was pleasant looking, reminding me more of my grandfather than of an Indian indigenous to the region.

I grasped a leather-like hand and thanked him. His English was good, but somewhat broken. I was thankful that I chose British Guiana, where English was the primary language in lieu of Venezuela or Brazil where I would be facing Spanish or Portuguese natives.

We agreed that he would be back in the morning so

we could head into the bush to prospect. With our brief conversation over, he left. Pena looked at me in approval at our meeting.

"Is that his full name," I asked. "Shanks?"

"His Christian name is Andrew Shanks," he answered. "But Shanks is what he is known as."

"Tell me a little about him."

"He lives in the vicinity of Kurupung, with his son," he replied.

"His son?" I repeated, thinking he had an older son.

"His son is ten, and goes with him on many trips."

"Tomorrow?"

"No, just you and he."

"How old is he?" I asked inquisitively as it was hard to judge from his appearance.

"He is seventy," he replied, "but very strong."

I learned from observing him in the days that followed that his strength and stamina were those of someone half his age.

When I asked Pena what it would cost me to hire him.

"Nothing," he stressed.

I was amazed at his answer and repeated what he said.

"He is my friend," he said firmly, "and you and I both have an arrangement."

I nodded in agreement, but was still surprised.

"What equipment will I need tomorrow?"

"Nothing for now," he answered. "You have a spade and a machete."


Early the next morning, as he promised, Shanks was back carrying the usual prospecting tools. In addition, he had a long stick made from a tree branch and hacked smooth.

"We will need this," he said, offering it to me.

I took it, wondering what use it would be. Before the day was out, I learned its importance.

Pena supplied me with some canned meat and dried fruit that I shoved into my baggy GI patch pockets. He also filled my canteen with what he called bush tea. It was a concoction steeped from some local plant. I actually grew to enjoy it every day.

We began our trek down one of the narrow paths out of the village and into the surrounding jungle. Shanks trudged ahead on wide leathery feet, deep into the green foliage and away from the river. At first the path was clear, but the farther into the jungle we got, the more tangled it became. Shanks swung his machete at overhanging vines as the sounds of the village gave way to the calls of jungle birds and monkeys screeching in the trees. Distance in the jungle is deceiving because of the overwhelming sameness around you, but my rough estimate was that we had gone anywhere from one to two miles from our starting point. Ahead, I saw a small stream and heard some voices in the distance.

Shanks turned to me, *"pork-knockers,"* he said. "We go farther."

When we reached the narrow stream, we saw three or four of them shoring up timbers on the bank adjacent to the water.

As we passed them, Shanks noted, "No good, stream overflows with rain."

I wondered at our destination as I had heard, and read, that diamonds were prospected in riverbeds.

*Why,* I wondered, *are we moving away from a stream instead of along one? Perhaps there's another one ahead, and he wants to be as far away from other prospectors as possible.*

I said nothing, relying on his judgment and on Pena's selection of a guide.

The farther in we trekked, the more obscure the path became.

I swung my own machete in unison with Shanks. When it appeared that the path ended, he held up his hand and indicated a direction for us to travel.

"We go here," he said, raising his machete and hacking heavily at the vegetation that blocked his path. I followed and tapped him on the shoulder.

"How far?"

"Not far now," he answered, motioning toward another, much narrower path that angled off from our own.

"This is the *line*," he said quietly.

The term *line* was used from that point onward and meant some sort of path that was difficult for me to see, but nevertheless was there.

We moved more slowly than we had before because of the tangle of vines and branches before us. Although the mosquitoes were ever present, I hadn't given them much notice until we began slashing our way through thicker foliage. There, they seemed to descend like a black cloud, clinging to the sweat that trickled down our faces and glistened on our arms.

After about an hour — or more, since time is difficult to judge in the jungle — Shanks stopped abruptly in a partial clearing near a muddy creek bed.

"We stop here and look," he announced as he dropped his equipment to the ground.

*Look where?* I wondered. I saw no water nearby and had no clue as to where we would start our hunt for diamonds.

He took the long tree limb from my sweaty grasp and started probing into the ground around him. After several attempts of probing into the soft earth beneath him, he stopped and held up his hand again.

"We try here," he blurted out. He began excavating a small hole near the soggy creek bed.

I unloaded my own gear and asked him where I should dig.

"Not ready yet," he said, stopping me.

After a few minutes, having reached a depth of a foot or more, he stopped digging and moved to another spot. He repeated the procedure on a second hole. After a similar excavation, he tested the soil between his fingers and stood up. He looked up at the trees that towered above us and slowly inspected the area around us.

"This is good. We dig here," he said.

As he spoke, he etched an eight-foot square onto the ground. He then started hacking at the foliage and small trees inside and around the square. I followed his example, and within a short time, a sixteen-foot space had been cleared, except for some larger trees.

"We come back for those," he said simply, and started to sink his spade into the soft decaying vegetation. He directed me to do the same, and after a few hours, we were standing in a dampened hole almost three feet deep.

Shanks straightened up and looked at me, taking in my sweat-drenched shirt and the spade I clenched in my hands.

"We do good work," he said, "but we come back tomorrow."

I nodded gratefully, my hands tingling from grasping the rough surface of the shovel.

The trek back was no easier than the trek in, and when we reached the stream where the *pork-knockers* had been, they were gone. Although it was not yet late afternoon, it was dusk above the small stream. The jungle is always in perpetual twilight.

I glanced at the small pools of water that apparently had formed when heavy rains caused the stream to spill out of its banks. Inside the pools, I noticed several fish under the surface. I nudged Shanks and pointed at the fish, which ranged in size from a few inches to a foot in length.

"Good to eat?" I inquired.

He shook his head and pulled me back away from the pools.

"No," he said emphatically. "*Perrai.*"

*Perrai*, I learned was the Indian word for *piranha*.

# 9

Pena wanted to know how we fared on our first day out and especially how I managed on our first pit.

I grimaced slightly, trying to conceal their stiffness, as I opened and clenched both hands.

"Fine," I said, trying to assure myself more than Pena.

"You are young and strong," he noted. "You will get used to the work."

Shanks nodded and said he would return again the next morning.

Pena introduced me to a young Guianan, who worked in the trading post and had arrived after we left that morning.

"This is Silva," he said.

He was small and slight of build but was very helpful not only to Pena, but to me. He frequently cooked our nightly meals, which became more exotic as time passed. Whether the different foods were prepared because of my presence or whether they were typical of what they usually ate, I didn't know. However, whatever hot food was put before me, I ate without question. Truthfully, much of what I ate was bizarre and tasted strangely. On occasion, it also had an odd odor, but nevertheless, I never let on that I didn't particularly find their offerings appealing. I knew I had to eat to keep up my strength for the grueling tasks we performed every day in the jungle.

The next morning, Shanks appeared with a black *pork-knocker*.

I was a little surprised, because he hadn't mentioned bringing anyone else along.

"This is Captain," he announced. "He will help us today."

He resembled all the others that I had seen: floppy fedora-type hat, loose-fitting short-sleeved shirt and cut-off pants. I glanced over at Pena, who stood nearby.

Sensing my indecision, he quickly spoke up.

"He is trustworthy," he said firmly.

I acknowledged his endorsement, and the three of us headed out of the village on the same path we took on the previous day. Shanks led, with me in the middle and Captain following. I learned later the significance of his name.

We approached the same stream where we had seen the *pork-knocker*s the day before. They were still occupied with shoring up the side of the pit bordering the river. It rained a little during the night and the level of the water had risen slightly. I glanced over at the pools of water with the *perrai*. Others floated lazily nearby. I had always heard that the voracious *piranha*, or *perrai* as Shanks called them, were only a few inches in length. As Shanks' continued my daily education about the bush and its denizens, he taught me that the *perrai* could attain sizes of up to a foot long. I would see the results of their attacks on more than one occasion.

Our trek inland covered the same territory as it had the day before, but it seemed easier because the *line* was freshly hacked. Also, although my guides were not particularly talkative, our sporadic conversation made the time pass more quickly. The mosquitoes, however, did not abate, and I was constantly warding them off. Neither Shanks nor Captain seemed particularly bothered by them. Either they were used to them or the mosquitoes didn't swarm around them as much.

When we reached the pit, Captain inspected the area

and indicated to Shanks that he would clear some of the larger trees in the vicinity. Shanks and I resumed our digging and within a short time had gone down another two feet into the soft earth. Periodically, we encountered tree roots that had to be hacked with our axes. The lower we got, the more water stared to trickle into the bottom. Soon, we were standing in mud. Shanks motioned that we should climb out and help Captain with some of the larger nearby trees. Before we climbed out, however, we stopped to chop at a thick rotten tree stump that protruded into our workspace. When my blade hit a soft spot nearest to me, large black scorpions came boiling out and down into the low water at the base of the pit around our legs. I cursed and began swinging at them, trying to smash those round me before they climbed up my pants. Shanks, who was barefoot and also wore cut-off pants, moved even faster and swung at them more viciously. Within a few moments, we killed at least a half dozen of them, and the others disappeared.

Captain, who worked nearby, heard the commotion and witnessed our frantic efforts. By the time he came over to help, the action was over and he made some brief joking comment to Shanks. Shanks responded in kind and began to help Captain as if nothing had happened. I was not quite as nonchalant about the episode. Before long though, I, too, would face unexpected situations and then just get on with my tasks.

With the trees cleared around the pit, my guides seemed satisfied. They inspected the pit again, and after evaluating its depth, Captain lowered himself into the hole. Shanks handed him the long pole. He took it and started to probe into the muddy base, which now was filled with several inches of water. After a few attempts, he stopped and nodded to Shanks.

"Gravel," he said. "We must bail the water and dig more."

We all took turns digging and bailing until we hit a depth that they both agreed was acceptable. We were down to about six feet, with water filling up almost as fast as it was being taken out.

Shanks spoke first.

"We come back tomorrow."

Captain looked at the pit and the fading light.

"Tomorrow is good," he said. "We can finish up what we have to do."

I questioned what he meant, since up to that point I had no idea the scope of diamond prospecting.

"We have to build up the sides of the pit with logs and then build a *plan* to work it," Captain replied.

Before I had a chance to ask him what a *plan* was, Shanks chimed in, "There is much work to be done yet, but there is good progress."

After our return to the village, it started to rain. My guides shook their heads almost in unison.

"This is not good," Shanks said. "The water will rise, and the pit will fill up."

"You mean the stream?" I asked, referring to the sluggish-moving water that we crossed.

He nodded his head. Captain added, "And our pit, too."

"We will still return," Shanks insisted. "There are three of us."

After they left, Pena asked how I did, noticing that I extended my fingers awkwardly to keep them from rubbing together. When I held them palms up, he saw that I had blisters that had broken open and become raw open sores.

"I have something to help," he said, locating some salt that he mixed into a bucket of water.

I shoved my hands into the strong briny solution, and after the fire subsided, found some minor temporary relief. The next day, however, was worse. There was no respite from the digging and the chopping, and I couldn't ask for any from either of my companions. The following night, I repeated the salt soak ritual, and by the end of several days, my hands had toughened.

That night, though, as I lay in my hammock with my hands still throbbing, rest didn't come readily. As I tried to fall asleep, I heard scurrying movements above me. I looked up at the rafter that ran the length of the shack and saw two large rats running across the beam. The noise never woke Pena, and when I mentioned it to him the next day, he shrugged his shoulders.

"They don't keep me awake," he said.

All the while I was there, the rats were there also. Although I was initially concerned about their balance directly above me, I soon learned to ignore them.

Shanks and Captain arrived again early the next morning in the midst of a light drizzle, and the three of us headed out of the village once more. We saw some *pork-knocker*s preparing to leave as well, but not as many as there usually were.

"They don't like the rain," Shanks noted. "But where we go, it will be almost dry."

As we trudged under the protective canopy of thick foliage, it was as he said, "almost dry." However, when we reached the partial clearing of the stream, both men held up their hands to stop. I heard the sound of water flowing over rocks. What had been a slow-moving stream the day before, was now a swiftly cascading river.

My guides approached the enlarged stream and examined its banks.

"We cross here," Shanks noted, indicating a spot with some flattened rocks protruding above its surface.

He plunged bare-footed into the warm water and motioned for me follow. The stream had risen to two or more feet, and as I sloshed across in my boots, I glanced over to where the shallow pools had been the previous day. They were gone, swallowed by the river. I saw only a solid mass of moving water and no *perrai*.

I had always been of the impression that *piranha/perrai* would only attack if there was blood in the water to attract them. Shanks told me that a pregnant — and temperamental — *perrai* could initiate an attack that would produce the necessary blood.

On the far side of the stream, which Captain managed to ford with some difficulty because of slippery rocks, Shanks held his hand up to a position high on his chest.

"Sometimes this high," he commented, pointing to the water. "When rains are heavy in the mountains — and sometimes higher."

Captain grunted agreement and shook his head at the thought.


The pit was, as they both warned, more than half-filled with water. Fortunately, they brought an extra bucket with which to bail, and while Shanks and I dumped the contents, Captain felled small trees to line the sides of the pit. After that, one of them started to dig a trench to siphon some of the water away from the pit, while the other cleared a top surface near its edge. I assisted where needed but constantly had to wrap and rewrap my hands with rags I brought along to protect them. If either one of them noticed, they said nothing. Neither did I mention it.

Finally, after hours of work, we reached a stage where it appeared there was nothing that remained to be done in our preparation.

Shanks was the first to stop and motioned for Captain to do the same. Both surveyed the pit and agreed that "tomorrow we start," although water still remained at the bottom.

On the trek back, we reached the stream again and saw that it was more swollen even than earlier. Further inspection by Shanks revealed another location to cross. This time the water was almost waist high in sections where there were no rocks, but I moved as well as I could. My thoughts of *perrai* were secondary, as I wanted to cross as quickly as possible. We regrouped on the far side of the stream and looked back at it. If the other two had similar thoughts to my own, they never mentioned them.

The next morning my guides were back, carrying additional equipment that I was unfamiliar with. Captain hoisted a large box while Shanks lugged a square piece of iron with holes in it. These would both be necessary in the prospecting process.

Although it did not rain during the night, the stream was still high, but not to the extent it had been at our last crossing. Shanks also pointed to the pit beside the water where we had first seen the three *pork-knockers*. It was completely flooded out. Shanks shook his head slowly from side to side, as if to say, they should have known better.

When we arrived at our own site, we all concentrated on emptying it as soon as possible. I had been told that below our pit lay gravel, which is where diamonds often could be found.

Once we reached the bottom of the hole, the dirt, sand and gravel were laboriously scooped up and shoveled onto the level area, the *plan* Captain referred to. He placed the large box at the front of the *plan*, on the level area near the pit. Using a hoe, the contents of the pit were forced through openings in the box and the holes in the flattened iron that Shanks brought. The remains were then forced-fed into another low box placed at the edge of the pit. The contents — by now considerably reduced — were finally shoveled into a large circular mesh sieve. From this point on, Captain and Shanks took turns meticulously swirling and pumping the sieve. Theoretically, diamonds — and gold nuggets — work their way to the bottom of the sieve. Although I knew gold was found in exactly the same manner as diamonds, I hadn't thought much about it. Diamonds were my goal.

The process took hours, and at the end of each operation, each of us carefully inspected the bottom of the sieve for either diamonds or yellow nuggets. After a considerable period where both of them worked continuously,

Shanks asked if I would like to try. At this point, the pit had filled with water again, but I gladly immersed myself in it to try my luck. After watching them closely for hours, I felt I could do it. My heart raced with anticipation as I finally reached the stage of inspecting the sieve.

There was nothing — no gold and no dulled diamonds — at the bottom of the sieve.

Captain suggested I try again and gave me some pointers on how to handle the sieve. Still nothing.

Both again took turns with the same results. All the while, the pit kept filling up and had to constantly be bailed out.

Hours passed and twilight settled in around us. My guides agreed that we were getting nowhere, and should abandon the pit. I couldn't understand why we couldn't continue. I felt let down.

Heavy rains, they stressed had soaked the ground and ruined our pit. The constant saturation of incoming water was diluting our efforts and we were literally wasting our time.

I grudgingly admitted they were right and picked up my own gear as they did the same.

I looked around at the cleared jungle that surrounded the pit and vividly recalled the efforts that were put into our excavation.

"We will try again on another pit," Shanks assured me.

Captain said he was sorry that he couldn't help us, but Shanks said he understood and nodded toward me.

"He knows how now."


At the stream, before we began to cross on our return to the village, Shanks, who had been scanning its flowing movement, suddenly held up his hand for us to stop. He walked a slight distance from where Captain and I stood and pointed to an object that appeared to have wedged on some rocks near the bank.

As we approached the spot, his brief comment was, *"perrai."*

Judging by the curved tusks that protruded from its bony head, it appeared to be the remains of a wild boar. But all that was left was the skeleton — picked totally clean.

# 10

The next morning Shanks returned, and we headed back into the surrounding jungle. This time, however, we were not loaded down with the large box and flattened iron. Instead, we carried our usual digging tools and, of course, our machetes. Mine was now as finely honed as Shanks', and it took little effort to slash through the smaller vines in my path. Our ultimate destination was new, although the first part of our trek took us toward the stream we had previously crossed several times. Just before we reached the rapidly flowing water, Shanks motioned that we parallel the stream and cut back toward the Kurupung River again.

At least an hour out, Shanks stopped in a partial clearing near another muddy creek bed, and held his hand up.

"We try here," he said simply, dropping his load to the ground.

I mumbled agreement and gratefully dropped my own implements.

It wasn't as if I was tired of lugging our equipment and perpetually swinging a machete, it was more a relief to know that we were going to start digging for diamonds again. After a week there, my hands had toughened up considerably and the sporadic back and shoulder pains I felt at first had subsided to dull aches that I could handle.

While Shanks repeated the probing procedure to decide where we should dig, I scanned our new area.

Although there is always a sameness to the green vegetation in the jungle, this particular spot that Shanks had chosen appeared to be more open than our previous site. There were fewer small trees around us, but the larger trees that towered above us, had an abundance of low-lying limbs that extended over the jungle floor.

While Shanks moved about the area testing various locations, I was absorbed in rubbing both arms. He glanced up and noticed me vigorously scratching. He stopped his probing activities and came over to me to see what the problem was. Slowly, he inspected my upper arms, carefully examining the small reddish welts and then nodding his head.

"*Miburi,*" he announced matter-of-factly, returning to his work.

*Miburi,* I learned, were minuscule parasites that infect the underside of leaves and vegetation. When exposed skin then brushes against the leaves, the parasites transfer and burrow unmercifully into the skin. Indians, I also learned, were not immune to the *miburi*. However, unsuspecting foreigners were more susceptible to the annoying effects of the parasite, as they were to many of the other afflictions and diseases prevalent in the tropics. Fortunately, Shanks made me aware — every day — of jungle remedies the Indians used to counteract many of these afflictions or diseases. In addition, because I became an enthralled student of his teachings and knowledge, he also passed on a great deal of Indian beliefs and practices, many of which I would have used without hesitation in an emergency.

One unique — if not bizarre — remedy for poisonous snakebite involved earthworms. The Akawaio Indian remedy was to grind a large earthworm into a pulp-like mass, place that concoction into water and then drink it.

On two separate occasions, one especially, I came close to being a victim — too close. If I had been hit either time, I immediately would have put into practice what Shanks taught me. I figured since his people were there long before the white man, they knew what to do.

It didn't take Shanks long to pinpoint a likely spot for us to begin digging. His probing stick encountered the rasping sound of gravel a few feet below the surface of the nearby creek bed. Although I knew by now that diamonds weren't found in all gravel deposits, I knew they were found where there was gravel.

We followed the same procedure we had with our first hole, working in unison to a shallow depth. This time, however, Shanks was satisfied with our dig and began to enlarge the site almost immediately. While he did that, I cleared the smaller trees that would hinder our expansion. He chopped at tree roots that protruded into the beginnings of our new pit. I then joined in, hacking at the stubborn roots with my own ax. It was difficult going. Frequently, the ax bounced off the roots of the larger trees because the wood was so hard. After several hours of labor we were bathed in sweat and standing in a two-foot-deep pit, half filled with water that came mid-way up our calves.

We stopped briefly to survey our work. Peering up at the trees near us, Shanks pointed at a small limb that extended overhead and indicated that it should come down. Immediately, I chopped at it, bringing it to the ground near the pit. In doing so, however, the vibration dislodged a small boa constrictor that tumbled, writhing into the water at our feet. In reflex, I yanked my pistol from its holster and took aim. Shanks shouted for me to stop, and I looked questioningly at him before reholstering it.

"It's OK," he said. "Small boa. No harm."

He gently lifted the twisting greenish coils of the four-foot snake and threw it out of the pit. I watched as it slithered away.

When I queried him afterward as to why he stopped me from killing it, he merely said, "Not bad snake," but didn't give it a name.

Weeks later, after my return to the states, I found out that it was an emerald tree boa, a small South American species that was very rare.

With the boa dropping in on us to briefly interrupt our work, we agreed that it was a good time to eat. As Shanks sat down to eat what he brought and I wolfed down my own canned food, he began what my daily lessons about the bush and its denizens.

"*La baria*," he began, "is poisonous snake — very bad." He stretched out his hands to indicate a length of about five feet.

"Small?" I asked.

"Some," he replied, "but fast." He extended his forefinger and middle finger in a downward curve to show its fangs. With his two fingers he repeatedly jabbed at his arm to show the unusual striking abilities of the *la baria*.

It was a name I had never heard mentioned before, but I assumed it was the deadly South American *fer de lance* snake, and the name Shanks used was probably the Indian name. In subsequent conversations with the *pork-knockers* in the village, they referred to it as the "snake of last cigarette." When I asked what they meant, they said, "if it hits you, you might as well smoke your last cigarette, because after that, you're dead." Unlike other poisonous snakes, these snakes reputedly injected venom with each strike. That amount of venom undoubtedly accounted for the quick fatalities of its victims.

Noting my concern over his description of the *la baria's* movements, Shanks commented on boa constrictors.

"They are slow-moving," he continued, "but watch the trees." He motioned for me to look at the thick limbs of the trees overhead.

I nodded, recalling our recent incident.

"Do they drop?"

He shook his head, but then added, "Sometimes."

"How big?" I wanted to know, remembering my boa kill in Costa Rica.

He pointed to a nearby fallen log at least fifteen feet long and made a large circle with his hands to show their thickness. "Sometimes bigger," he added.

"What about the water boa constrictor, the anaconda?" I asked.

"Very big," he said slowly, pointing to a much larger tree on the ground. "In the river, you must watch. They are bad."

When I asked what he meant, he told me that frequently they would crawl up on floating logs or branches to sun themselves. If an Indian dugout were on the river's surface, the anaconda could not tell it from a log and would flop its coils on the small boat. Obviously, its size and weight would be disastrous to the occupants of the dugout, as the murky rivers teemed with other unfriendly creatures.

With Shanks' brief discourse on bush life over, he rose and eyed me silently for a moment.

"More, another time," he said.

The balance of the afternoon, we continued to dig and shore up the sides of our pit to prevent it from caving in. By the end of the day, even Shanks' leathery skin glistened with perspiration. As for my own condition, the underside of my gun belt was wet from sweat. Although I could have removed it to make it easier to work the pit, I never did. The security of having it on far outweighed the discomfort.

We saw no other *pork-knockers* near the stream on our return and were glad. We wanted our new pit to be away from the prying eyes of others

# 11

Later that same day, as I recounted the earlier events to Pena inside his shop, two *pork-knockers* stopped to buy supplies. Although they appeared interested in the snake story and added similar experiences of their own, they were more interested in my activities as a prospector. Was I experienced? Where did I come from? How long would I be there?

I fielded their general questions with vague responses. I didn't like the directness or rapidity of their inquiries, so when they zeroed in on where we headed each morning and how successful we had been, I avoided answering and continued my conversation with Pena. They refused to be ignored, however, and started to comment on my attire. One said he liked my combat boots and would like to wear a pair like that. The other, not to be outdone by the first, silently stared at the pistol in my holster and quietly announced that he would like one exactly like that also. I tried to ignore the remark, but he shifted his gaze from the pistol to my eyes and in a louder and firmer tone announced, "I want that gun!"

I was taken aback by his sudden statement, but not enough to be silent.

I touched it easily and returned his intense stare.

"The only time I give this up, is when I'm dead."

They both left without a word.

"You and Shanks will have to be very careful now, my

friend," Pena said somberly.

That night, as I lay in my hammock watching the two rats run the length of the beam overhead, I shifted my boots, which held my gun belt as I slept. I had always kept my boots directly below my hammock, but now I shifted them closer to Pena's hammock, as well. From one boot, I extracted my hunting knife and slipped it into the front of my pants again, a habit I had given up almost a week earlier.

The next morning, Pena told Shanks of the incident.

He nodded knowingly. "I will watch," he said.

On the way out of the village, we took a more circuitous path to our pit. Periodically Shanks would stop to listen. I heard nothing but the usual screeching of birds and monkeys overhead and the occasional crash of trees to the jungle floor. It was a sound I had become accustomed to hearing and was a continual danger. Shanks had warned me that falling trees and limbs were probably the number one cause of fatalities and injuries in the jungle.

Our trek in proved uneventful, and during the lulls in our working routine of digging, bailing and chopping, Shanks resumed educating me about the bush.

Had I heard of vampire bats at night, he wanted to know?

I admitted that I knew the night air was filled with bats and that Pena had advised me to leave the lantern on when I first arrived. Other than that, I never questioned him about the reason. I knew nothing about vampire bats.

"They are real," he said. "If you do not have the lantern on and there is no light around you, they will feast on you," he continued.

I must have looked dubious.

"It is true," he insisted.

He went on to explain that the bats land on unprotected skin at night, make their puncture wounds and then lap up the blood. When I remarked that a person must be able to feel the puncture of the bats' fangs before they begin their feast, he held his hand up.

First, he explained, they deaden the area with a type of needle-like insertion that is a preliminary to the fang punctures. A victim, he noted, could have a vampire bat land on him, and be unaware of its presence. I was amazed at what he told me.

"That is not all," he continued. "Some have paralytic rabies."

After that, I always made sure I had oil in the lamp and the wick in operable order.

That knowledge would be of little use to me in the very near future when I was faced with a situation that was beyond my control.


We labored the rest of the day until it appeared we were at the final stage of preparation.

Shanks threw his shovel out of the deep pit. It was water logged and at least four feet deep.

"Tomorrow, we bring box and iron," he announced.

"Good," I acknowledged, eager to see what our new pit would bring.

On the journey back to Kurupung, Shanks periodically stopped to listen for any unusual sounds. Hearing none, he then motioned me forward again.

As we entered another partial clearing, he stopped briefly and held his arms up to prevent me from walking near a large tree. Before I had a chance to ask why, he pointed at a football-sized clump at the base of the tree.

"*Anni*," he said quietly. "Do not step here."

I stared at the mound and saw several large ants emerge from it.

"Poisonous," he exclaimed. "Very dangerous."

After we carefully made our way around it he told me the ants' venom was second only to a snake's and that they grew to enormous sizes. He held up his thick flattened thumb to stress the point.

I nodded appreciatively.

"Tomorrow," he said, "I show you."

The next morning I awoke to a great disappointment. It had rained steadily throughout the night, and when Shanks showed up at his usual time, his statement was short and to the point.

"Too much rain," he said, gesturing around us. "Not good to dig."

I grudgingly agreed, remembering the futility of trying to dig the last pit while it filled with water faster than we could bail.

"We talk more," he said, leading me to an overhang outside Pena's shack to stay as dry as possible.

"*Anni,*" he began, referring to the large poisonous ants we saw the day before, "are not the only bad ants. There are the *marabunta.*"

*Marabunta*, I soon learned, were voracious army ants that periodically go on rampaging marches through the jungle. Tens of thousands cut a wide swath of destruction through leaves and vegetation — and anything else in their path.

I had read an account of that and had seen some Hollywood movie about the devastation they wrought but really hadn't given it much thought. At least until Shanks made it a reality.

After allowing that information to sink in, Shanks pointed to a nearby spider on the outer wall of the building.

"Not bad spider," he announced, "but some are."

When I questioned him specifically, he answered, "*ting ting* spider."

"*Ting ting* spider," I repeated, intrigued by the name and also aware that I had never heard of one.

"They jump," he said, indicating a distance of about a foot from him to my arm.

"Poisonous, also," he stressed.

I nodded and asked him for a description. He mentioned it had some type of distinctive markings.

"Black widow?" I asked.

Although he nodded, I'm not sure he understood

what I said since he went back to talking about the *marabunta*.

"They have pincers and are this long," he said holding up his thumb and forefinger to demonstrate the size of the inch-long ant.

I winced as I pictured it.

"Not like *pingos*," he said. "Climb tree to get away from *pingos*. No can climb tree to get away from *marabunta*."

*Pingos*, I learned, were small wild pigs that traveled in packs of hundreds. If you were caught anywhere near them, you'd want to get away from them as soon as possible. Wild boars, on the other hand, only traveled in small groups of five or six. Those five or six, however, with their highly sharpened tusks, were even more vicious than the sheer mass of smaller *pingos*.

The two local constables interrupted our brief discussions. They had been away in the bush and had heard of my arrival in the village.

One introduced himself as Corporal Paton and the other simply as King. Both were from Georgetown and appeared to be in their early- to mid-thirties. The corporal had an easy manner about him and seemed to be genuinely interested in my welfare. King, on the other hand, was a hulking giant of a man with an abrupt way of speaking. I called him King Kong, and to my surprise, he relished the comparison and would use it whenever he greeted me. Since I was the only white man in a village of a hundred black *pork-knockers*, they both cautioned me, especially after I relayed the comments from the two *pork-knockers* of the previous night.

"I can take care of myself," I reassured them as I patted my gun belt.

"We hope so," they both added seriously before leaving for their own hut at the edge of the village.

Shanks left to talk to Pena. When he returned, he stated that he had to attend to something for Pena. I told him I understood and would tend to my own affairs. I reentered the shack to get out of the rain and decided to re-oil my weapons and sharpen my machete.

Pena, who had been busily tending to *pork-knockers* for their food supplies and other implements, stopped in the back of the shack. He eyed me silently for a moment as I methodically worked the guns over.

"I must ask a favor of you," he announced quietly.

"Just name it," I answered. "I owe you much."

"I have to go down river within the fortnight, and I would like you to accompany me."

I agreed readily, and when I gently questioned him as to the reason, he did not hesitate.

"I have diamonds that I must take to Tumureng, and I need you to guard me."

I jumped at the opportunity to ride shotgun for him.

"Gladly," I said loudly.

When he noted the enthusiasm in my voice, he smiled.

"It is only to take the diamonds to the syndicate."

When I raised my eyebrows questioningly, he explained that he did it periodically to sell to European buyers from Holland. *Pork-knockers* had given him the diamonds in trade for supplies — until, of course, they made their big hit. Although, he explained, none of them had made a big strike in a while, he had accumulated about six hundred carats in raw diamonds to take down river. The syndicate then paid him the equivalent of a hundred dollars per carat. It didn't take much figuring to realize the small fortune he was transporting and the five-figure amount he would realize.

He noted me silently mulling over the transaction and nodded.

"Perhaps," he said slowly, "when you return home, we may be able to do business together."

The enormity of his offer took awhile to sink in. Before I had a chance to answer, he was interrupted by someone entering the front of his shop.

"We will talk of this again," he said.

The balance of the day I thought about the potential of

his oblique offer and, if sincere, how I would handle it.

The next morning, Shanks was back with the additional equipment to finish working the pit. This time, however, he had a young Indian boy with him, his ten-year-old son.

"This is Dudley," he announced proudly. "He has helped me to carry the box and the iron, and he will help us with our work."

I nodded appreciatively to the young Akawaio youth with the unlikely English name and stuck out my hand.

He grasped it without hesitation, and with a firm little squeeze, gave me a small quick shy smile.

I immediately liked him, a fact that Shanks noted, and we were soon on the path out of the village and into vegetation that dripped heavily from the previous day's rain.

I didn't like the possibility of what we might face in our second pit, having remembered our first one.

Neither of us was surprised at what we saw. Water had filled our pit. Shanks just shook his head as he dropped his equipment to the jungle floor.

"We must bail quickly," he said as he extracted a second pail from one he carried.

For the next hour or two, we both bailed as much water as we could from the pit. Dudley, too, at his father's urging, took the pail from me and followed suit.

Finally, Shanks decided it was time to prepare the *plan* at the top of the pit. The large box was again placed at the lower end of the *plan* with the flattened iron — he now referred to it as the *tom iron* — below that. He then shoveled the contents of the base of the soggy pit onto the *plan*. He directed me to use the hoe. It was a repeat performance of the first pit. We took turns sifting the wet dirt through the sieve to look for diamonds while one of the three of us constantly bailed water from the slowly filling pit.

After what seemed like hours, with the mounting water constantly diluting the soil in our shovels, Shanks abruptly stopped.

"No good," he said in frustration, as he climbed out of the pit. "Too much water. Too much rain."

He looked as disgusted at our progress, as I felt.

We both sat on a nearby log watching the water from the surrounding earth slowly trickle back into the pit. Dudley, too, sat quietly on a fallen tree, eyeing the two of us.

After an interminable period, Shanks stood up and slowly looked around.

"We go," he said, as he picked up his equipment. "We try again somewhere else after the ground has dried more."

I was disappointed at having to abandon a second pit, but I trusted Shanks' experience and grudgingly relied on his judgment.

We took the same *line* back to the village as we had on our prior trek before the rains came. Shanks stopped near the same tree again with the telltale clump of earth at its base and motioned the two of us back. With the tip of his machete, he sliced open the mound and from it boiled numerous angry large black ants.

"*Anni*," Shanks said in a hushed tone, holding his fingers to his nostrils.

A strong scent of ammonia permeated the air. I mentioned it to Shanks. He nodded, pointing at the split-open mound, and then gesturing that we should move quickly in another direction.

A short distance farther on and somewhat off the narrow *line*, Dudley, who had been following us, suddenly yelled out to his father.

We both turned to see him frantically pointing to some object at the base of a large tree. We responded quickly, stopping to stare at the crumpled object that had led to his abnormal behavior. It was a human skeleton — or what remained of one — with its arms and hands outstretched before it. The legs seemed to fold beneath it. Vegetation grew through the bones. Matted, decaying cloth clung to the body in tatters, but was unrecognizable as clothing.

"*Pork-knocker,*" Shanks muttered, as he fingered the shreds of clothing.

Dudley, his eyes still wide open, stepped back silently to watch us inspect the scene.

Shanks, who had been carefully examining the area around the tree, reached near the skeleton and extracted what appeared to be a shortened arrow.

He held it near his lips and gave a short puff of air.

"Blow-gun," I said in amazement, and he nodded.

"Wai Wai," he grunted, jabbing the air toward a section we had not yet explored.

# 12

Pena listened intently as we described our discovery of the remains of a long-dead *pork-knocker*.

He shrugged his shoulders when I asked whether I should report it to the local constables.

"It is your decision," he said casually, "but..." he added slowly, "I doubt if they will look into it, as it sounds as if Indians from the mountains took care of him."

Shanks, who stood nearby, nodded agreement.

"*Pork-knockers* come and go all the time. Some disappear," he said with a shrug of indifference. "Nobody ever knows."

I thought about it a moment and agreed.

Pena returned to the front of his shack to serve a *pork-knocker*, who had just walked into the trading post. Shanks and I joined Dudley, who waited for us on a crude bench in front of the building. He tilted his small head up at his father with a questioning gaze.

"We stay awhile," Shanks answered his gaze, motioning for him to remain seated.

"What mountains did he mean?" I asked, referring to Pena's earlier comment.

"Watabaru and Mt. Perenong," Shanks answered without hesitation.

I repeated the names aloud and waited for further explanations.

"Watabaru is plateau," he said, pointing off in the distance. "It is seven miles from village. Perenong is peak and is farther from village."

I wanted to know if the Indians that Pena spoke about lived in that area. Shanks nodded.

"Wai Wai," he continued, "live on top of Watabaru."

I remembered that he had used that name when we found the skeleton and gave him a sign of recognition.

"They are head hunters," he said seriously.

I looked at him in surprise.

"If they are head hunters, why didn't they take his head?"

Shanks shook his own head slowly from side to side.

Dudley, who had been listening to the conversation with rapt attention, silently moved closer to us as his father continued.

"When we are in bush and see Wai Wai, stay close to me."

I smiled and patted my holster reassuringly again.

"You stay close to me," I stressed.

"No," he insisted, "too many of them. You cannot kill all. They have blow-guns," and held his hands up to his mouth holding an imaginary weapon.

"Whatever they want you to do, you do," he said.

I asked what he meant.

"If they give you food, you eat," he said simply.

"If they want you to drink, you drink," he continued in the same tone.

When I questioned him again, he answered as if I should have known.

"Do not make enemies," he added. "If you do not make enemies with them, they will not bother you."

I nodded in understanding.

"If we do meet them," he went on, "they will not harm you if I am with you."

His comment was comforting and sincere, and I believed him.

He directed his attention to his young son.

"We go now." He directed Dudley to gather some of

the equipment propped against the building.

"We be back in two days if no rain," he said. "And we try further in bush." He gestured toward the mountains.

For the next couple of days, I stayed near the village and explored. I was becoming acclimated to the jungle and almost had a feeling of invincibility. I had overcome recent hardships and difficulties in a hostile environment and had prospered from my experiences.

Then one night those feelings were set back slightly when I experienced an unexpected event that could have had dire consequences.

As I wrote a daily entry into my diary by the light of a kerosene lamp on Pena's crude table, I heard a loud commotion through the open window. A *pork-knocker* was yelling and repeatedly beating the ground with a heavy stick. When I ran outside to see what was happening, I saw the still-twitching writhing coils of a dying snake on the path near the edge of the building.

As I questioned the man about his actions, he breathlessly pointed to the large open space beneath our shack and then to the long snake that lay before it.

"*Bushmaster*," he said aloud, "was going under Pena's building."

I saw the slowly contorting coils of what appeared to be at least a ten-foot *bushmaster*. It was the largest and reputedly the deadliest venomous South American snake, and it was the first time I had ever seen one.

Pena, who had been elsewhere in the village, also came running when he heard the commotion near his shack.

When we entered the small building, Pena took me to the table beside the window where I always sat and then pointed to the widely separated boards on the floor directly behind me.

"You are lucky mon," he said. "He might have come in building."

Although I had been constantly aware of my surroundings, that incident sharpened my perception of what could happen if I became too nonchalant. In spite of that heightened awareness, however, a similar situation arose on a nocturnal hunt in the not-too-distant future.


Three days later, Shanks and Dudley appeared minus *tom box* and *tom iron.* Shanks held his palms upward and looked up at the blue sky through openings in the towering trees above us.

"No rain," he said. "Good to dig."

I hoped his prediction was accurate because I was becoming more than a little frustrated with our progress.

The now-familiar trek out of the village took a turn when Shanks set out in a new direction.

I tapped him on the shoulder indicating that I knew the *line* we were now on was one we had not hacked through before.

He half-smiled, acknowledging that I was right. He pointed ahead.

"Toward mountains," he said.

"Watabaru?" I said apprehensively, recalling all too vividly where the Wai Wai lived.

He shook his head, and Dudley, who walked between us, looked a little relieved as well

"Not far as Watabaru or Perenong," he announced.

We hiked through the dense bush swinging our machetes. Finally, after what seemed to be a greater distance than we'd ever gone, we came to a partial clearing. Shanks stopped and pointed ahead through a break in the trees.

"Watabaru," he said almost proudly.

Ahead of us, although still at a great distance, loomed a massive plateau with sheer rock sides that dipped into the jungle. It rose several hundred feet and was bare of trees, or seemed so from our vantage point. To the left, I saw a craggy peak that I assumed was Mt. Perenong. Shanks confirmed it, and Dudley, who apparently had never been to this section before, stared in awe at

Watabaru.

Shanks dropped his implements to the ground and motioned for me to do the same. Again, as at the previous two pits, he searched for what he considered an appropriate spot by probing the soft earth.

For the next three days, our working routine was the same as it had been on the previous two pits. Dudley was very helpful and volunteered to do some of the smaller tasks without his father's urging. Meanwhile, Shanks and I labored constantly in the dampened earth. The more we dug, however, the more water we encountered. Although the surface of the ground was a little drier than we had experienced before, because of the slight increase in elevation, the lower recesses of the pit were no different from the others.

On the night of the third day, after we returned to the village, it rained slightly. Shanks and his son had already left me in Kurupung to return to their own dwellings and were not with me when the rain started. But I knew — or rather feared — what we would face again the next day having seen what happened before.

The rains that we continually encountered were not normal for the season. That was the very reason I had chosen to prospect for diamonds at that time of year. Supposedly, the months of August through October were the dry period. That was not the situation I now faced, and my level of frustration rose. This was my third pit, and I had yet to see a diamond, although I had become experienced in the whole procedure and looked forward to working the sieve. Just to have discovered some would have made the whole trip worthwhile. I knew that some prospectors had hit pockets of them, and at first I thought I would do the same. With the reality of prospecting behind me, I would have been satisfied to hit a few. I knew exactly what to look for, and in response to my early queries to both Shanks and Captain as to what a raw diamond looked like, I was told, "You'll know when you see one."

They were right.

When I did view diamonds in the rough, there was no mistaking what they were. They looked precisely like diamonds, but without the brilliance. It is the cutting and polishing that gives them their fire.

The morning of the fourth day Shanks again appeared with Dudley, but said very little before we began our trek inland once more. He appeared to have a slight limp and when I asked about it, he just shrugged it off.

By the time we reached our pit, our worst fears were realized. The night's rain, however light, half-filled our pit and we both looked at each other silently before we started to bail in unison. Although it didn't take us long to empty it, the continual seepage slowly filled the bottom of the pit and hampered our digging and scooping process. The water trickled off the shovels and made the process of placing the dirt on the *plan* virtually useless.

After what seemed like hours, with Dudley doing what he could to assist us, Shanks shook his head again. I saw the futility in continuing what we were doing without any results and shook my own head in agreement.

We climbed out of the pit, gathered all our equipment and headed back toward Kurupung.

# 13

Pena was half-apologetic as he told me that his "woman" was to return on the biweekly supply boat the following day.

Although I had expected her back sooner or later, as Pena had first mentioned it to me on my arrival, it was the sudden announcement that caught me off guard. I had become used to our living arrangement and felt secure in his shack, especially at night while I slept.

Pena noticed my concern and added that she would be there but a few days and that our eating arrangements would not change. Silva, he said, would still prepare the majority of our meals, but his Indian woman would do some cooking.

I nodded and gestured toward my hammock, intending to ask him where I would hang it in the interim. He anticipated my question.

"It is all arranged," he said. "You will sleep in the constables' shack."

Although I had never been in their building, I had noted that there appeared to be two sections to their large shack. The constables conducted their duties on the right side of the building, and they apparently slept in that section, as well. The left side, I learned, was for visitors. It was sort of an open-air bush hotel.

"Silva will help you with your equipment," Pena said. As an afterthought, he also mentioned the settlement at

Tumureng, my prior one-night stay-over.

"After my woman leaves, we will go down river to meet the syndicate."

The disappointment of our recent washed-out pit coupled with the unexpected announcement of the arrival of Pena's woman suddenly dissipated with that information. I smiled broadly at him.

"I'm sure you'll find it interesting," he said.

I welcomed that down river diversion. The thought of his recent business offer concerning the diamonds began to fill my mind again. But it was the idea of riding shotgun that really appealed to me.

As promised, Silva helped me move some of my gear down to the constables' shack. Corporal Paton greeted me and led me into the vacant section, indicating where I could hang my hammock. The only items in the barren room were a chair beside a crude table with a kerosene lamp on top.

"King is in the bush now on police business, and I will be leaving shortly," Paton announced. "We will be gone a few days, but the place is yours," he said, gesturing around the nearly empty room. He turned to leave.

I thanked him and looked around at my new home. Other than the table and chair and the ever-present lamp, there were only a few hooks on the walls. Nothing else. There were two openings for windows on either side of the building. One faced the pathway that skirted the porch on the front, and the other window looked out the back on a sparse clearing with thick jungle behind it.

After some brief entries into my diary and acclimating myself to my new area, I wandered back to Pena's shack for the evening meal. The few *pork-knockers* in the village who noticed me nodded recognition or made some type of appropriate comment, since I was more or less one of them. If there were any type of antagonism toward me or any looks of envy concerning what I had, it was not apparent. I did not see either of the two *pork-knockers* who had made no bones about wanting my personal gear a few days earlier. However, the one who liked my boots did appear in Pena's shop after Pena and I had our meal.

He did not repeat his comment about my boots or comment about any other item of my attire or equipment. To relieve my concern of his outspoken companion, I questioned him about the man's whereabouts. He shook his head indicating ignorance, but did mention he had not seen him for a few days. In reply to Pena's persistence, he only responded that he thought he had gone up river. Pena glanced at me with a look of satisfaction with the answer.


Back in the constables' shack I prepared myself for the night. I hung my hammock, checked the wick on the oil lamp and placed my personal gear and my equipment near me as I had done each night. Before I lit the lantern, however, I lifted it to see if it was full. To my amazement, it seemed almost empty. I hurriedly scanned the area for more oil before darkness set in. There was none. I checked the constables' area to see if there were any containers. There were none, and their interior section had a log door with a lock. I thought of returning to Pena's shack to see if he had any extra oil, but discounted it because of the distance. I also did not want to bother him for something that trivial. I thought that the oil in the lamp would certainly last the night. Unfortunately, it did not.

Midway through the night, I woke to pitch-blackness and sensed fluttering noises in the shack. I groped for my flashlight and flicked it on. Its bright beam illuminated the table and the darkened lamp, and I eased myself out of the hammock to inspect it. It was cold to the touch indicating that it had been off for a while. I didn't know how long I slept in the darkness and instructively brushed both arms to verify that no bats had alighted on me. I glanced at my watch and knew that several hours of darkness still remained. I also realized that I had to have light in the room, so I did the only thing I could think of. I dragged the heavy log table away from the open window and placed it alongside an adjoining solid wall. On the table itself, I put my still illuminated flashlight facing the wall so it cast an eerie dull light against the flattened surface. I was satisfied that it would do the job, and although I tried to stay awake, I could not.

At the crack of dawn, I immediately awoke and glanced over at the table. The flashlight had gone out, but apparently it had done the trick because, as far as I could determine, I had received no puncture wounds.

Months later, my description of that episode earned me a twenty-five dollar check from Ever-Ready Batteries. The company used my account in advertisements in various men's magazines to demonstrate the effectiveness of its batteries in warding off vampire bats.

That morning, when I related the story of the previous night, Pena expressed concern about my welfare. But he complemented me on my ingenuity. Shanks also was impressed when he heard the tale later that morning. When I noticed that he still favored his leg, I asked him what happened. His only reply was that he had "injured it." He said, however, that we would resume our prospecting after our return from Tumureng.

As expected, the supply boat arrived later in the day, and with it, Pena's woman. Her stay was as he indicated, "a few days," and she returned to Tumureng on the same boat. Although Pena and I also were scheduled to leave, Pena had a security problem with his trading post and did not want to head out until the constables returned to the village.

Two days later we boarded a much smaller boat for the trip. The vessel more closely resembled a large canopied dugout with an outboard motor. It was unlike any watercraft I had ever seen. There were only three of us — Pena, me and the helmsman — my former prospecting companion on my second pit, Captain. We renewed acquaintances and also discussed my bad luck on the washed-out pits. When he asked if we had ever picked up any gold in our pits, I shook my head. I had not really thought of that possibility as I had my mind set only on diamonds. However, I had been told that gold nuggets and even specks were found in the same manner. When I questioned Captain about the possibility that I might have overlooked the gold, he shook his head. He repeated what he had told me earlier, "You'll know it when you see it," and then added with a slight smile, "Shanks wouldn't let you."

The trip up the murky Kurupung River seemed faster this time than on the night of my arrival, and I had more opportunity to examine the encroaching thick vegetation on the riverbanks. I also noticed smaller tributaries that emptied into the muddy river. On one such sluggish tributary, a few miles from the village, I saw what appeared to be a small, shallow abandoned dugout caught on some undergrowth. I tapped Pena on the shoulder and pointed to the object. He motioned for Captain to pull in closer to the dugout. As we approached it, we saw shreds or pieces of clothing floating near the shore. Captain reached out to retrieve what he could and held it up to examine it more closely.

"*Pork-knocker,*" he said quietly, throwing the items back in the water.

"Maybe your friend," Pena added with a slight smile, and then motioned Captain forward again.

As the small boat glided into the wide expanse of the Mazaruni River, I saw individual shacks and huts dotting the riverbanks. Dogs yapped as we approached them. Small Indian children played near the water's edge.

The Mazaruni seemed wider than I recalled from a few weeks earlier. Perhaps it was because of the relative width of the Kurupung or maybe because we were going up river. It was just as murky as the Kurupung, however, and I was more aware of the creatures that lurked beneath its surface. I did not, as Shanks had warned, spot any anacondas swimming near us, although I did occasionally see some stretched out or coiled on shore. The crocs, as usual, raised up and slid into the river as we noisily motored by.

Finally, Tumureng appeared in the distance, and

Captain gestured ahead at it. Pena nodded and leaned toward me to be heard over the sound of the motor.

"When we are in the village, stay nearby and be alert."

I nodded agreement and asked him about the men from the diamond syndicate.

"When are they coming?" I asked.

He looked toward the village.

"They are already there," he said. "They have been there since the supply boat left our village."

"They've been waiting two days," I noted.

"It is to their advantage to wait for me," he added, patting the small satchel where he had stashed the raw diamonds.

Captain guided our boat to the same small muddy embankment from which I had left earlier and from which the seaplane landed and took off.

On shore, two middle-aged white men strode toward our boat to warmly greet Pena. He introduced me as a friend and fellow prospector, and they accepted the description without question, though they glanced at the gun on my hip. They spoke with Dutch accents and led Pena to a nearby shack that appeared empty. Pena quietly indicated that I follow them up to the building and then remain outside while they conducted their business.

Their meeting took less than an hour. Pena emerged first and motioned that we return to the boat and to Captain who awaited us. The Europeans then emerged, looking pleased, and waved toward Pena.

"Is that it?" I asked him on our walk back down the muddy slope.

"That's it, my friend," he answered nonchalantly, patting the satchel again. "We will talk more of our own possible business arrangement when we are back in Kurupung."

I nodded agreement, but wondered how well he did with the syndicate. I was sure he would confide in me since he always seemed so open with me.

On the trip back down river, although it was early

afternoon with the blazing sun still high in the sky, I took no notice of the heat or our surroundings. I was lost in reverie about ways to enter into a business arrangement with Pena so I could sell his diamonds on my return to the States. Obviously, he would want some type of long-term guarantee, and a good — or better — profit than he had been receiving from the Dutch syndicate. Also, there was the all-important part of the business deal — my own profit. I came up with no ready answers but knew I would have to think it through before Pena and I spoke again.

Before long we again were at the mouth of the Kurupung River and moving rapidly toward the village. The same abandoned dugout came into view, and I stared at the bleakness that surrounded it. Neither Pena nor Captain glanced in its direction.

By the time we pulled into Kurupung, it was late afternoon. A few of the natives greeted us and inquired of our trip and of Tumureng. The only mention of any mishap to any *pork-knocker* was a brief comment by Captain to the fact that there was an empty dugout a few miles down river if anybody needed one.

On our return to Pena's shack, Silva told us of Shanks' visit and his message that he would return the following morning.

That night, as I once again lay in my hammock in Pena's hut, watching the rats that scurried overhead, I wondered about our next pit and whether or not it would turn up any diamonds — or gold.

That dream, would remain just that, a dream.


The next morning, Shanks was back but without any equipment. When I asked why, he had replied that "there was too much water" and that our efforts "would be useless."

I must have shown some disappointment because Pena, who stood nearby, stepped in to offer a suggestion.

"Perhaps he would like to hunt," he told Shanks.

That word triggered an immediate reaction in me that I had not thought about since I had hunted in Central America.

"What game?" I eagerly asked both.

Shanks was the first to respond. "*Pingos*, boar, jaguar..."

Before he had time to mention another type of game, I stopped him.

"Jaguar!" I repeated aloud.

"Yes," he answered. "All types." He rattled off a string of Indian names with their descriptions. One variety he mentioned was an *achebana*. The name intrigued me, and I wanted to know more about it. I had heard of none of those he cited, and was only aware of the one type of jaguar, the spotted variety that more resembled a large leopard.

"When?" I wanted to know.

"There is danger," Shanks added.

I shrugged at the comment and Shanks looked at Pena who held up his hands to indicate that it was up to him to decide.

"Tomorrow morning," he said in a low voice, "early is best — very early."

# 14

Early the following morning, as the first rays of the sun penetrated the *mora* trees at the edge of the village, Shanks was there. He had his machete, as usual, and also carried an old single-barreled shotgun, devoid of most of the bluing on its surface. In contrast, I carried a double-barreled 16-gauge shotgun, and of course, my own machete and .357 magnum pistol.

From a clearing near the huts, Shanks pointed toward Mt. Watabaru, the rock-like plateau seven miles from the village that was to be our destination. He believed that the big cats were to be found in that vicinity, and I looked forward to the challenge.

At that stage of our journey, little did I realize that the hunt for a kill would encompass a grueling three full days — day and night — to accomplish.

It was a matter of minutes from the warm brightness to the dampness of the jungle that swallowed us. Overhead, I saw only the trees' foliage that blotted out the sunlight like an eclipse. Shanks trudged ahead of me, swinging his razor-like machete whenever the brush made it necessary. Watching his slight limp as he moved ahead at a steady pace, I felt a little sorry for forcing him into a hunt merely to fulfill an impulse. However, he never mentioned his leg, and I didn't want to raise the subject.

After a mile or more, he abruptly left the narrow *line* we had been following and ducked and hacked his way farther into the bush. I mimicked his movements as I gripped my shotgun in my left hand and swung my machete with my right. Rotten limbs and trees, perils that I had become accustomed to, crashed near us. Shallow creeks interrupted our path, but unhesitatingly Shanks' leathery bare feet easily waded through. My clumsy GI boots sloshed heavily across them, weighing me down. In some sections, where the ground looked solid, we'd sink a foot deep in thick mud. All the while, the ever-present mosquitoes, gnats and flies buzzed incessantly around us. They didn't seem to bother Shanks as much, and I should have been used to them, but I wasn't. In sections where we had not been before, thorns and sawgrass ripped into my hands and arms and only caused the insects' unceasing attacks to intensify.

The *miburi*, those molecular insects that infested the leaves, burrowed themselves in my arms, burning and itching skin that wasn't already torn. To add to the discomfort, small but potent red ants that also clung to the foliage, swarmed over me, inflicting miniature stings that felt like tiny drops of acid. I began to wonder if it was all worth it. The deeper in we got, the more tangled it became and the harder it was to see clearly. Visibility and effectiveness for a good shot were cut to about thirty feet — sometimes less. At intervals, whenever we came into partial clearings, Shanks would hold up his arm for me to stop, and then would blow a peculiar series of notes on a crude tin whistle. The first time he did it, I questioned him quietly.

"For the *acouri*," he said in a low voice.

I knew they were the wild rabbits of the jungle, but didn't know the connection between the *acouris* and the jaguars.

Shanks must've anticipated my question.

"If jaguar hears sound, he come too," Shanks added.

With that pointed comment, anticipation built within me, and all the skin irritations that I experienced became secondary.

Each time he blew the notes, I released the safety on my shotgun and stood and waited as my eyes continually searched the green wall of jungle that surrounded us. Each time, I expected to see a jaguar break through that wall — but it never happened. Even the *acouri* stayed out of sight. Each time, Shanks dejectedly shook his head and silently motioned me ahead again.

The closer we came to Watabaru, the tougher the trek became. The terrain sloped upward, and as the climb became steeper, I periodically lost my footing, my slick boots causing me to slip on the moist vines underfoot.

Shanks, who had been continually scanning the ground, stopped short and bent down. He pointed out a jaguar track as large as my fist. My blood raced at the first sight of my quarry's prints. He also found the solitary tracks of a *pingo*, the abundant wild pigs prevalent in that area. Undoubtedly, the jaguar was on the prowl for a meal. However, half a mile later, it became dense and matted at the base of Watabaru, and the rains and mud had obliterated everything. We had to abandon our relentless stalk.

The hunt continued the balance of the day. By the time we both wearily and silently trudged back into the settlement, we had trekked twelve miles. My shotgun felt like a lead pipe in my grip. I gladly laid it down inside my hut.

Late that afternoon, as we both sat outside Pena's building, other native *pork-knockers* approached us and wanted to know of our luck. We recounted our day's experiences, and they all told of episodes they had, or had heard about, with *tigres* in the past. One of the older natives started his tale and mentioned glimpsing an unusually large black one a month earlier. Intrigued by his description, I quickly questioned him. His reply was in their typical repetitive jargon.

"Him was big, big."

"How big?" I wanted to know.

"Maybe seven foot," he answered, indicating the length from its head to its tail. "Maybe more."

I looked at Shanks, who gave a slight nod.

Where had he seen it I asked?

"It go toward Perenong," he added.

The jagged peak of Mt. Perenong lay another seven miles from Mt. Watabaru. I realized it would be too much for Shanks to hike because of his leg. My tiredness and my aching body became secondary to my new goal, and when I asked him if he could take me to the area again, his excuse was weak. I glanced questioningly at the others, but none volunteered. Shanks remained silent as he looked around the group. I repeated my request for a guide. Finally, one of them blurted out the name, "Frenchie," and then assured me, "Him can. Him hunt good."

"Is he in the settlement?" I wanted to know.

The native said that he was and would try to find him. I stepped back inside the hut to tell Pena of my new plans and asked if he knew anything about someone named Frenchie. He said he did and that he seemed OK, but that he would check with Shanks.

A short while later, an almost ebony-black native entered the shack, and when I told him I needed him, his somber expression changed to a toothy grin.

"Me try. Me see," he told me.

I learned that he was from French Guiana, on the northeast of the South American coast, and had done much hunting there. We briefly discussed the hunt and where I wanted him to take me, and he agreed.

"When can we go?"

"Very late tonight," he answered.

I hesitated a moment. I didn't relish the thought of entering the jungle at night. He was adamant about the necessity of a night hunt, and when I questioned it, he was equally confident of its success.

"*Tigre* hunt at night, and we hunt *tigre* then," he said simply.

The time was set at three-thirty in the morning and I readily agreed without thinking. He then left as quickly as he entered. As I stepped outside again, Shanks and the others gathered around me. When I told them of my arrangement, some of the men shook their heads. Shanks, who had spoken briefly with Pena, was the first to speak. Frenchie, he said, had charms to protect him against snakes, but that I had none. He reminded me of the fever from the mosquitoes and of all the poisonous insects he had told me about, which I had seen in the daylight. At night, I would be able to see nothing, not even the jaguar I would be hunting. I was naturally concerned, but not enough to be dissuaded. They all wished me luck and left, but Shanks lingered. He said he wanted to go with us. Although I wanted him, I knew his injured leg would torture him. I tried to minimize the dangers and told him that he had taught me much, and I would be constantly aware. He looked at me steadily for a moment and then reached into his tattered cutoffs, pulling out what appeared to be a hardened root of some kind.

"Protection against jaguar," he said, as he placed it in my hand. "It is pumpkin's stem with pins in it."

When I asked what it all meant, he replied.

"Akawaio Indian charm. Pins prevent jaguar claws from closing."

I thanked him, and placed it in one of my patch pockets. His hand firmly grasped my arm and squeezed before he turned away silently and left.

At four-thirty in the morning, Frenchie rapped on the door of our hut, and came in. He quietly apologized for oversleeping. I said I understood but was a little annoyed. He had been the one to set the time, and I had been ready and waiting an hour for him. My pistol was loaded and checked, and I picked up my canteen and strapped it on. Instead of water, it contained "bush tea," a mixture that I had grown to like. I pushed a small loaf of bread Silva had prepared and two cans of sardines into one of my GI patch pockets. Into the other, I put additional shotgun shells. Because I had a double-barreled shotgun, I carried two types of British charges. One called SSG for the jaguar and a lighter load called BB for the snakes and smaller game. I broke open the shotgun, jammed an SSG into the right barrel, the BB in the left and clicked it shut. I glanced back toward Pena to see if there were any movement. There was none, and I was ready. We left.

Outside, clouds covered the moon. It was pitch black. There was no sound in the village, except for a couple of barking dogs at the far end. Rain fell lightly, and my body felt sticky. We flicked our flashlights on as Frenchie led the way. A short distance from the shack and we were at the edge of the settlement and on the brink of the jungle. It resembled a cave, a blackened cave of dripping vegetation — and the unknown.

A swollen creek, from the night's rain crossed our *line*. Frenchie stopped momentarily and sloshed through. I did the same. My pants, from the knees down, clung to my legs and the warm water seeped through the mud-laden boots and trickled over my feet and toes. When I reached the opposite side, I started to climb over a rotten log. Suddenly, my foot slid out from under me, and the butt of my shotgun slammed down hard on the top of the log, breaking my fall. Without stopping, Frenchie looked back to see me push myself to my feet. He continued weaving and ducking limbs and branches as we probed deeper and deeper into the jungle. Mosquitoes droned and stung my entire body without letup. Insects that clung to the leaves during the rain, invisible to me in the darkness, crawled over me. Macaws screeched in the night. Howler baboons passed overhead and set off their strange wind-like noises. Crashes in the jungle even made Frenchie stop to listen twice. For the balance of the night, I followed him into that unrelenting dark zone. The meager beams of light that darted from our small flashlights stabbed the inkiness that surrounded us and danced crazily with our erratic movements.

When daylight finally sifted through the trees, I tapped Frenchie on the shoulder to let him know that I wanted to lead. Although he knew the way at night, after countless days of trekking *lines* during daylight hours, I felt I could also discern the narrow paths in the jungle. I also wanted a first shot if and when we would raise a jaguar. After just a short distance, however, it became so tangled and overgrown that I couldn't see the *line*. Frenchie noticed my hesitation and motioned that he would go ahead again. I grudgingly acquiesced. That unanticipated sudden change in our positions proved to be an unexpected life-saving incident for me.

Frenchie had traveled less than a dozen steps or so when he stepped up on a fallen tree that blocked our path and prepared to step over it. Before he had a chance to place his foot on the ground, he abruptly stopped short and threw up his left hand to ward me back. Because his motion was without warning, and because I was literally on top of him, I almost pushed him forward. As he braced himself against my movement, he also lashed out with the machete in his right hand at something on the other side of the tree.

Frenchie's swift action neatly severed the head of a venomous *la baria* that was coiled and ready to strike. I heard the thick lifeless body thud heavily to the ground before I actually saw it.

He glanced at me momentarily, and I nodded appreciatively to him.

Had I been in the lead, I might have seen it first and acted accordingly — and then again, maybe not.

About eleven o'clock we came across a shallow creek bed to quench our thirst and decided to eat. As we sat on a fallen tree and I propped my shotgun beside me, we looked at each other silently. Frenchie broke the quiet by mumbling apologies for not being able to raise a *tigre* for me. I optimistically told him our luck would change after we ate.

"Me try," he told me again seriously.

From my pocket, I took out the soggy stale bread, pried open the sardine cans and wolfed it all down. Then I washed the food down with the half sour "tea" from my canteen. At that point in the hunt, a steak dinner couldn't have satisfied me more.

All the while I sat and ate, I constantly looked around half-expecting to see a jaguar break from the bush toward us. Frenchie must have had the same feeling, because he did the same, cradling his shotgun in his lap.

As we stepped out again and moved in the direction of Mt. Perenong, I felt disappointed with the hunt so far. Although my arms were raw and bleeding, they didn't bother me half as much as the fact that we hadn't caught so much as a glimpse of a big cat.

Suddenly, my daydreaming was interrupted as the solid, tangled bush that hugged the narrow *line* we were on crackled and splintered. I jerked my head to my right and saw a huge, black form parallel to me and less than ten feet away, crash back into the jungle. From the rear, which stood almost three feet off the ground and was about two feet in width, it resembled a bear. Without thinking, I pulled my shotgun to my shoulder to fire, and squeezed the trigger on the heavy load I had in my right barrel. It clicked harmlessly. Unbelieving, I adjusted my safety simultaneously and pulled it again. Same result, nothing happened. It was jammed. Before I could fire the lighter load in my left barrel, the dark form disappeared from sight in overgrown thickets. I cursed the gun, as I threw it to the ground and yelled for Frenchie to follow me. I yanked my pistol from its holster and plunged into the bush after it. Frenchie circled away from me and headed in the same general direction, but the form had eluded both of us.

We returned back to the *line*, and Frenchie told me our prey was a *barim,* an anteater. I had never seen one that large, in or out of captivity. We both examined my shotgun, and Frenchie commented that I must have shaken something loose when it broke my fall earlier in the hunt. I didn't know if it affected both barrels and removed the lighter load from my left barrel to test the firing mechanism. Happily, it worked. He looked it over again and thought he could fix it after we returned to the village.

There also was the possibility that the shell itself was defective.

I was thankful that we saw a *barim* first, and not a jaguar. A defective shotgun, especially the barrel that contained a heavier charge, would have been useless to me when I needed it.

Fifteen hours after we began our nocturnal hunt, we trudged wearily back into Kurupung, at night again. The kerosene lamps that glowed eerily from within the huts were a welcome sight. Natives that were usually in their own huts milled around Pena's building. All were amazed at seeing us. They told me that some of the others and Shanks had searched for us even after the sun set. They had given me up as lost or dead. Shanks and Pena emerged from the shack and greeted me like someone risen from the grave.

That night I slept like I never had before. I was usually aware of any noises during the night and would immediately wake, but not that night.

The next morning, Frenchie stopped by to check my shotgun again. If a mechanism was loose, he couldn't find it, and we both double-checked to see if it would fire without a shell in the chamber. All seemed well. We both believed it to be a defective shell — or so we hoped.

Frenchie also told me he was going down river for about a week and was sorry he couldn't take me out on another prowl before he left. I knew Shanks' leg still troubled him so I circulated the word around that I wanted another guide. I waited for a response, but again, none volunteered.

That evening, as I sat outside my hut and oiled my guns, a native I knew only by sight as De Freitas, wandered by and stopped. The double-barreled shotgun intrigued him, and he wanted to inspect it. In the course of our broken conversation, he told me he originally came from the Brazilian border and of his hunting prowess there. I listened intently. When he casually mentioned that he had shot at a *tigre* the day before, I interrupted him and made him retell the entire episode. He told me that while he was hunting for a *pingo*, he spied and shot at a *"labba tigre,"* more commonly called ocelots, a smaller spotted species of cat. The color and size became secondary, only a kill was important to me now. He had wounded it and tracked it until the bush became too thick and twilight started to darken the jungle. That's when he abandoned the hunt and returned to the village.

I asked him if he would take me to the area again, but he refused. I pulled out some shotgun shells, offered them to him and promised him still more if we could locate the small *tigre* again. He thought about it a moment, and then eyed me silently before his outstretched hands greedily accepted them.

Dawn had faintly illuminated the moistened jungle as De Freitas rapped on the door of the hut. As Pena let him in, three small dogs rushed in wildly, yapping their heads off. Pena's continued concern was somewhat lessened when De Freitas advised him that they were the, "best hunters in Kurupung." To me, they didn't look like they could stand up to an *acouri*, much less a wounded *labba*. None of them stood over a foot high and at the most were two feet in length. De Freitas, too, didn't present an awe-inspiring picture. He carried a rusted, single-barreled shotgun and a long bayonet-type knife at his hip.

On the path to the Kurupung River, his face was expressionless as he asked me whether I was an accurate shot. When I dispelled his doubts, his face still remained blank. The three mongrels reached a small low Indian dugout and eagerly jumped in. We cautiously climbed in the still-rocking boat, and De Freitas pushed it away from the muddy bank.

From the settlement to our preliminary destination at Tacouba Creek, we paddled and bucked the tide upriver for about three miles. Unused to paddling, my arms and shoulders ached from pulling against the current as we swung off the Kurupung River and glided a quarter of a mile or so up Tacouba Creek. As soon as the dugout neared the muddy bank, the three dogs scrambled out and ran into the dense jungle that skirted the creek. De Freitas led the way, carefully following his footprints of the day before. Unlike Shanks and Frenchie, he wasn't quiet. When I questioned him about it, his answer was direct.

"*Tigre* smell dog, him come."

If the *labba*, or any other *tigre* were within miles of us, the dogs' scent would attract them, he said. As an afterthought, he also added that the section we would cover was known to have larger species of *tigre* and also a greater abundance of them.

His last statement was the most encouraging, and it was hard to curb my impatience.

For the next two or three miles, De Freitas moved slowly along his old path. It was off the *line*, and because the bush was so thick and he was without a machete to chop our path, we ducked and twisted our way. Vines as strong as ropes held us back. Thorns tore at my arms and enmeshed themselves in my shirt, scratching my chest and back.

Finally, we reached the spot where De Frietas had wounded the cat he told me about earlier. He stopped and pointed at the ground. I could barely make out a patch of reddish coloring that brightened the leaves on the damp jungle floor. The dogs sensed the blood and darted forward, barking and sniffing the earth.

We followed the dogs, and De Freitas reminded me of facts I had already learned from Shanks: to watch low-hanging branches as well as fallen trees that formed an angle with the ground, and also the tops of huge boulders that were weirdly interspersed in the overgrown jungle. All were know to be favorite spots for jaguars to rest and wait for quarry.

While we walked, De Freitas periodically whistled for *acouri* on a whistle similar to the one Shanks had used. Each time we would stop, listen and wait. After several of these attempts, we heard the dogs' barks change to distinctive yowls, and we knew they had located something. Noises in the distance drew closer, and we both stood motionless, hardly breathing. There were crashes in the jungle directly ahead, and we both raised our guns. Instead of our anticipated wounded *labba*, however, four or five *acouris* bounded in front of the excited dogs. Disappointed, I lowered my gun and De Frietas did the same. He called them back and sent them out again. We trailed them once more.

After following our zigzag pattern for a mile or two more, the dogs concentrated beyond us and their tone again indicated game. As soon as we reached them, we learned their reason. They stood amid hundreds of *pingo* tracks that had rumpled the mud and leaves. All three raced around in a frenzied state trying to smell out those of the jaguar. Finally, the oldest and smallest of the three singled out an imprint, and they all yapped out running, ready for a kill. Whether it was our wounded *labba*, or another jaguar we didn't know, but we forged behind the dogs as they led us toward Saganong Mountain.

The air was stifling, and hordes of unrelenting insects settled on us and clung to my clammy skin. The never-ending barking ahead of us drove us faster in quest of our quarry. The farther in we hiked, the swampier it became. We trampled through flat, oozing marshes that took too much time to go around. At the far side of one such patch of brownish ooze, De Freitas stopped and pointed out a jaguar pad as large as the sole of my GI boots.

"The *labba*?" I asked De Freitas in a hushed tone.

"Too big," he answered before starting out again.

As the slope toward the mountain increased, short steep hills rose around us. I knew that jaguar were also found in this type of locale, resting or looking for their own prey. Once on the move, streaking down one of those hills, a jaguar is like greased lightening. As the morose De Freitas stopped at the top of one such hill and looked around carefully, he told me of something I didn't realize.

The remnants of a dead pig might lay buried in the leaves of the lowlands we had just pushed through. If we had walked over or near a half-eaten carcass, a *tigre* might race down on us. They always take a vantage point near any meat that they've killed until they feel the urge to finish their meal.

After climbing ten to fifteen of such matted and knotted, greenish mounds of earth, De Freitas stopped suddenly and knelt down. He showed me a different set of jaguar tracks. I was amazed as I looked at the depth of its impression. Its imprint in the mud sank twice as far as my own. It must have been three hundred pounds or greater.

I didn't know whether this set was the same that the dogs had initially sensed among the *pingos*, or whether it, too, was different. This meant that we were tracking either two jaguars or three, a contingency I had not bargained for. De Freitas was unusually silent as he examined this latest set more closely. He calculated it had passed about twelve hours earlier. As he stood up and moved ahead slowly, he indicated the tracks of additional *pingos*. They had joined with the first group, evidently banding together for protection. All tracks headed in the same direction, toward the mountain.

It had been six hours since we began our hunt, and we decided it was a good time to eat and rest. Once the dogs got the call from their master, they came running back, panting with their tongues dangling out of the sides of their mouths.

De Freitas sat nearby on a log and started to feed the two younger ones, while I leaned against a fallen tree and propped my shotgun beside me. As I opened a can of sardines, the oldest dog came over to me and begged for a handout. I dug into it with my pocketknife as a fork and had just leaned toward her, when I stopped. There was a heavy crackling in the jungle behind us. I turned, by instinct, to see what had fallen. The sight that greeted me stunned me momentarily. Less than sixty feet away, crashing out of the bush with its head held low was a black jaguar, barreling toward the dog and me. I threw the can and my knife down and grabbed for my shotgun. It happened so fast that I knew I wasn't aiming accurately. I jammed the gun against my shoulder, yanked the trigger on my right barrel and fired. I didn't have time to even think about whether the shotgun would fire properly. The gun roared as the heavy load caught him in the head and shoulders and his body flipped over heavily. One of the younger dogs rushed forward, followed by the older one I fed, and then the other.

As the first dog reached the jaguar, the big cat sprang back on its haunches and lashed out savagely with its flashing claws. The sudden vicious attack caught the dog by surprise, and it screamed in pain as the jaguar ripped its neck open, almost tearing its head off. The other two held ground growling at the wounded animal. The jaguar bared its fangs and gave out its own throaty growl.

I sensed its momentary indecision and gripped the shotgun tightly into my shoulder, taking careful aim. I squeezed the trigger on the lighter load and the blast hit its neck and chest. It dropped back to the ground, with a deep gurgling sound welling up from its throat.

While I watched and waited, I saw the sides rise and contract in spasms as blood trickled from the mouth and the buckshot in its head. To put an end to its misery, I pulled my pistol out of its holster and put a final shot into the massive skull. The twitching stopped.

We both approached the dead form and marveled at its eight-foot length, from head to tail.

At that moment, if I had discovered a lost Amazonian city or hit a diamond strike, my dream of success wouldn't have been more complete.

# 15

It didn't take long for the word to get around the settlement that I had killed a "giant black *tigre.*" All were impressed and made a point of stopping by Pena's trading post to congratulate me and to view the huge hide. There were now numerous offers to guide me on another hunt for whatever game I chose. However, I was satisfied with what I considered a challenging kill and didn't find the need to repeat it again soon.

As soon as Shanks heard, he was back in Kurupung to see how I fared and to hear all the details of the kill. Exactly where were we when we saw it? Were we near Watabaru or Perenong? Was it on the move, or was it looking down at us from a resting perch? Then, an important question to him: what type of jaguar? Was it an *achebana*? That was the exotic-sounding species of big cat he had previously mentioned, and one that was said to inhabit that mountainous area. If it was, I answered, I didn't see any white stripes. It was just a big black jaguar. It looked more like an African panther, only larger. My answers satisfied him, and the subject was closed.

It wasn't until some time later that I learned that Akawaio Indians do not kill jaguars. They believe that if they do, one in turn will kill their children. I wasn't aware of that superstition before Shanks and I engaged on our first day's hunt. However, I did wonder about it afterward. I realized he was only acting as my guide, but would he have actively participated in the shoot if it became necessary? If there was a question of mortal danger to him or others, would he act contrary to his belief? I thought he would, but never raised the issue. I knew that Frenchie and De Freitas had no such qualms because they were black natives who specifically hunted *tigre*, not Indians indigenous to the region who had specific ingrained superstitions.

The week or so following my jaguar hunt, we did not resume our diamond prospecting because of intermittent light rains that would have made the task formidable, if not impossible. Also, Shanks' leg still seemed to trouble him, although he never complained. I just took in stride my inability to resume my digging and instead occupied my time hunting small game to eat. Not only did I provide *acouris, pingos,* and occasionally a macaw or two for our table, but also for the others in the settlement who came to Pena and me because they had little to eat. Some of the *pork-knocker*s did not plan well, but I still felt obliged to help them. Most appreciated my assistance.

One evening, a couple of days before the supply boat was due to arrive on fortnight, and on which I was scheduled to leave, two natives approached our shack and wanted to know if I wanted to see "the Great Falls." I didn't know what they were talking about and asked Pena for confirmation. He just shrugged his shoulders.

"Where?" I wanted to know.

"Saganong River," they said in unison.

Pena looked at them in doubt, and I dug out my large detailed topographical map and spread it out before them.

"Where?" I demanded as I jabbed a finger at our section.

They both examined it carefully and excitedly pointed to a stream on the map.

"Saganong River here," they said aloud.

I followed the place they indicated and while I saw

Saganong River, I did not see "the Great Falls." Neither did I see a mention of any other falls near the river. They were very insistent as to its existence, however, and even persuaded Pena of their sincerity.

"If there is a Great Falls there," he said to me, "they should know. They've prospected that area."

"You're sure?" I asked them.

They nodded their heads vigorously in agreement and kept repeating, "Great Falls, Great Falls," while they wildly waved their arms in the air.

"OK, I believe you," I said half-heartedly, trying to calm them down.

Although Pena seemed convinced, I didn't see how it was possible that there was a waterfall in that area since my very detailed map didn't show one.

"When can I see this Great Falls?" I asked mockingly.

They looked at each other questioningly, apparently waiting for the other to set the time.

One said "tomorrow," and the other nodded his head in affirmation. A time was set.

The next morning they both appeared, machetes in hand and we set off. I hadn't seen Shanks in a couple of days to ask his opinion, but it was worth an exploration as it was in an area I had not seen before.

The sun shone brightly until we entered the canopied covering of the jungle. Both natives hacked a path so there was little for me to do but follow. The direction they chose was unfamiliar to me, but the thick green vegetation surrounding us was not. I could tell that we were moving in the general direction of the mountains because the terrain slowly started upward. Before long, the new *line* that we were on suddenly changed to a steeper incline. I saw nothing ahead of us but trees and saplings perched on a sloping giant hill. They moved slowly forward bracing themselves carefully so they would not fall backward as they climbed. I was directly behind them, watching their tortuous ascent while trying to maintain my own balance on the slippery ground with my heavy boots.

The more we climbed, the greater the slant became, until it seemed we were at about a sixty-degree angle and constantly pulling ourselves upward. Occasionally, one or both of the natives glanced back to see if I was keeping up with them, and I waved them forward.

After what seemed like a couple of hours — perhaps more — one of them stopped and held up his hand for me to do the same. He then pointed to his ear and motioned to the left of our climb. At first I heard nothing over my own labored breathing, but as I rested and listened carefully, I heard a very dull roar in the distance. It sounded like thunder, but there had been no clouds in sight before we left. In fact, I hadn't seen any clouds in the sky that day whenever I looked up through the trees.

They both moved ahead cautiously, clutching at the small trees to pull themselves upward. I did the same while trying at the same time to keep the sling on my shotgun from sliding off my shoulder.

After a relatively short steep climb, they stopped in a partial clearing and anxiously beckoned me ahead to where they stood. I saw them outlined against the blue sky, and when I managed to reach their spot, I heard an awesome sound like that of a locomotive in the distance. Its dull roar, which was barely noticeable earlier through the protective barrier of the trees, was no longer muffled. It was now a gigantic crescendo of rushing water nearby. Both natives pointed excitedly in the direction of the tremendous roar.

"Great Falls, Great Falls," they exclaimed again.

Immediately to our left, and almost on the same level as we now stood was, as they described, a Great Falls, gushing over a precipice in huge torrents of water plunging downward.

From our vantage point, all I saw was the upper section of the waterfalls. We had not yet reached a stage where I could see its total drop, and I couldn't really see its full width at the top.

I stood transfixed at the beauty of blue cascading

water in the middle of green foliage.

The natives, obviously pleased at my reaction, again motioned me forward toward the falls themselves.

The closer we got to the waterfalls, the bigger it seemed in both width and volume of water tumbling downward. However, we still could not see how far it plunged to the creek below.

Finally, after perhaps another half-hour or more, with the three of us constantly hacking our way toward our goal, we were behind the falls. We were now on the top of a plateau and could see its source. The water apparently originated from some stream or river fed by some type of spring. It then poured into an immense holding pond from which the falls flowed over the side.

We located a shallow, narrow point in the river and successfully crossed to the other side. The huge pond, itself, was in the middle of a large grassy field, and we worked our way toward the edge of the plateau at the top of the falls. The deafening sound increased to the point where we could no longer communicate to each other without yelling.

The three of us cautiously approached the precipice over which the water tumbled downward. Looking below at what must have been Saganong River was even more of an awesome sight than I had first beheld. In the distance, I saw a valley of endless green foliage that was hard to fathom as being the tops of trees. A sparkling ribbon of blue water snaked through the valley. From the enormous pond — small lake was probably a more accurate description — water spilled over the edge of the summit to the main falls. The width at the top of the falls was a couple of hundred feet across, and the first spillage of water that fed the falls was an initial drop of about five or six feet. From this almost inconspicuous miniature amount of falling water, there was a funneling of water into the gigantic waterfalls at our feet. As I looked below at the rushing torrent of water, I calculated its descent to be at least three times higher than our own Niagara Falls. It could have been much more, but having no reference on my map to go by and only judging from looking straight down the cascade, I could not tell.

I was awestruck by the vision of what lay before me and had momentarily dismissed the thought of prospecting for diamonds as unimportant. Even the successful outcome of my jaguar hunt was temporarily pushed out of my mind. I couldn't visualize the sheer volume of water that would plummet over its summit in rainy season if what we now saw was the Guiana dry season.

The trek back to the settlement was accomplished in about half the time and was done in silence. The natives returned to their own huts and were satisfied that I was pleased with what I saw. Pena was not surprised.

"British Guiana is largely unexplored," he said. "Not many white men have been here. You may have been the first to see and climb the Great Falls."

At the time, I was too amazed at what I saw of something that shouldn't have been there, to think much about its "discovery," but would as time went by.

With the arrival of the supply boat, while I was out, came my first letter from home, and with it a copy of another long article that appeared in the Sunday supplement of the *Ft. Lauderdale News.*

Apparently, my foreign venture was still making news even though I was not around. I was naturally pleased when I saw the large spread by staff reporter Joe Bryant, a reporter I had never met but who evidently followed my progress via my family's news.

Below the catchy heading:

## "POSTAL CLERK SEEKS FORTUNE"

was a smaller subtitle:

### "No Diamonds Yet, Just Blisters"

Below the headline was a half-smiling photo of me looking confidently down at a machete in my hand. Beneath the photo was:

## "MARTY ROLAND
### ... he's still digging"

Although I never recalled posing for that particular shot, I had to admit it looked intriguing and certainly would pique the readers' interest.

The very informative story said in part:

"Ft. Lauderdale's diamond-hunting postal clerk, Marty Roland, has gathered a wealth of knowledge but no diamonds during the first month of his six-week expedition into the jungles of British Guiana. In a letter which arrived here this week, 10 days after it was dispatched by riverboat from his inaccessible camp, the 28-year-old veteran of World War II voiced the dream that spurs all prospectors onward.

"You never know when your spade will turn up a fortune," he wrote from his camp 200 miles in the interior near Kurupung, Mazaruni District.

Roland is the only white man in the settlement of 100.

The one interest of all 100 is diamonds, he wrote.

"'*Pork-knockers*', as the native diamond prospectors are called, live and breathe diamonds here. Everyone digs for diamonds, sells them and goes back in again. They've all hit a few times — different size stones ranging from one to five carats. There are some who have hit pockets and taken out hundreds of carats of valuable stones. A couple of them dug a couple of thousand carats out of one pit."

## "HIGHEST QUALITY

"This is the country for it. Diamonds of the highest quality have been found in this area." Roland said that for the two weeks he had been in this mountainous region he had worked long and hard. Up early each day, he hikes two and a half miles back into the jungle, swings his machete, axe and shovel for eight or nine hours — usually working in foot-deep mud and water — and then hikes back to camp.

"The first week was rough. I had blisters on top of my blisters and my arms, legs and back felt like somebody gave me a good working over. But I'm in good shape now."

"Insects are plentiful," Roland reported. "There are all types of animal life here and the rivers are filled with fish and creatures that aren't social — but I don't make a habit of swimming anyway."

Supplies are brought into the settlement twice a monthly by riverboat and everything seems to get scarce in the last few days before the packet arrives, he said.

But the adventurous clerk has found native food to his liking.

"After the time I've spent here I can eat anything that's not alive," he wrote.

"Eating native and Indian dishes and wild game, I've gained a few pounds."

His part aborigine guide is educating him in Indian beliefs and practices and "everything I should know about the bush.". . .

The lengthy article then delved into my diamond hunt being the "Latest in a Series" of adventures and went into my prior travels and my background.

At the conclusion of the article, the reporter closed out his piece with:

## "PLANS BOOK"

"Whether or not his diamond hunt is successful isn't too important to Roland. In fact, other than maybe buying out the Post Office Department, he has given little thought to how he would spend a fortune.

When he returns he plans to write a book about his adventure.

And he'll be back at his parcel post window in the main post office, he said — until his next vacation.

Incidentally, the roving Roland is not married.

"I could never get away on something like this if I were," he explained."

When I showed the newspaper story to Pena, he was amused.

"You are a famous mon," he said.

"I'd rather be a rich man," I replied more seriously.

"Time will tell," he said, and then added, "I hope you've thought about a possible business arrangement where we both can make money on the diamonds."

I nodded my head. "I'm working on it."

As I turned to leave, Pena called out to me. "Have you seen the three Englishmen yet? They arrived on today's boat."

# 16

I don't know who was more surprised, the new arrivals or me. Here in the middle of nowhere, in a dense rain forest, they come across a lone American prospector. For my part, I fully expected to be — and wanted to be — the only white man in a *pork-knocker* village. Instead, I had company.

They were a bit taken aback by my appearance. I had a month's growth of heavy black beard, was wearing muddy, disheveled army fatigues and had a gun belt with a large pistol on my hip. Even the shoelaces on my constantly water-soaked boots had rotted and were pieced together.

They, on the other hand, were all clean-shaven, and had on knee-length pants and low cut shoes. Two of the younger ones carried cameras and equipment, while the third man carried a new shotgun, or so it appeared. It was not like the other old rusted shotguns I had been used to seeing in the village, and it wasn't as weather beaten as mine had become.

The older man had sandy hair, was slight of build and of average height. He appeared to be in his mid- to late-forties and had an easy smile after he introduced himself.

"I'm Bill Fleming," he said, "here from England to take photos for my book."

We shook hands, and I introduced myself.

They all seemed a bit relieved when they learned that I was not some renegade bandit who had taken over the village.

Fleming introduced the two younger men who accompanied him.

The older of the two, holding one of the more expensive cameras, immediately sized me up for a picture.

"We can use him in the book," he enthusiastically told Fleming.

Fleming nodded.

"You're welcome to tag along with us, if you like."

I didn't relish the thought of other whites being in what I considered my village, but as I thought about it, I reconsidered.

Their cameras are better than my solitary one, I thought, and I could use some good photos.

Although I knew I had brought a fairly good professional model in with me — a Rolleiflex — their equipment seemed far superior to what I had.

"Thanks for the offer, I just might do that."

"Today, we'll probably just stay around Kurupung and get some local shots, but tomorrow we'll head out into the surrounding bush," he said.

The lead cameraman mulled it over.

"Sounds good to me, Bill. You're the boss."

That evening, I told Pena of my plans and asked if he had seen Shanks lately.

"No. Captain told me that his leg was bothering him more, but that he would try to see you soon."


The next morning, the three Englishmen appeared outside of Pena's shack.

"Would you like to accompany us today?" Fleming asked.

"I'm ready whenever you are," I answered.

"Now is a good time as any," he said, gesturing to the two cameramen behind him.

I retrieved my shotgun and a canteen of rainwater, and as I was exiting the shack, I buckled on my gun belt.

"Good photo," the cameraman said aloud as he snapped a quick shot of me outside the building.

It was the first of many photos he would take of me over the next day or so. Sometimes, they were unexpected, as this one had been, and sometimes they were posed for effect.

Look this way, or that way, he would say. Let's get a close-up shot of you with the trunk of that *mora* tree in the background, or of the river, or of any other scene that he thought was dramatic or representative of the jungle, especially if my pistol or shotgun were in view.

In response to a question by Fleming as to what else in the area would be worthwhile to appear in his book, I mentioned the Great Falls.

All were intrigued by my description of it, especially the lead cameraman. At the time, I was not concerned about sharing my knowledge of the Great Falls, in spite of Pena's comment about my possibly being the first white man to view it.

I advised them that it would be a difficult climb with their equipment, but nevertheless they were eager to see it, and I arranged the trek with the same two natives.


The following morning the six of us were back on the same trail I had trod two days earlier. It was almost as grueling on my second trip as it had been on my first, but the time seemed to pass quicker. Fleming, who apparently had been in the bush before, was in good shape for someone his age, and handled the climb well. The cameraman and his assistant, loaded down as they were, did not.

Finally, when we reached the level where we could see and hear the loud rumble of the falls, they were amazed at the sight and sound of it. Countless pictures were taken to satisfy all involved before we moved clos-er to the Great Falls. Fortunately, the path had been recently hacked by us and the approach to the river was made in record time. We crossed in the same location as before, and the three of us led the others to the same site where we had stood and gazed out and down. For a moment, they were speechless, but it didn't take long for the photographers to shoot every conceivable angle of the falls, and us in the foreground.

Before our rapid descent back down the mountain-side, Fleming thanked me profusely.

"Copies of some of the photos, are thanks enough," I assured him.

"I'll remind them," he said sincerely.

However, it never happened.

When we got back, Pena was busy in his store arranging supplies that had just arrived on the boat. Before I entering the shack, however, I noticed the boat had moved from its original mooring spot to another place on the riverbank. There also was some activity around it.

"Is something the matter with the boat?" I asked.

"It needs some minor work," he answered, "and they will remain here a little longer."

I was a little concerned, as I had given the pilot that flew me to Tumureng, an approximate date to pick me up.

"Did they say when?"

"The repairs should be finished today, and they will be ready to leave tomorrow," he said.

"I hope so."

"Did you give the pilot an exact date?"

"No, I allowed a couple of extra days as I didn't know how far I would be from Tumureng."

"It will be fine, then," he assured me.

"Any word on Shanks?"

"He told Captain to tell me he would see us

tonight."

"Good, I'll miss him. He taught me a lot."

"I'm sure he'll miss you too, my friend," he replied, and then added, "I regret your prospecting was not profitable."

"Me too," I said slowly as I shook my head. "It was the off-season rains."

"Speaking of the diamonds," he continued, "are we together?"

I nodded enthusiastically.

"All I have to do is find an investor with money who's willing to invest in diamonds."

"Do you expect it to be difficult?"

"I don't think so," I replied confidently. "There's a lot of money in South Florida and..." I continued, "...I have had a lot of publicity on my expedition."

"If I haven't already told you," he went on, "we will share fifty-fifty in the profits."

I smiled at his offer.

"You know how little I make from the syndicate," he said. "I feel sure that there is more money to be gotten from your country."

"It's worth a try," I said.

"However," he cautioned, "it would have to be long term, as once I leave the syndicate I will not be able to return."

"I'll do my best," I said, firmly shaking his hand.

"I'm sure you will my friend. I trust you."


For the next hour or so, I gathered whatever meager gear I had spread out in our sleeping area because I wasn't sure when the boat would leave.

It was still light enough to be outside so I took a short walk to say my good-byes to those I knew.

When I returned to the hut, De Freitas, my guide on the third day of my successful jaguar hunt, had stopped by to see me. He always stopped in whenever he was in the vicinity. Apparently, there was a closer bond between us than he shared with other *pork-knock-ers* because of our recent hunt.

The topic, as always, was of *tigres*. Did I intend to go out again or would I continue my prospecting?

As he had not heard of my departure plans, I told him.

"The diamonds are not good now because of the rains," he reminded me, "but hunting is."

"I must leave, though."

"It is too bad," he said. "You are a good hunter."

"If I have time before I return home, I'll try the Rupununi District," I said.

I had heard that jaguars were plentiful in that section of country before I decided to head into the Mazaruni District. However, because diamonds were my priority, I decided to concentrate on the upper part of British Guiana.

As soon as I mentioned Rupununi to De Frietas, he spoke glowingly of the section. He spoke in stilted English and occasionally lapsed into Portuguese. It was in the southern part of the country near his native Brazil. The *tigres* there were the biggest and most ferocious because of the cattle in the low-lying area.

His descriptions and his vivid accounts triggered my urge, again, to hunt *tigres,* and I made a mental note to fly there from Georgetown for a few days before I returned to the states.


As promised, Shanks stopped by that evening. I noticed that he was in pain with his leg.

"I am sorry that I have been unable to spend more time with you to tell you more of the bush," he said. "Also...I am sorry about the diamonds."

"It's not your fault," I assured him. "It was the rains."

He nodded in agreement.

While we spoke, I saw him grimace periodically as he silently clutched at his leg.

"I hope you heal soon."

He smiled slightly and reached into his tattered shorts.

"These are for you," he said, extracting two items for me.

The first one was a thick, yellowed fang about two-and-a-half to three inches long, that I assumed was from a jaguar.

He held the large tooth up to his mouth in a downward position to indicate where it came from.

"Wear it around your neck for luck," he said, pointing to a small hole drilled near its base.

The second item that he placed in my hand looked like a small chunk of hardened tar.

"*Curare*," he said. "It is for the tips of arrows or spears."

I had heard of *curare*, the poison that Jivaro Indians used to slow down, or kill, game they hunted — or their enemies.

"It can be melted down to use whatever amount you need," he explained.

When I thanked him, he simply rose slowly and grasped my hand and arm.

"I must go now," he said with finality.

I never saw him again to bid him goodbye. I never received a letter from him after my return to the states, either.


It was early afternoon before I again boarded the same supply boat that took me there a month earlier. There were a few *pork-knockers* at the landing to wave me off, as well as the Englishmen.

Fleming said he appreciated the trek to the falls, and the photographers promised me copies. Although I gave them my address, I neglected to get theirs, or for that matter, for whom they worked. It was a big mistake on my part, because they never kept their word, and I was unable to follow-up.

Pena was the last to see me off and shook my hand warmly.

In it, he placed a small, thick brown envelope.

I looked at him questioningly and started to open it.

"Not yet," he cautioned me. "Open it when you get to Georgetown. There are some diamonds," he continued, "and gold dust from the *pork-knockers* for all you have done for them."

"It was nothing," I said. "I did what I could."

"We will be in touch," he promised.

Unlike my initial trip, the boat was not loaded down with supplies and livestock. I was one of only a few passengers going up river, and was immersed in my own thoughts as we chugged up the Kurupung and then into the Mazaruni.

When the settlement of Tumureng finally came into view, I realized I was not looking forward to disembarking. I had actually grown accustomed to my environment and to the daily challenge of life in the jungle, and knew I would miss it.

# 17

The stillness of the jungle was disturbed by the ever-increasing sound of an approaching airplane overhead. Its steady drone changed to a loud hum before it splashed down noisily on the Mazaruni.

Natives, who steadily watched it make its steep descent over the trees, gathered at the water's edge as it taxied toward the landing at Tumureng. The roar of the Grumman Amphib's engine drowned out the yapping of the dogs in the village until the pilot cut its power and it rocked to a bobbing stop in the muddy river.

I was part of that group of natives who awaited the pilot as he exited his aircraft.

He stared at me momentarily in disbelief.

"You've changed," he said briefly, as he looked at me.

The last time he saw me, I was clean-shaven and wore neat fatigues with fully laced dry boots.

This time, I was the grimy disheveled prospector that the Englishmen saw when they arrived in Kurupung.

"Been waiting long?" he asked.

"A day or so," I answered.

"As soon as they unload and load up whatever goes back, we'll be off," he said.

"I'm ready, whenever you are."

"Probably an hour, maybe less," he noted, as he observed the natives unloading his plane.

I nodded acknowledgment and moved out of the way

of the activity to sit on the bank beside my own gear.

With the last of boxes and my own equipment lashed into place on the plane, the pilot motioned for me to board.

"You're my only passenger today," he said. "I'm sure you'll find it a little different than your last time." He was undoubtedly referring to the native woman who threw up in the aisle.

"I didn't think you'd remember I was a passenger then."

"It was a flight that's hard to forget. And one I hope doesn't happen again," he said, pinching his nose.

I found an empty seat near the window so I could see the riverbank and the natives moving away from the seaplane as the engine kicked over. Its fuselage sat low enough in the water that if there was an open porthole, I could probably have touched the water.

At first, the plane moved slowly across the river, and then it picked up speed as it sought to lift itself from its watery path. Waves churned beneath it, heavily slapping the lower section of the aircraft and temporarily obscuring the window. Suddenly, the pilot pulled back on the controls and we were airborne. The plane rose quickly to avoid the surrounding trees and banked sharply to head back to the coast.

I glanced out the window and saw the village of Tumureng rapidly disappear from view. Once more, we were over thick, impenetrable jungle. This time, however, I was not in awe of what sprawled below me. Even if for some reason we were forced down into that tangle of unyielding foliage, I knew I could survive.

The drone of the engine was hypnotic as I tried to recall all that I had seen and done — and learned from Shanks. The longer we flew, however, the more my thoughts were replaced by plans to head into the Rupununi District for one more jaguar hunt. I wondered about the cost of chartering a new flight and when it would leave. I made a mental note to check with the pilot when I deplaned since I didn't know the Guiana Airways office hours.

With those plans temporarily resolved, my next thought was of returning home. I hadn't accomplished what I wanted. I wasn't coming back with a fortune in diamonds as I hoped I would. For some reason, however, that fact no longer seemed important to me. I had seen much, done a lot and learned even more. I realized, looking out at that endless expanse of unbroken jungle, that my experience was invaluable, and that no amount of money could buy that.

As soon as that thought crossed my mind, I recalled the small brown envelope that Pena had pressed into my hand. I took it from my patch pocket. When I carefully opened it, not wanting its contents to spill out should we encounter any rough flying, I saw what appeared to be several small diamonds at the bottom and a miniature brown envelope. I gently fingered the small stones, trying to determine the number in the envelope but couldn't. I then slowly lifted the miniature brown envelope to the top of the larger envelope without removing it completely. It was lumpy and sealed with tape. *It must be the gold dust,* I thought, replacing it in the envelope. I returned the entire packet to my pants pocket and smiled to myself as I patted it reassuringly. *I wonder how much it's worth?* I thought.


We had been airborne over two hours when the pilot, whose door was open, yelled back to me.

"Georgetown!" he said, pointing ahead.

Through his windshield, I saw the outlines of the city in the distance.

He pushed forward on the controls and the seaplane began its slow descent toward the Demarara River that sprawled beneath us. It continued its gentle downward movement until the pilot banked it hard to be directly in line with the wide river. Within minutes, he set the aircraft down on the water, and we bounced along on its rough surface toward the hangar that skirted the river at Guiana Airways. The pilot cut the Grumman's engine and we settled low in the water.

I looked at my watch and saw that it was mid-afternoon. I wondered if the office was open for information. I didn't see much activity.

The pilot confirmed that it probably was, although it was Wednesday afternoon, a comment that I assumed meant Wednesday was not a good day to arrive.

As soon as I scrambled off the plane and retrieved my gear, I asked the pilot if there were flights to Rupununi. He assured me there were, but that he did not personally fly into that district. The office would know the schedule, he said.

I found someone sitting behind a desk but also saw several people waiting for service. I chose not to wait and instead hailed a nearby taxi to take me back to the Tower Hotel, the place I initially checked into a month earlier.

If I appeared a little strange to the driver, he didn't comment. He only eyed my guns. Undoubtedly, he was used to seeing odd characters board and disembark from the craft at Guiana Airways.

The people in the crowded lobby of the hotel and the desk staff were another story. They all looked at me as though I were an alien who had just arrived on their planet. The desk clerk asked if I'd like to check my guns in their office.

I closely examined the small office that adjoined the front desk and didn't see any security for my weapons.

"No," I said. "I think I'll keep them with me."

"As you wish," he said, and handed me my key. "Is there anything else I can do for you?"

"Yes, I'd like to check out the suitcase I left here before I went into the bush."

It contained casual clothes I wore on the flight from the states, and I didn't want to take them into the interior.

He entered the adjacent office, looked around at the various cases, located mine and came back with it to the front desk.

While I awaited his return, I glanced at a nearby mirror and got a good look at my reflection. I didn't realize I looked as rough as I did, nor had I given it much thought until I was back in civilization.

*No wonder I drew all those stares,* I said to myself. *I look more like a renegade or a mercenary than a prospector.*

The clerk noticed me rubbing the beard on my face and pushing my fingers through my thick hair.

"Was there something else?" he wanted to know.

"Where can I get a haircut and a shave?" I asked.

"I'm sorry," he said. "Today is Wednesday, and the shops are all closed."

I figured as much. I retrieved my bag and took the elevator to my room. It was small but clean, with a small balcony that overlooked the city. As I unbuckled my gun belt and threw it on the bed, I sat down to remove my grimy boots. Unburdened of a load I had worn for a month, I walked back over to the open window to look around. I noticed a nearby hotel about a block away and saw two young females standing on their own balcony frantically waving at me to get my attention. Amused, I waved back, but because of the distance I couldn't tell what they looked like. Besides, I had a girlfriend back home. My immediate thought was a hot shower, not socializing long distance.

After a very long shower, I took another glimpse of myself in the bathroom mirror. Although I was cleaner, I didn't look any better and decided to rectify the situation. All I had in my bag was a safety razor. I had no scissors. With the safety razor only, I hacked away at the heavy month's growth of beard. It probably took me close to an hour to remove the thick bristle from my face and under my chin.

When it was done, the skin on the face was very tender, but I almost looked normal. I dressed in the casual clothes I had brought, hid my guns as best I could and went down to the lobby to find somewhere to eat. The same clerk who checked me in didn't recognize me, but obviously felt a little relieved and was more relaxed when I identified myself.

Although I had only been in the bush a month, and should've easily adjusted to being back in civilization, it still felt a little strange. Even after a leisurely hot meal in the hotel, and a cool beer, I was not quite as relaxed as I expected to be. I sort of half-missed some of Silva's meals that he prepared for Pena and me, especially a type of hot cake or pancake he frequently made.

Before returning to my room, I realized it was too late in the day to contact Guiana Airways about Rupununi flights for one more jaguar hunt.

Unfortunately, it was not in the cards.

Early the next morning, I called their office to inquire. There were no flights leaving until the following week, and the cost was more than I could afford. Disappointed at the news, I decided I would return to the states earlier than I had planned and booked a flight for the weekend. Armed with the specifics of the flight, I wired my family of the news. By the next day, I received a return telegram telling me how overjoyed they were and that "everybody in town" was told.

Since I still had two days remaining in Georgetown, I wandered around playing tourist again. On one of my walks near the hotel, I saw a tailor shop that made custom suits and stopped to ask about the cost and time element. They set a very reasonable price that I couldn't turn down and guaranteed delivery before I left. Measurements were taken, and I chose a suit and a sports jacket. The suit was a lightweight beige fabric, and the jacket was light blue. I had heard of custom-made suits done in Hong Kong that were extremely reasonable, but wasn't aware that British Guiana tailors were equally proficient and low cost. As promised, they both were ready before my flight was scheduled to depart, and I was not disappointed in the result. The beige suit cost twenty-eight dollars, and the blue jacket twenty-five dollars. They both fit like a glove.

On the plane back to Miami, I was pleased with myself and feeling more relaxed. Not only had I made a good purchase, but also my solo expedition into British

Guiana's uncharted interior was an adventure that few could imitate. Truthfully, however, I was slightly disheartened about not bringing back the fortune in diamonds that I had sought. The *Argosy Magazine* article by some Italian count who discovered a half million dollars worth of diamonds, had inflamed my imagination. It was his story that triggered my own venture in the hope of duplicating his prospecting success.

My own unique successes I felt — or tried to convince myself — exceeded his efforts in the Venezuelan jungles. *Besides*, I said to myself, *I do have some diamonds*.

I was tempted to take out the brown envelope and inspect the diamonds that Pena gave me but decided against it. Counting diamonds in an airliner, however surreptitiously, was not a wise move. That action would have to wait until I got home.

As long and tedious as that flight was, my daydreams of the potential of the joint partnership arrangement with Pena filled much of my thoughts, as did my recollections of the entire trip.

"Approaching the Florida coastline," clicked in over the intercom, and I strained to see the white sandy beaches.

"Kindly fasten your seatbelts," the pilot intoned. "We will be landing in about twenty minutes."

The Miami International Airport came into view, but instead of the pilot placing the aircraft on a downward leg, I noted that the airplane began a wide sweeping circle of the airport. I dismissed it temporarily, but when his initial circle was completed, he began a second one. Some of the other passengers looked a little concerned as the plane moved away from the landing strip. Before any of the passengers could ask the stewardess what was happening, the pilot clicked on again.

"I'm sorry for the delay," he said calmly, "but we are experiencing a little difficulty with our landing gear."

The stewardess, who had been summoned to the cabin, returned after a few minutes.

"Nothing to be alarmed about," she said to some of the passengers who asked exactly what was happening. "It should be resolved shortly."

However, "shortly," did not materialize.

On our third sweep of the airport, we were directed to fly in at a lower altitude over a remote runway.

As the aircraft banked over the area, we all saw emergency vehicles with flashing red lights racing toward our landing strip.

The pilot came on the intercom again.

"At the present time, we are still unable to get the landing gear down. However, preparations are being made on the ground to minimize our landing," he said in a controlled voice. He then added in a more assured tone, "We are still attempting to rectify the problem."

There was no panic among the passengers. In fact, the cabin was strangely silent. All eyes stared out windows, trying to see the activity below.

The only thought that crossed my mind was, *Great! I fly deep into the Guiana jungles without a mishap only to have a crash landing when I arrive home!*

However, the crash landing never happened. Somehow the pilot managed to get the landing gear down and locked into place before we touched down.

We did learn that the "preparations being made on the ground to minimize our landing" included foaming the runway, a contingency that we thankfully didn't have to use.

After the pilot and the crew were congratulated on their skill and professionalism, the airplane rolled to a stop and the cabin door was opened for us to exit the aircraft.

Before any of the passengers had a chance to disembark, a representative of the airlines boarded the plane first and called out my name.

"Would Mr. Marty Roland please step forward and follow me."

Amazed, I looked at the other passengers and wondered what was happening. From the puzzled expressions on their faces, they were wondering as well.

The smiling representative led me to the bottom of the ramp where an eager photographer stood, camera in hand and began to snap my picture.

# 18

The days that followed my return home were hectic, with an endless cycle of parties, talks and newspaper interviews.

The first welcome-home event was, of course, the house party to which my family and close friends were invited to see and talk to me about my experiences.

That relatively small reception was followed by a noisier group of supporters who welcomed me back at my local hangout, the Elbow Room, a Fort Lauderdale Beach bar at the corner of E. Las Olas Boulevard and Ocean Drive.

So many of my friends and acquaintances crowded into that small drinking establishment that someone decided a more formal reception would be more appropriate.

A small hotel with a pool was suggested and arrangements were made to hold it a week later.

Food and drinks were available for all those who wanted to officially meet "Fort Lauderdale's own diamond hunter."

In the interim, the *Miami Herald* ran two full-length articles on succeeding days mid week.

The first article showed a serious-looking close-up photo of me that the photographer had taken at the Miami airport. Below the picture was the appealing caption:

## "MARTY ROLAND
### . . .gems in his pocket"

The large headline of the story:

## "ADVENTUROUS POSTAL CLERK
## COMES HOME WITH DIAMONDS"

had a smaller sub-title below it:

### "Vacation Breaks Even"

The very informative piece read:

"FORT LAUDERDALE — Marty Roland, the adventurous postal clerk, came home from the jungle Wednesday with diamonds clinking in his pocket.

He had three fair-sized stones that he estimated would make one carat and five or six smaller ones that would go about another carat.

"That may be about $1,000," Marty said.

He's going to a jeweler's Thursday morning to see if he's right. If he is, then he's just about broken even on his vacation, which cost him about $900.

Marty expects his trip deep into British Guiana to continue paying off. He made arrangements with a native to market any stones the native finds. They find them fairly often.

He had to admit he didn't find the stones he brought back. The biggest was given to him by a native who sympathized with him because he wasn't having any luck finding them himself.

Others he bought at "bush-prices."

"You just give them what they consider fair price," he said. He indicated that wasn't much.

Marty flew to Georgetown, British Guiana,

on the first leg of his vacation trip six weeks ago. He had read about rich diamond finds in the hills west of Georgetown and he decided to try his luck. He advertised in Fort Lauderdale for a companion but none turned up.

From Georgetown he flew in a British Guiana Airways plane for 175 miles westward, to Tumereng, then took a riverboat. He acquired a native guide at a little town called Kurupung who took him to an area owned by natives who had dug around in the hills and stream beds for diamonds.

Marty was given a shack to live in and permission to dig. He dug like mad but didn't find anything. He had to hunt to provide food for himself and the guide — wild pig, bush turkeys and a kind of pheasant — and they fished.

The natives liked Marty and he made an arrangement with one which he thinks may turn into a pretty fair source of revenue.

He's been knocking around in unlikely places on vacations for several years. British Guiana was all right, he says, but "I've had it." He's not going back right away.

He'll be at the parcel post window in the main post office again Monday."

The only discrepancy in the article was the mentioned that I bought some of the diamonds at "bush prices." All were given to me by the natives who appreciated my efforts for them and were sorry that I was unsuccessful with my own pits.

The reference to "bush prices" dealt with my private deals with Pena.

The second article, even longer, and remarkably detailed had a picture of two men and me.

Below the photo there was a description of the scene:

**"DIAMONDS HE FOUND** in the jungles are examined through a microscope by Marty Roland with the help of jewelers Morris Walters, left, and Herman Davis."

At the top of the long piece was an intriguing caption that would catch the reader's eye:

## "British Guiana's Interior Is Enough to Frighten You

"FORT LAUDERDALE — The interior of British Guiana is the sort of place where your reflexes are always prepared for the appearance of poisonous snakes, tarantulas, jaguars, centipedes and a myriad of stinging insects.

"It only takes a couple of days for you to learn to see things out of the corner of your eye," says Marty Roland, one-man diamond-hunting expedition.

"You may be looking up in a tree and at the same time a snake may move on the ground, but you see it anyway. You get so that you're conscious of any movement around you.

"You wake up every two hours or more often at night to check around for snakes or insects."

The forest blacks out the sky. Snakes, exotic birds, monkeys, the big cats, vicious insects and natives live together in a continuous cold war conducted in a twilight world. Only rarely is there a break in the forest roof that permits a glimpse of the sky.

The natives manage to survive with homemade remedies used for centuries, to protect them from the effects of snake and insect bites. Marty, who spent a month with them, took along a snake bite kit.

"I had it the first day and then threw it away," he says. "The natives have herbs and their own medicines and they're better."

Even taking a bath is dangerous. It has to be done in streams which contain fresh water sting rays, giant electric eels and *piranha*, vicious small fish that attack just about everything.

"You go in up to your waist and keep a careful watch while you bathe, says Marty. He saw an electric eel about six feet long. The shock from one of them could momentarily paralyze a man.

When walking you don't keep your head down to see where each foot is going to avoid stepping on a dangerous snake. You just keep looking and if there's a snake there, you become so alert that you'll see it, he says.

Marty, who made immediate friends with the Indians and lived among them while he hunted for diamonds, came back with six diamonds that are now in New York to be appraised. He found none himself, but was given the largest and purchased the rest from the Indians.

He went there on vacation from his job at the parcel post window in the main post office. He's now back and awaiting the results of a deal he worked up with an Indian under which he'll market diamonds the Indian finds."

By the time the weekend rolled around, there were very few in town who had not seen the stories — and it seemed most of them showed up at the pool/reception party.

As a result, there were probably as many "gate-crashers," who didn't know me, as there were those who did.

Human nature being what it is, I learned that even after the extensive coverage the newspapers gave me — before I left and after my return — there were those who didn't believe what they read. One particular "gate-crasher" to whom I talked, didn't know who I was and was adamant in his reaction to all the stories about me he had heard or read.

"I don't believe any of it," he insisted. "Nobody would be crazy enough to do all the things that this guy said he did."

Without revealing my identity — although I was tempted — I couldn't convince him that there were indeed people like that in the world, of similar temperament, who acted on their inclinations regardless of difficulties or dangers involved.

Fortunately, his disbelief was in the minority because I was asked to give talks to local fraternal and civic groups, and even to a PTA meeting at an elementary school.

Shortly after my return, mail that had been sent to the Tower Hotel in Georgetown was forwarded to my home address in the states.

One such memorable letter was from my long-suffering mother who had constantly endured the "abnormal" youthful activities of both her sons. (My kid sister was fine). I was the first to try to enlist in the Navy at the end of World War II while I was sixteen. (They made me wait until I turned seventeen). Then, while I was overseas, my younger brother took my birth certificate to fraudulently enlist in the Army. Although he succeeded, there was a myriad of problems after both our discharges because he refused to change back to his name at birth. To complicate the situation further, I was receiving a disability from the Veteran's Administration while he was medically retired from the Army because of injury.

The letter, in part, read:

"You have no idea how everybody constantly inquires about you. Including all the prayers and candles lit for you. However, diamonds or no diamonds, I'm sure you'll get a royal welcome. Everybody's anxious to see you back safely since we all miss you." The balance of the letter was of family news of my brother and of my sister, who was going to make me an uncle. My mother then closed out her poignant letter by writing that she had spoken to my girlfriend, a "few times," and that "she truly is sweet." — a fact I never disputed. However, my very concerned and overly patient mother felt compelled to add:

"And know if you'll marry her, will be very happy. And am quite sure she will be the one to have you settle down to a normal life. Can't stand any more of this coming and going. . ."

The marriage, however, never happened, nor did the "settling down to a normal life" — much to her dismay.

An even more interesting letter greeted me when I returned to work the following week. It was addressed to "Jungle Marty Roland" from a Bill Smith, a man who claimed to be in the Latin America export business.

His short note read:

> "You left here too soon, the fellow you read about in the *Reader's Digest,* Jim Angel, that discovered the Angel Falls in Venezuela and found the big gold mine — just arrived here and flew on charter plane back in the jungle. He might have taken you along."

The individual that Smith referred to in his letter was the renowned explorer, Jimmy Angel, who discovered the 3,000 foot waterfalls in South America — reputed to be the world's highest — that was subsequently named in his honor.

His discovery had only occurred a year or so earlier and had been in the same general area as my own Great Falls.

Angel Falls was situated in the extreme eastern section of Venezuela, while the Great Falls lay in the far western section of British Guiana. However, I never checked the proximity of both falls, as I was unaware of the location of Angel Falls before I initiated my own solitary expedition. Subsequent inspection of topographical maps of the region revealed that both falls were on the same general latitude. My own "discovery" and exploration of that unknown and uncharted falls in British Guiana was a recognition that I sought years later  but, unfortunately was unable to perfect.

Although the publicity of my venture died out within a few weeks, the flames of that notoriety did not die out within me. Before I was able to plan, or even think about, any future junkets, however, I had to concentrate on the business arrangement — concerning diamonds — that Pena and I had discussed before I left Kurupung.

It wasn't long before I was reminded of our association.

# 19

In a short letter, dated 29/9/55, (the day always preceded the month) Pena anxiously responded to a post card I had mailed him from Georgetown:

"I received your card with no address so I am replying to your last address. Don't know if it would reach you. Yes, I really imagine something was wrong with you. Anyway I am please to hear that you are alive and strong. So sorry that you were not keeping in touch with me. The men shot about eight jaguars here which you could of got the skins. Let me know as early as possible if you are still interested in the skins. This is a fine season for you to be out here. Everyone who knew you, were please to hear of you.

With best regards and hoping to hear from you early."

In a continuing effort to keep me informed of his ongoing activities, he also forwarded me a copy of a formal request he sent a week later to the Officer-in-Charge of the River District in Stewartville.

In the same format, it was dated 5/10/55, and read:

"Sir

I hereby beg to apply for a Permission to own and carry a revolver. I am carrying on a shop in this District and have to be conveying Diamonds and other valuables from here to Tumureng, which is quite a long distance, and think it necessary.

Thanking you in Advance.
Yrs. Respectfully
Lionel A. Pena"

Although we had been fairly close in our short association, I was unaware that his first name was Lionel. He had never used it in my presence and had never addressed me by my first name.

Even in all our future letters, he would use the formal salutation, "Mr. Roland." Perhaps, it was his proper British training, but it was a practice that spilled over to the natives and Indians in the country. Shanks, my guide, always used his last name, although Andrew was his first name.

Pena wasn't the only one who initiated writing letters to me. In a very cordial letter, dated 23/10/55, Pena's servant, Joseph De Silva, wrote me a thank-you note that was addressed to "Mr Marty Roland:"

"Sir

Hooping the arrival of these few lines may find yourself and Mrs quite well. At presant thanks God I am still Alive. I received the parcle what you sent for me. But one peice of goods missin that is the cloak Sir I must thank you evour so much for your kindness you bestoed on me Sir. I am glad to hear from you of you return home safe It is fortnight Here and I am sitting and writing at the same time Our time is 12 oclock Midnight

> Good Night"

The verbatim simplistic letter shown above in no way denigrates the writer but is realistic of the very basic education afforded natives in more under-developed countries. His primitive writing style and word usage is overshadowed by his sincerity in expressing his gratitude to me for sending him a package from Georgetown before my departure. I knew there were items he needed and was unable to afford.

The reference to a "Mrs." in his note was his belief that I would be married upon my return home. It was a conviction that I not only shared with him and Pena but with the two constables, in the village as well.

A much longer letter from Pena, dated 4/11/55, showed his continuing interest in our business agreement and reflected my own persistent efforts to raise cash:

"Dear Mr Roland

I received your last letter and the other written in Geo.Town safe along with the articles sent which I must again thank you for. I hope by now you got the one that was addressed to you in Geo.Town from me. I note what you mention RE various calls and visits that is just what was expected, I only hope you would be compensated as you had a month of hustling here. The folks here think you quite an exception as you were so punctual to your promises.

About our proposition, I think it quite easy to get cash to me and the Bank would be able to certify what I receive and what was sent to you, the balance would be left to confidence. I hope you won't think that I am forcing you into this business, it is just that I see a way where we can earn some money, so if you can see anything doubtful in it I won't encourage you so it's all left to you.

My pit won't be finish before about the 15th of Dec as we took in another piece of land and estimate the whole to produce about 300 carrats. I read what you mention about prices in the States, although you did not mention the figures but according to what you wrote I can only imagine. I would expect to hear from you early then we should be definite about it.

Hopeing Yourself and family are in good health. With best Regard from all you know here.

Sincerely,
Yrs
L.A. Pena

N.B. Mr Flemming ask to be remembered he is doing some prospecting."

When I finished reading his letter, I could see that he was becoming even more concerned about the delays at my end in being unable to raise money to promote our diamond deal.

I was also unaware that he had his own pit that was being worked by one or more *pork-knockers*.

Undoubtedly, from the tone of his letter, his optimism about his pit made him even more anxious about selling the diamonds to the States.

On a happier note, I received my first letter from Corporal Paton, the constable in Kurupung, dated 1/11/55.

He must have transmitted it to Georgetown in his official reports, because it wasn't postmarked from Georgetown until 16 Nov. 1955.

His upbeat letter, although short, was amusing and newsy:

"Hello Pal,

Yours received. Glad you have arrived safely, but by now got rid of those pests, reporters etc., etc. I shall like to have a picture of you after your honeymoon to see your condition so I can send a piece of *"labba"* and *"wild cow"* to put back some of what you lost. We all missed you a lot, such a distinguished visitor in B.G. jungle we seldom have and to see you adapted yourself to our custom make we missed you more. You are a man of two world. I personally missed some of the wise "cracks" you pulled over sometimes on big buddy king. Hope to see you back in our jungle soon. Sorry you did not make the trip to our Rupununi District, you might have been fortunate with the tiger. Be good to yourself and take care of the "Doll" don't try to over-do the do.

Your Pal
Corporal

P.S. Up to the time of writing I haven't received the camera. P."

In his letter, his reference to the "doll" was a term I always used when I spoke of my former fiancé. It was a descriptive word that appealed to him, and he also adopted it for usage.

His postscript mentioned that he had not received a camera that I sent him from Georgetown. It was one of several items I promised and forwarded to those I had befriended in Kurupung.

However, the journey from the capital in Georgetown to the bush was a long way and the dependability of the mail was uncertain, especially in regard to desirable items being shipped.

I received two more short letters from Paton. The first one, again sent from Georgetown, was postmarked 12 Dec. 1955:

"Hello Marty
Seasons Greetings.

My November Holiday is finished and now back to station. I thought I would have heard from you in reply to my letter, but I conclude owing to the advent of your matrimonial bliss you are deeply engaged in your preparation but never-the-less you can spare a few minutes off and send those pictures if they are still good. I still have a piece of preserved "*labba*," would you like to have it?..."

His second letter, dated 31/1/56, was a short note advising me that he was "no longer in the jungle," and gave me his new address as the River Police Station in Georgetown. He also let me know that he had finally "received the camera and film intact, thanks for same." I was relieved at the news, as we had developed a friendship while I was there.

My third letter from Pena, dated 17/12/55, began in the same formal vein but was more sympathetic to the problems I encountered in finding a backer. At the same time, it told of his successes:

"Dear Mr. Roland

Yours of the 16th Nov received about nine days after you wrote, it must of detain some-where, of course you know how we are situated here so it shouldn't be surprising.

You mention about what we propose which I consider a bit too strenuous on your part to carry out immediately, you having your hands filled with so much other important matters to get fixed. So I suggest that you hold on a bit until your side is settled, which won't be before some time next year, except you get some capitalist interested, as you see two thousand dollars can only purchase one stone which may be about six carrats or a little over so you see that won't pay, so I think its best to wait until you can get about it in a payable way even if you have to come over yourself. What I mention is just my suggestion but you may be able to see or sum up in a different way, as you are playing the most important part.

About my pit now we only started washing last week and we are getting up to now twenty carrats per day and expect to finish before the second week in January and believe the production would increase, and should not get less than four hundred carrats which would work out around twenty thousand dollars.

Fleming has been enquiring of you. I told him what you mentioned. Silva and others join in sending their regards and wishing you a happy X'mas and a Prosperous New Year.

Yrs.
Sincerely
L.A. Pena

N.B. Expecting to hear from you soon am tired and sleepy, can't write anything more now and I don't want to loose this opportunity."

Regrettably, it was the last letter I received from him.

Whether he became discouraged at my lack of progress in locating financing — or whether something happened to him — I never knew. However, I still continued my efforts.

I received two more letters — interestingly only from Silva. The first one dated, 15/1/56, was consistent with Pena's last letter, and while child-like in composition was flowery as well:

"Sir

I must thank you eavery so mutch for your kindness as to remember me a poor Creaiture Sir I don'nt no if you are married as yet if so you can give my Respect to the Mrs for me I received the Post Office Notice that a Parcil Com for me. But it is a Bartica Post Office And I have to send $9.00 to Redime the Parcil from Bartica Post Office I have not Received the Parcil as yet till the Next mail Boat or so But I am Sorry that you did not stop to See the Boss pit wat was working it coming to Be a Close up to this letter to this date Nearly four Hundred Cararts and we have two more week work But the diamonds are fine and the large stone is a Two Carat up to now the Same time I received the mail note for the parcil I received a New From Home that my Brotherin Law is on dying And I Can'nt go home Because the work Hav'nt finish Nothing More

At Preasant
Joseph De Silva"

The letter, while readable and understandable, appeared to be more a stream-of-consciousness letter than his last one to me. I didn't attribute his run-on sentences to anything unusual until I read his second one and his reference to liquor. It was written six months later with an 18

Jun 1956 postmark form Georgetown. Although it mentioned Fleming's name, it never mentioned Pena's name. I thought it a bit unusual as Silva had worked for him. That omission lent credence to my belief that something might have happened to Pena in the six months between January and June.

Silva's final letter was basically the same type as the one he wrote in January, with less structure to it. It was also much shorter:

"Dear
    Sir Hooping the arrival of these few lines may find yourself and family shading under the Branches of Good Health by God Grace as it leave me sic But not in Bed. I went with Mr. Flimin to Prospect But we did not make out Good a the Kuruping Montain It has some Positible But on acount Rashing when I say Rashin I mean food Because when we start to Get some Diamonds the shop hav'nt Got food to Sell So all we can do with diamond sell and drink Rum with it so I had to leave them and try to catch Home afer spending so long time from my home

                        Joseph De Silva"

Although I didn't hear from Pena after his letter of 16 November, 1955, I did receive one from Silva on 15 January, 1956, and knew that Pena's pits were still being worked. I also was aware that they were producing diamonds. On the strength of that continuing information, I kept up my efforts to locate investment money. Unfortunately, my sources dried up, and I decided to write, and attempt to publish, an upbeat how-to technical pamphlet in order to generate public interest and — I hoped — the elusive income I needed.

I contacted several local printers to see about having my pamphlet printed up in minimum quantities and even included numerous photos to enhance salability.

My finished product, although on hindsight was amateurish, was impressive (at least to me), and I didn't see how it could fail to stir up attention in the men's adventure field.

# 20

### "HOW TO DIG FOR
## SOUTH AMERICAN DIAMONDS
### by Marty Roland

They say "Diamonds are a girl's best friend." As far as I'm concerned, it should be the other way around. Once a guy, any guy, has enough of Mother Nature's sparkling rocks in his possession, the material things in life he desires can come as a matter of course.

I flew over 3000 miles alone in quest of my rare commodity, and actually dug into the pot at the end of my legendary rainbow. That, in conjunction with a source of contact I now have, will enable me to attain the same ends, and I do know the whole procedure necessary to acquire a fortune that is not so elusive as most people force themselves into believing.

The only ingredients required for a business venture of this nature are a little guts, a lot of patience, and a willingness to be able to put up with and do a tough job.

The South American country I chose for my operations was British Guiana. There has been very little written about it, or as far as I could determine before I left, very little known about this English Colony. It lies sandwiched between Dutch Guiana and Venezuela on the upper part of the continent of South America. Below it is the vast expanse of Brazil. I could have chosen Venezuela or Brazil for the same job, but I knew that competition would be less due to the simple fact that because of its relatively unknown-ness, prospectors and even tourists gave it a wide berth for reasons known only to themselves. The area known as "La Gran Sabana" region encompasses the countries of Venezuela, British Guiana and Brazil, and it is this same area which is "diamondiferous" — or loaded with diamonds, to the untechnical layman.

In order of importance, the first step necessary is to obtain a passport which can be done at the "Passport Division" of any Federal Building. The next is to secure the required shots for immunization against diseases prevalent there. Since I'm writing about British Guiana, any Federal Health Agency will supply the vaccination against "Smallpox," a "Typhoid Injection," and one for "Yellow Fever" also. "Aralen" tablets are the newest preventative against malaria and can be used as a successful cure. A doctor's prescription will enable you to pick it up at a pharmacy. Vitamin pills containing iron I took with me also. They're optional. The next question that is bound to arise is "What'll I take with me?" As for myself, I took G.I. fatigues. Dungarees or anything on that order will suffice. Don't do as I did. I regretted it all the time I was there. I only had one pair of G.I. combat boots. I should've had an extra pair. A pair of sneakers will be sufficient for a short stay. The best type of shirts to take are the "T" shirts — tight fitting at the neck. As long as you're not setting out to make a solitary safari or try to act like a "Jungle Jim" or a "Frank Buck" as

I did, a shotgun is all that's necessary — preferably a double-barrel. Light and heavy charges can be used in it at the same time. The only other piece of equipment you'll need from the States will be a canteen. In my case, at first, it was one of the most important items I had.

From the states to Georgetown, capital of British Guiana, is a detail the airlines can arrange for you. At Georgetown itself, the procedure is as anything, once you know how, simple. I entered the colony cold. All I knew was the fact that I was in diamond country and I wanted them. Nothing else.

Any type of firearms may be brought into the country without a previous license or approval, with the exception of a 45 caliber automatic. The Customs Department at Atkinson Field, which is Port of Entry, hold them in bond until your trip into the Interior and they are then released to you. The next stop is to notify Central Police Headquarters in Georgetown of your intentions with the firearms and their use. A fee for the permit and license is only a couple of dollars. From there the "Bureau of Lands & Mines furnishes you with a "Prospector's License" for $5.00, and a "Mining Privilege" for an additional shilling ($ .24). This Mining Privilege gives you the legal right, should the occasion arise, to work in somebody else's claim. They also furnish you with all pamphlets necessary and a detailed map. In my case, one of the Wardens there told me of sections which are known to be proficient in diamonds and gold both. It is equally known to contain the valuable yellow dust. Once the above necessary rules have been followed, the game is no longer a mystery or foreign to you. British Guiana Airways schedule charter flights into the Jungle or "Bush" as it is called. The longest round trip is roughly $60.00, which is a one way 200 mile airborne trek, and, as was in my case, far enough. Then you notify the Customs Department of your intended departure. They, in turn, levy a 36% deposit on the firearms. When you leave their country, it is refunded.

The above information and other trivial matters, which could have been eliminated if I'd have had the know-how, cost me five days of talking, walking and waiting, and an increase in my blood pressure.

Once everything has been accomplished, take a sigh of relief, buy a hammock and mosquito netting, and climb into the Grumman Amphib that takes off at the edge of town from the Demarara River. The rest of your supplies can be obtained from the settlements in the Interior.

The jungle below may look wild and desolate, but just lean back and think of diamonds. Feelings of the forthcoming venture will be varied according to the individual. Others have done it and come back and are doing like myself — writing and hoping that my experiences will be of assistance to all those who read about it and are interested in a business trip that could be worth a fortune and is far from being legendary or farfetched.

Men have written for centuries about jungles in every corner of the universe. Once, and the sooner the better, you can learn to adapt yourself, you have 90% of your troubles behind you.

Indian guides are easily found in any section of British Guiana and are found to be reliable and trustworthy. The black native, or *"porkknocker,"* as he's called, has been prospecting for diamonds for years and know the little things that count. If you should encounter one, use your own judgement picking one to help you work. If they promise you the moon and diamonds clinking in buckets, forget about them. If they had the opportunity, no matter what excuses they may offer, why should they make a two-way split when they can have it all?

The necessary tools and implements are as follows: a machete, an ax, a spade, a hoe, a sieve, a bucket, a Tom box and a Tom iron. Last, but not least, a probing stick. I'll explain these all in detail along with their application in the work involved.

The tools and implements are in order and either your Indian guide or the *pork-knocker* are ready to take you down your plush corridor into your future office. You may have read accounts in the various men's magazines of how easy it seemed. All you have to do is dig in the river beds and fortune is yours — as easy as that. As I mentioned earlier, the natives have been in the jungle for years and working diamonds all that while. The most accessible and easiest places are done first. The tough part, but which contain just as many of the glittering pebbles, is the jungle itself, or rather below the floor of the tangled green cobweb of trees and vines.

The idea to plaster in your mind is that diamonds are found in gravel. The probing stick, that although I placed at the end of the list of tools, is the first you use, with the exception of the machete. It can be cut from a tree sapling the same thickness as a pool stick, and about a seven to eight foot length. With this preliminary implement, once you've wandered around the jungle and found any type of trickle of water, the process is started.

The probing stick will sink into soft ground

and mud as your finger will into soft butter, but when it hits gravel - - there is apt to be a rasping, grating sound. The deeper you press the harder it will be to do so, and at the same time you'll be able to determine the depth of the gravel. It will vary in thickness from a few inches to a foot or more.

This is the part where the speculation and investigation ends and where a back-breaking tough grind begins. A dirty, grimy job when in the future days to come you'll wonder why you ever tackled it. Days where your hands will blister and be raw and when your fingers will cramp up from grasping a shovel. Endless days when you'll be bathed in sweat up from the mud and water you might have to work in, to the top of your head. As quickly as the strangeness of the work gave you the feelings and sensations involved, it will pass and you'll only think of it as a daily job — a job where any time your spade will turn up diamonds and a fortune, to make the task well worth the effort.

Away from the initial location of the gravel, use the probing stick a few more times to determine the extent and direction the gravel lies. It's then that you use your machete again to hack a clearing of all vines, shrubs and small trees within a twenty to thirty-foot diameter. There are only certain things a machete can and will be successfully used against. After that you have to rely on your ax. In that same clearing, all trees, no matter what size, have to be felled and dragged out of the way. With two or three men working, yourself included, it may take two or three days to reach this stage. If it sounds rough so far, it is, but you also have to remember that anything worth while in life, no matter what it is, never comes easy. Diamonds are no exception.

As I noted earlier, there will be a small trickle of water or a muddy creek bed, or even a pool of water, where you started your original exploration. From this point, enlarge a trench or "tail-rec," as it's known, to lead all water away from the origin and outside the clearing that has been chopped away. The purpose is to have the clearing as dry as possible and at the same time, have the "tail-rec" on hand so that when the time comes — and it will — to be able to drain all water from the future pit you'll be working in.

With the rough clearing you've formed, except for occasional tree stumps, the ax again is the order of the day. The upper layer of the jungle floor, which will include vines and tree roots, is cut. Situate this as close to the original source of water as possible so that soil may be thrown into the water to absorb it. For two or three men working, a good excavation is approximately a ten by ten foot pit. The depth of the pit will vary according to the depth that the probing stick has determined the gravel to be below the surface of the ground. The first foot, and in some cases down to about two feet, is the worst part. Tree roots which feel like they've been welded into the earth will defy your ax, but remember a covering such as you may be removing might be nature's protective armor against the wealth that may lie beneath.

At this stage, although the most grueling part is behind you, you'll care less about winding up a tycoon than you ever have in our life, but you'll continue because it'd be stupid and foolish to quit at this point.

Although you'll move as if you're a robot or a machine, you'll grab your spade. The earth will be soft and you'll have to dig and scoop the remains out and place them along side your pit.

After a certain amount of earth, you strike mud, and below the mud will be your worst foe - - water. Water that seeps into the pit from the water you've made an ally and neighbor of. Water that will seep in after rains and have to be bailed out and thrown into your "tail-rec." Before you reach the depth where you're forced to dig mud and earth out of the water "pawling" a pit is the next step. "Pawling" is placing tree limbs and leaves behind them on all four sides to prevent the ground from falling into your glorified hole. When it's completed it'll resemble a mine entrance, only the direction will be down instead of the customary walk-in type. Before any constructive future digging can be accomplished, the pit has to be constantly bailed out with your bucket and thrown into the "tom box" which is a three-sided rectangular frame about four feet long. The "tom box" is placed over the edge of the pit and extends into the "tail-rec." They both have to be cleared of mud, sand, and any other obstructions that may prevent the natural flow of the water.

Sand is the next element that forms a part of the lower recesses. Shoveling sand is easier, but in conjunction with bailing multiple buckets of water from the "tail-rec" and the "tom box," the task is harder. The tedious monotonous job of bailing bucketsful of water is a necessary evil. Keeping the base of the pit as dry as possible makes the immediate job of shoveling easier and the next step of hitting gravel more effective.

Gravel is found below the level of the sand but in order to provide a resting place for pay dirt, you have to make what is known as a "plan." It merely consists of leveling all sand and earth away from one side of the pit to allow for the "waste," as gravel is called. In a pit such as I described, five-six feet back is ample room.

Below the sand may be "fools gravel." It is coarse gravel which is unmistakable in composition, inasmuch as the chunks are large, and is mixed with sand, which is whitish in color. Diamonds are occasionally found in the "fools gravel," but are few and far between. The probing stick again is used as a beckoning finger pointing the way and gauging the distance below the surface to the pure gravel. Digging and bailing is more cautious but just as steady. The pits I worked in had pure gravel about six inches below coarse gravel. It may vary, and the case may be that below the sand will only be pure gravel, with no coarse gravel.

After endless hours and days of using your spade like it was a third hand, it's a pleasure throwing the gravel out and onto the "plan." You're supposed to handle the semi-precious stuff as if you were scooping sugar from a small bowl with a large spoon. As the "pork-knocker" told me, that I worked with on my first pit, "easy man, there may be diamonds in there!"

There have been instances when gravel that stuck to a person's boots, or legs, or even some that splashed back in someone's face, contained assorted sizes of diamonds.

The thickness of the pure gravel, as a rule, is usually only a few inches and below that will be clay. Pale-greenish in color, it is also called "waste" from the pit. Diamonds settle into this clay and although its weight is like lifting gold bricks into the "plan," the value of each shovel could equal or exceed it. A depth of eight inches to a foot is enough allowance to play safe.

With the base of the pit neatly and carefully stripped of its hidden contents, you can finally give way to nature and have water seep back in until it's full. The "waste" from the "plan" is shoveled into the "tom box" and a "tom iron" is inserted into the base nearest the pit. The "tom iron" is a square metal plate with circular holes cut into it. As water is mixed with the gravel and clay you use a hoe to haul the contents to the "tom." Larger particles stay behind and the smaller ones are forced thru the "tom iron" into a "box." Any type of wooden box will do. The contents of the "box" are then put into a "sieve." This "sieve" is about the diameter of a section of a barrel. Its sides extend about six inches in thickness to hold the gravel. The base of it is finely-meshed wire.

The last part of this operation — that of working the "sieve" — while you're standing, sometimes, waist deep in water from the pit — is the most delicate and ticklish. The "pork-knockers" main fear is that they might be throwing diamonds away. In many cases, that's exactly what happens when other natives rework or "wash the gravel" and find diamonds their predecessors had thrown away carelessly in the worked over gravel.

Two tree limbs stretched across the top of the pit hold the "sieve" while it is being loaded with gravel from the "box." It's then immersed in the water in the pit and "pumped" - - an up and down motion - - slowly and a few times. Then the "sieve" is "jigged" - - a swirling motion clockwise (or counter clockwise) - - a few more times. It's removed from the water, put back on the supports and you'll find the heavier particles have all settled in the lower section of it. Sand remains on top. It's scooped off carefully and the procedure of immersing the "sieve" is repeated; then withdrawn after it has been "pumped" and "jigged." The upper layer is again removed, as well as the outer fringe. This process is done four or five times, and as I said, carefully and as exacting as if you were threading a needle. On its final withdrawal from the water, very little gravel will remain.

The heaviest particles which are diamonds, as well as "indications" will be in the center and bottom of the "sieve." "Indications" are what are known as "forerunners of diamonds." Their texture and composition, and sometimes even their size, resemble black pencil lead. Whenever there are these same "indications," there are bound to be diamonds in the vicinity. On the other hand, diamonds may be resting comfortably on the bottom of the "sieve" and there hasn't been a trace of an "indication."

The "sieve" is constantly filled and emptied in the above procedure until all of the "waste" has been "washed." If you're lucky, fortune may turn her gaze on you. You never know.

The questions I asked before I started will be the same that you and others after you will ask.

"What do they look like?"

"How will I know one when I see it?"

The answer they gave me, I'll pass on to you.

"You'll know."

There's no mistaking a diamond. Even in the rough it looks like what it is — a diamond. The only difference at first sight is that the fire and brilliance in it is dimmed down more than those you would see at Tiffany's or any other jewelry store.

In the course of my prospecting I came across one native who hit a pocket and took out over 2000 carats in one pit. Countless others came upon hundreds of carats in a pit and other "pork-knockers" dug their way into their share of wealth. There is nothing mythical about a fortune in diamonds in South America.

A six weeks' business venture that cost me $900.00 is in the process now of skyrocketing many times my original investment. Whether you decide that the stakes are worth the gamble and whether Fate steps in to lend you a helping hand, you'll never know until you try it.

Nothing ventured, nothing gained.

If you should — "Good luck."


Sadly, not only was the cost of printing the pamphlets more that I could afford on a civil servant's salary, but monthly advertising rates in the men's adventure magazines were way out of my league. In addition, it was impossible to locate any investment capital I could use as seed money to get me started.

The only source of potential income I could come up with was the writing of my various experiences as short stories for the men's adventure magazines.

In that era (the 1950s), there were a slew of such magazines on the market, and they all catered to my field. *True* and *Argosy* were the primary ones that paid top prices for a piece of several thousand words: $3,000 for the former and $2,500 for the latter. Other second-rate magazines — with stories just as fascinating and set in locales just as exotic — were *Cavalier* and *Outdoor Adventurer.* Their payment scale topped out at about $1,000. Then of course, there were numerous others that were fairly new to the field. They were open to tales of danger in the great outdoors and were receptive to new writers. Unfortunately, these lesser-known periodicals paid on publication rather than on acceptance, and their scales were far less than the max of $1,000 paid by the likes of *Cavalier* and *Outdoor Adventurer.* It was in this third category of magazines that I managed to finally break into the publishing field. However, by the time I was paid for two stories of my British Guiana experiences, it was far too late to be of any monetary assistance in the business deal between Pena and me. Those payments — even if paid on acceptance —

would hardly have paid for a raw diamond chip from Pena.

My first story of my three-day jaguar hunt I titled "*Achebana.*" The publisher, Weider Periodicals, had several magazines in its chain, two of which were *Safari* and *Fury*. It appeared in the October 1957 issue of *Safari* magazine retitled as "I Challenged the Biggest Jaguar," for which I was paid $100.

My second story, of my discovery and climb of the Great Falls, I titled, "The Falls That Weren't There." I never knew what title the publisher had finally given it or when it was published. A letter I received from Joseph Weider on March 7, 1957, advised me that although the article was left out of the magazine twice, they expected "to run it shortly." I was only paid $75 for that piece.

I was fortunate, however, in subsequently having my jaguar story translated into German to appear in European periodicals. Dr. H. Tschudin of Basil, Switzerland, was the agent/translator who titled it, "*Ich Forderte den Jaguar heraus,*" for which I was paid an additional $25.

It didn't take a genius to figure out that even when I sold my short stories, I was not going to make the money that I expected as a great writer and would never be able to promote or support my South American diamond deal.

Although I eventually wrote seven such adventure short stories depicting various aspects of my Central and South American exploits, acceptance and recognition were long in coming.

Before I made my first sale, I accumulated a hundred and ten rejection slips from various magazines and newspapers, representing those seven pieces. Of course, many of those stories went back to the same magazine as their editorial requirements constantly changed.

In the months after my return from South America I was becoming frustrated with the lack of progress I was making in my diamond financing and short story sales. Someone suggested I write a book about my British Guiana experience, but when you are in your twenties, doing a book is too time-consuming. I didn't have the time or the patience to pursue it. Instead, I decided on a different approach to my problem. I needed a well-known author to write my book, which I tentatively had titled "British Guiana Diary." Who better to accomplish that project than "Papa" Hemingway.

It took a while to locate his new address, since he moved from his home in Key West to Cuba sometime in 1956.

The fairly long audacious handwritten letter, although very complimentary of his past successes, did mention that "although others had said he was slipping, I didn't believe it." I not only had the nerve to ask if he would write the book, but suggested that if he would ghostwrite it, I would gladly pay him a sizable portion of the royalties. As a reason for my unusual approach, I told him that I was "too busy" to do justice to the book.

He never responded.

With the passing of months, I decided on a new trip for the summer or fall of 1956. Although I had heard that Borneo was a good place to explore next, because diamonds were also reputed to be found in the jungles, I was forced to alter any plans about that Pacific destination. Distance and expense were my primary reasons.

I was still unsure of my next trip, but knew that it had to be as exotic and challenging as my last ones had been. Also, I realized that to "make my mark" as a writer/adventurer/explorer I would have to surpass prior exploits.

Accordingly, I placed the following ad in the personal section of the *Miami Herald* in mid-March 1956:


"Am willing to go anywhere in the world from Madagascar to Mongolia, on any assignment for any individual or organization." P.O. Box 326 Ft. Lauderdale, FLA."


The nine responses I received ran the gamut from acceptable to bizarre.

# 21

Three of the replies were on postcards from Fort Lauderdale.

Four of the replies were either in letter form or on other cards from Miami, and one letter was from Texas.

The two cards that were postmarked locally, I discounted as being from my buddies.

Amusing as they were, I didn't appreciate them, as they were not what I hoped for.

One of the local cards said:

> "In answer to your ad, if it's travel you want, ask for Peaches at Elbo on beach. Am always interested in trysts around the world. Anxiously, Peaches."

Elbo was my frequent off-hours hangout, the Elbow Room at Fort Lauderdale Beach.

The second local card, aiming at a little more intrigue, read:

> "Dear Sir:
>
> I am looking for an undercover agent in Greece. Think you will meet all requirements.

Write Box 1332."

The third postcard was very brief, and was probably put in that format to pique my interest:

"Regarding ad, phone JA2-9542 9-5 daily. Ask for Ralph."

The first of the three cards from Miami sounded more mysterious but had no name or return address:

"Saw your ad in the Herald and it made me wonder if you could be H.K. Williams. If so, you will find Pretzil in the same little cottage where I lived when I first met you."

The second Miami card, from a lonely female who stressed she was a "Miss" and gave a General Delivery address, obviously was bored and looking for a little excitement:

"I read your ad in today's *Miami Herald* which states 'will go anywhere in the world.' If I had the chance, I would, too."

The final Miami card also appeared to be seeking something but wanted me to find it for him.
He gave a name and a return address, which I declined to follow-up:

"Dear Friend,
If you should run into something that doesn't

interest you and might interest me, how about
letting me know about it."


The next piece of mail was a single-spaced bizarre letter from an individual in Miami. Although many of the
facts he mentioned were fascinating, and might have been
worth pursuing under different circumstances, it appeared
that he had lost touch with reality — especially in regard to
the wearing of a "rubber plastic uniform" as protection
against "ten thousand snakes." He certainly was not the
type of person I wanted for a partner, even if he would be
willing to foot the entire cost of an expedition.

For the reasons cited, I did not attempt to contact him,
although he gave his name, address and phone number.

The following letter appears in its entirety:


"DEAR SIR: I HAVE SEEN YOUR ADD IN
THE MIAMI HEARLD I WAS WONDERING IF
YOU MIGHT BE INTERESTED IN TREASURE
HUNTING FLORIDA AND SOUTH EASTERN
UNTIED STATES I HAVE ONE TREASURE MAP
AND CAN GET SOME MORE I KNOW OF VAR-
IOUS LOCATIONS AFRICA LOST CITIES WITH
TREASURE AND CENTRAL AMERICA LOST
CITIES MILLIONS IN GOLD BACED ON A
STORY SOUTH AMERICA LOST CITIES WITH
MILLIONS IN GOLD AND JEWLES I KNOW OF
A EXACT LOCATION IN SOUTH AMERICA
PURU A STORY BACED ON TEN THOUSAND
SNAKES GUARDING THE TREASURE I THINK
IF I COULD MAKE A RUBBER PLASTIC UNI-
FORM I COULD GO RIGHT IN AFTER IT PLAS-
TIC HOOD CLEAR WOULDENT COST TO
MUCH SUPPOSED TO BE THOUSANDS IN
INDISTIS TREASURE FLORIDA HAS MANY
ISLANDS OF MILLIONS IN TREASURE I AM

SHURE I COULD GET THAT TREASURE IN PERU I ALSO KNOW OF A SHIP WITH A MILLION GALLONS OF OIL IN IT THE SHIP LIES UPSIDE DOWN IN TWENTY SIX FEET OF WATER IN LAKE ERIE IN OHIO I ALSO KNOW OF A LOST CITY IN INDO CHINA WHERE THERE IS SUPPOSED TO BE THOUSANDS OF DOLLERS WORTH OF EMBERLADS AND RUBIES IF A PERSON CAN AFFORD A START WHICH SHOULDENT COST OVER FIVE THOUSAND DOLLERS A PERSON COULD WORK ON UP THERE ARE MANY ISLANDS WITH PIRATE TREASURE THERE IS PIRATE TREASURE IN COLORADO ISLANDS NEAR HATIE CUBA WITH CAVES WHERE PIRATES USED FOR THEIR HIDE OUT IF YOU LIKE ADVENTURE PLEASE CONTACT ME I AM SUPPOSED TO GET MONEY BEFORE LONG NOT TO MUCH IF I CANT FIND A PARTNER I AM STARTING OUT MYSELF. I HOPE THAT WE CAN BE PARTENERS PLEASE SEND PHOTO OF YOUR SELF OR MAKE APPOINTMENT WITH TO SEE ME MY TELEPHONE NUMBER IS - - I HAVE MANY SUBECTS ON LOST TREASURE I MIGHT WRITE TO A CONSERN FOR MORE INFORMATION ON LOST BUIRIED TREASURE MANY LOCATIONS POINTED OUT SOME EXACT AND OTHERS APPROMIXLY. HOPE TO HEAR FROM YOU SOON.
     SINCEARLY YOURS"


The fifth, and last, letter from Miami was very interesting. It was from an individual I felt comfortable with and could easily have paired up with as a potential partner.

However, at that time, I wasn't seeking an equal-share partner but rather some source that wanted a specific task accomplished — and was willing to pay for it.

Regrettably, I had to pass on the following letter:


"Dear Mr. Roland:

As a fellow adventurer I salute you. I read your well-phrased ad in the *Miami Herald* and noted that you are a good deal like myself.

In the past I have inserted similar ads myself but seldom receive any replies that are particularly noteworthy. Invariably I end up backing my own expeditions in a quest for adventure.

In the fall of 1955 I spent a few months in Morocco living with the Arabs. This in itself is nothing exceptional but for the fact that the French-Arab was in process. With what delight I now recall those nights when the French troops searched in vain to find our little group in the Atlas Mountains?

What of yourself? Have you had any luck in finding an interesting pre-paid adventure?

With-in the next three or four days I will be off once more. This time I am planning an extended camping trip that will take me through many States and across Canada to the West Coast in a quest for adventure in nature. During this trip I will do a good deal of hunting — with a movie camera. Perhaps at the end of the journey I will be able to sell the film to cover expenses.

I would enjoy hearing from you. Particularly so if you should find need of a 'companion in adventure.'

Laurence D. Craig"


The final response to my ad was a neat well-phrased typewritten letter from Houston, Texas:

"Dear Sir:

This is with reference to your ad in the *Miami Herald* relating to your willingness to go anywhere in the world for any individual or organization.

If you receive an interesting proposition that you will not take yourself, I would appreciate it if you would pass it on to me. If I accept one of your castoff proposals, I'll send you $25.00 as a token of my appreciation (or whatever you feel would be equitable).

As of possible interest to you, and as strange as it may seem, the ALBUQUERQUE JOURNAL carries many ads pertaining to overseas work, if that's of any interest.

Yours very truly,
Don Vasque"

As willing as the party was to pay for any information I would relay to him, it, too, was not the type of answer I sought. Also, the newspaper source that he mentioned I did not follow-up as I believed it solicited foreign jobs. That was not what I was looking for, either.

There were no other replies to that insertion in the *Miami Herald*. Perhaps, if I had placed multiple ads in the paper or expanded my search to other newspapers, the results might have been more productive. However, from the type of responses that I received and from the additional expense required to advertise, I decided to concentrate on a more specific locale similar to my South American trip.

I chose the African Continent.

When my immediate family — especially my mother — learned of my new intentions, they tried hard to discourage me. On the other hand, friends and acquaintances quickly encouraged me. I needed very little persuasion to take the latter course of action since I had already made up my mind.

It didn't take long for the newspapers to get wind of my latest plans. When they did, a short article appeared in the *Miami Herald:*

## "EXPLORER PLANS TRIP TO AFRICA

FORT LAUDERDALE — Marty Roland, the jungle explorer who works at the post office between trips, is about to do it again.

He announced Wednesday that he's decided on the African jungles this time, and plans to leave early in September.

Last year the 29-year-old Roland went on what turned out to be an unprofitable diamond-hunting expedition to British Guiana, and before that he hunted game in the jungles of Central America.

Though he plans to do some hunting, Roland says his objective is going into the African wild is to get material for a book.

"I plan to go into the Kenya region first, then into French West Africa, and end up with a trip across the Sahara. I expect to be gone six weeks or two months."

If the postal clerk can get a sponsor for his trip, he'll fly to North Africa. Otherwise he'll have to settle for a tramp steamer.

Roland figures the trip will cost $2,000 or $3,000. He's been trying to find a partner who'll share expenses, but hasn't had any luck so far."

With the word out, there were innumerable comments or remarks about my prospective expedition.

One local reporter, Orville Revelle in his *Pass in Review* column had extensive comment of concern.

His cautionary article follows:

## "HE DREAMS OF AFRICA

MARTY ROLAND has the itch again. This itch can't be scratched. He must travel to get rid of it.

It was just last year he got the itch to try his luck in South America — for diamonds. Now he wants to cross Africa, alone. But to do this he must have a sponsor.

What's it going to cost the sponsor? $3,000

What's the sponsor going to get for his $3,000?

Marty says 30 per cent of everything that is realized out of the venture.

What will he realize?

HE says he will take motion pictures for television. He'll charge for lectures after he gets back. He may find some valuable gems — he hopes. If he kills any big game he'll sell the skins. If he captures any alive he hopes to sell them to zoos. He'll write for magazines and newspapers — if they will buy what he has to sell. He also plans to work along the way, and his sponsor will get 20 per cent of his salary.

And he wants his sponsor to know that he already has mapped out his trek.

"I'll enter through Dakar, at French West Africa," he says. "Then cross the Sahara into French Equatorial Africa. I'll pass through Sudan, Ethiopia, Kenya and Tanganyika. And I also hope to make stopovers in Somalialand and Mosambique."

DOWN through the ages there have been many Marty Rolands — dreaming of the day they could conquer new worlds. Many have sought sponsors to help them realize their dreams. Only a few scored. I'm afraid that if he waits for a sponsor to turn up, his dream will never come true. And since I'm led to believe he has a nice job in our local Post Office, my advice is to save up his money until he has enough to make the first leg of the journey and then chance it he can earn while he learns of Africa's darkest secrets.

It is unfortunate that Marty didn't get the opportunity to meet Bill Hart about a year back when the latter was seriously considering a trip to Africa.

At the time, Bill was looking for a companion for the trip — one who might be able to record with typewriter and camera, the highlights of the safari.

Maybe these two men can get together some day and make this trip both seem interested in."

Considering all the prior publicity I had received on my solo South American exploits, I fully expected some type of backing from some local sources. However, no one came forward to sponsor me, although I made my intentions fully known in the newspapers of how I was going to repay any potential sponsors. It wasn't as if I was an unknown quantity as to my ability to do what I said I would do, as my track record on prior trips bore out my contentions.

I knew that absent any sponsors, I was unable to afford another trip. Even though the maximum that my new six-week adventure would cost was only in the $3,000 range, for that time and era, it was impossible to raise. My salary as a Postal Clerk was slightly over $4,000 per year, and loans without collateral were equally unobtainable.

Although I became frustrated with the apparent lack

of financial interest shown toward my future endeavors, I was not discouraged.

If there was no one in South Florida to back me, I decided to expand my search. I wrote the following foundations of my intentions to cover the African Continent and tried to gain their sponsorship for specific goals that their organizations might like to see accomplished:

Ford Foundation
Rockefeller Foundation
Wenner-Oren Foundation for Anthropological Research
Carnegie Endowment for International Peace
Arthur Jordan Foundation
American Foundation
Smithsonian Institution
National Geographic Society

None of the organizations were interested. Some were good enough to inform me of their lack of interest, while others ignored the request.

In a continuing effort, I then contacted appropriate renowned individuals in the travel field. I sought specific concrete suggestions or advice on how to slant my African junkets. Specifically, I wrote Lowell Thomas, and his son, Lowell Thomas Jr., because of their reputations.

When that approach also failed, I first wrote, and then visited, the Explorer's Club in New York for the same information. It, too, was unsuccessful.

In one of my final bids for a foreign assignment, I sent a letter to The *Ethiopian Herald* in Addis Ababa, Ethiopia, and advised them that since I would be in their country, what would they like me to write about as an American explorer.

Again, nothing of value from their editor.

When I finally realized that my queries were asking someone for vague assignments rather than telling them of my specific goals, I changed my approach.

I then wrote the three top men's magazines with which I had previous contacts, and who either had seen or knew of my British Guiana pieces: *True*, *Argosy* and *Cavalier*.

Their replies, to my queries, were almost immediate, especially since I told them that I was going to:

1. Cross the Sahara Desert by camel,
2. Lion hunt with the Masai natives in Kenya, and
3. Climb Mt. Kilimanjaro.

However, their idea of an assignment was merely, a "look-see." There was no money advanced, as had been the journalistic practice in prior days.

The cutting back of advance monies also hit the television adventure/exploration shows.

My specific query to the CBS-TV show *"Adventure,"* to film archeological digs in two different sections of Africa that I had read about, also elicited a rapid response from the producers. If I could use a movie camera, they were very interested in my coverage of those newsworthy events. One was the discovery of long-dead giant soldiers in the sands of French West Africa and the other was the discovery of the "Dead Sea Scrolls" in Aden on the Red Sea.

The reason for their pronounced interest was the fact that their cameramen were all Jewish and were consequently not welcome in Muslim countries — especially Aden. Inasmuch as I was Christian and was available immediately, I was needed.

The only stumbling block to the assignment was the fact that they were no longer able to pay me any advance monies toward my travel to get to the Africa continent. If I could somehow manage to get to the places where they needed me, I would be reimbursed for my expenses.

Regrettably, I was still unable to raise the capital I needed to get to Africa.

As a result of my failure to do so, not only were my short-term gains thwarted, but any long-term gains, especially recognition, that I might have realized as a result of my connection with CBS, were stymied.

I had little choice but to abandon my African trek for 1956.

Although I devoted a great deal of my spare time to writing short stories, both fiction and nonfiction during 1956, it was not satisfying enough. I knew I had to schedule something — somewhere — as soon as possible, in order to maintain the momentum I had established.

The year 1957 proved to be almost as eventful as 1955 — and in some respects, more.

# 22

My continuing interest in foreign lands and travel to those far-off places never wavered, and because of my fascination — or perhaps it was my obsession — I constantly followed recurring events in world news. I felt strongly that it was just a matter of time before there would be abnormal events in those foreign countries upon which I could capitalize as a writer, adventurer and explorer.

It didn't take long for dramatic situations to materialize.

An article first appeared in the May 18, 1957, edition of the *New York Times* and mentioned mob violence consisting of anti-U.S. riots on the island of Formosa (Taiwan). The U.S. Embassy in Taipei was invaded, with destruction to property and the flag trampled upon. The reason: an army master sergeant had slain a local who had harassed and then threatened him. Follow-up articles in the next few days stated that thirteen Americans had been injured and cautioned all others to remain indoors because of the anti-U.S. sentiment. (I recalled that I had previously written that newly established nation — as I had many others — of my desire to work for them in some independent capacity.)

Because of my prior contact, it triggered a reaction in me to follow-up on that incident, as soon as possible, since I was still awaiting a reply to my original query letter.

On May 25, 1957, I wired the following cablegram to President (formerly Generalissimo) Chiang Kai-shek:

"Can successfully counteract unfavorable public opinion of anti-U.S. rioting by articles as a free-lance writer. Refer to April 29th letter. Available immediately."

As presumptuous as that cablegram was at the time, I had no doubt that I could accomplish what I stated.

On May 30, 1957, I received the following appreciative letter from the Government Information Office, Republic of China:

"Dear Mr. Roland,

Your kind letter of April 29 addressed to President Chiang Kai-shek was referred to this office.

With regard to your offer to be a war correspondent in Free China, the President wishes me to inform you that the government does not employ its own correspondents, such being hired directly by the newspapers, magazines and press agencies here in a private capacity. Those who come from abroad are sent here by their own newspapers or publications in their countries.

With regard to your offer to serve the government in any capacity in the absence of an assignment as a war correspondent, while we are appreciative of your good intentions, we are afraid it would be impossible for you to live on the meager pay of our government service which is barely enough to maintain a decent way of living even by oriental standards. And to keep the morale of our own people, we cannot very well make an exception for you.

The President hopes you will understand the difficulties involved and wait till better days when we return to the mainland. Meanwhile, we hope you will make full use of your writing abilities in favor of our cause and disseminate your writings through the American newspaper syndicates and television programs. To keep you informed on developments here, I have asked the Chinese News Service in New York to place your name on the mailing list for its weekly news release.

Sincerely yours,
Sampson C. Shen
Director"


In response to Director Shen's letter, I sent another cablegram to the Generalissimo and received an equally-appreciative letter from Shen again, dated June 13, 1957:


"Dear Mr. Roland,

You have perhaps received by now my letter of May 29 written on behalf of President Chiang Kai-shek in reply to yours of April 29.

I wish to acknowledge receipt of your cables to the President dated May 25 and June 1 respectively. Your offer to counteract public opinion in your country on the May 24 incident in Taipei and to work in our favor in general is very deeply appreciated.

You will be interested to know that besides the American correspondents permanently stationed in Taiwan, many flew in after the incident from Tokyo and Hong Kong to cover its aftermath. They all were briefed on the case during their stay here both by American officials and our government leaders.

The primary consideration now is not to delve into the whys and wherefores of the incident but how to prevent the international Communists from taking advantage of it and hurting the free world's anti-Communist cause. We all realize the grave implications involved and are working hard together towards repairing the situation.

I am also glad to tell you that things in Taipei have returned to normal and that relations between the Americans in Taiwan and our people are as friendly as ever. There have never been any anti-American sentiments among our people and please rest assured that there is none now.

Thanking you for your kindly interest in the welfare of our country,

Sincerely yours,
Sampson C. Shen
Director"

Satisfied that my prolific letter-writing campaign was beginning to take off, I awaited replies from other foreign dignitaries. At about the same time that I first wrote a letter to Chiang Kai-shek, I also offered my services as a correspondent to the following 14 rulers and leaders of their respective countries:

Emperor Haile Selassie I, Ethiopia
General Francisco Lopez, Portugal
Premier Ba Swe, Burma
President Achmed Sukarno, Indonesia
Mahendra Bir Bikram, Nepal
Maharaja Jigme Wangchuk, Bhutan
King Rama IX, Thailand
President Bayar, Turkey
President Ngo-Dinh-Diem, Vietnam
King Faisal II, Iraq
Prime Minister Abdullah Khalil, Sudan
King Ahmed ibn Yahya Hamid Ed-Dis, Yemen
Mohammed Riza Pahvlavi, Iran
King Hussein I, Jordan

In those days, my letter-writing campaign was considered neither derogatory nor unsavory. I merely stated that I was interested in gaining sympathy and attention to the country in my capacity as a writer. Although my impetuousness was questioned by some of my friends, my philosophy then was — and still is — "nothing ventured, nothing gained."

In addition to writing the foreign heads of state, I still had not forgotten about my original destination, Africa. At the suggestion of some of my co-workers, I tried a more commercial approach in resolving my initial plans of an African trek. On May 30, 1957, I wrote what I considered a masterful letter to the firm that represented Willy's jeeps and trucks, Weintraub Company — and expected a favorable response:

"Weintraub Co.
Chrysler Bldg.
New York, NY
Gentlemen:

How would you like to receive over a million dollars worth of international publicity within a short period of time, for your client "Willys Motors, Inc.?"

Does this future slogan appeal to you — "The truck that conquered Africa?" I can make these words become a reality with my future plans. I am ready, willing and able to drive a Willys, thousands of miles over the Sahara and across the African continent, beginning from "Dakar" and ending at "Diibouti," on the Red Sea.

My past experience on solitary ventures will be attested to by the enclosed newspaper clippings. In addition to the personal side of my nature, which the newspapers have brought out, I have further concrete abilities. I am also a Published Writer and Photographer and am able to use a movie camera competently, which would certainly prove beneficial to Willys, as well as to the trip itself. I could not only document the entire trip for a program such as "Bold Journey" on television but also any structural or mechanical phases of the Willys itself, if you so deem necessary.

The reason I chose a Willys truck was obvious after I carefully investigated the other makes and models. Its 4-wheel drive and off-road traction, as well as its unbelievable maneuverability and limitless visibility ruled out any other company because it consolidated all these features into its ruggedness and made such a trip a distinct possibility.

The "FC-Stake Truck" is perfect for the long haul. It's larger bed area and its frame sides are suitable to carry the necessary equipment on a trek of this nature. Although it is the newest and highest priced of the Willy's models, it could easily become the most in demand because of its unique accomplishment, with myself behind the wheel.

The AAA Auto Club has been most helpful in my preparation and if you are interested in this opportunity to put Willys in the spotlight of notoriety, I can combine your product with all their resources and thereby produce a successful and profitable project.

> Until I hear from you.
> I remain —
> Sincerely,
> Marty Roland"

Within two weeks, I received a very diplomatically phrased rejection letter advising me that my proposal was "most interesting," but that it was "not possible for us to participate in such an undertaking." Their very logical reason was that "every week we receive similar requests from all parts of the world."

As disappointed as I was, I knew I had many other "irons in the fire" and expected at least one of them to heat up. It wasn't long before my expectation was realized — at least partially. On June 8, I received an impressive-looking official envelope from Thailand, apparently in response to my letter to King Rama IX.

When I opened it, it showed an even more impressive letterhead of an oriental winged deity that resembled a Buddha. It also bore "His Majesty's Private Secretariat, Grand Palace, Bangkok" as the return address. Below that, it carried the date it was written, "May 31, E.D. 2500 (1957)."

The formal-sounding letter appears below:

"Sir,

I have been commanded by His Majesty the King, my Gracious Sovereign, to express His appreciation of the spirit in which you offered Him your services in various fields as mentioned in your letter of May 6, 1957, and, in reply, to inform you that under the present circumstances there is not yet any need for services in those fields.

I have the honour to be,

Sir,
Your obedient servant,
(M.C. Nikorn Devan Devakula)
Principal Private Secretary to H.M. the King."

A second response to my initial flurry of foreign letters arrived a few days later. Although it carried numerous stamps from India, I couldn't determine its origination.

When I opened the small letter, its place of origin appeared in the upper right hand corner: "Royal Palace, Kathmandu," with "Office of the Press Attache" in the upper left-hand corner. It was in reply to my letter to Nepal and was signed by, "Renu Lai Singh, Press Attache to H.M. the King":

"Dear Mr. Roland,

Your letter of May 6, 1957, addressed to His Most Gracious Majesty, was received and presented to His Majesty's gracious attention.

His Majesty has noted the contents of your letter and has commanded me to convey his thanks for the same.

Though just now there is no assignment suitable for you, your voluntary offer is appreciated and continued correspondence will be welcome.

By the way, may we know whether you have ever done any article on Nepal? Also, may we know how you happened to develop your penchant for Nepal?"

The tone of the letter was very encouraging and I sought to satisfy his written request for "continued correspondence" and to answer his question about my "penchant for Nepal." Intensive research at the local library produced my reply of June 26, 1957, and I believed it encompassed all aspects of that mysterious land:

"Renu Lal Singh
Press Attache to his Majesty the King
Royal Palace Katmandu, Nepal

Dear Mr. Singh:

Since the conquest of Mt. Everest, the mountain kingdom of Nepal has intrigued me. No other country in the world has been so veiled by mystery and yet has so much to offer.

The African Continent has been called the Land of Contrast but in truth it is really Nepal that surpasses this conception. What other country, or even continent, has the extremes of climate varying from the sub-tropical jungles of the Terai to the icy-cold of the Himalayas, the world's highest mountain range? What other country can combine the wild game of three other continents within its borders, for the hunter and sportsman? Where else can scholars learn from some of the World's oldest manuscripts, than through the ancient Sanscrit literature found in Patna University? Where else can archaeologists and related fields study the ancient cities of Patan, Bhadgaon and Dhankuta? In what other country in the world can an Occidental not only see Hinduism and Buddhism devoutly flourishing in its countless temples but also have the opportunity of understanding and applying the ancient Oriental concepts and beliefs.

I have not yet been fortunate enough to write anything of Nepal, however, should the opportunity present itself, I will be able to write abundantly of the various phases of your country, for the World's consumption.

It is not only unbelievable, to an Adventurer as myself, but disturbing as well, to think that so many people consider only China and India to be the countries of Asia and so few people to even know of the existence of Nepal, much less anything about it.

My penchant for Nepal has developed into an obsession and if I can be of service to His Majesty, I cannot only open the eyes of the Western World but also benefit Nepal, itself."


While I awaited some type of favorable response to my well-prepared letter — which unfortunately never happened — other noteworthy worldwide events were happening that kept me fully occupied.

The first substantial news item was of continuing violence between the French and the Algerians because of their quest for independence. Worldwide opinion against the French was mounting because of their retaliation against Algerian rebels and their violent tactics.

As a follow-up to that coverage, I immediately sent a cablegram on June 1, 1957, to President Rene Coute, Paris, France, similar to the one that I had wired to Generalissimo Chiang Kai-shek:

> "Can successfully stimulate favorable world opinion of your policies by coverage Algerian crisis as free lance correspondent. Available immediately."

Again, as before, I had no idea what I could do, but just knew that I could do something.

This time, however, there was no reply from France.

Also, earlier, there had been a small news item about the death of one of Haile Selassie's sons. That son, his second one and known as Duke of Harar was popular in his province and was killed in an auto accident south of Addis Ababa when the car he was being driven in overturned several times. Inasmuch as Haile Selassie was one of the rulers I had initially written two months earlier, I sent a follow-up letter that I considered appropriate to the occasion.

It was addressed in its formal style to:

"His Imperial majesty
Haile Selassie I
Emperor of Ethiopia
Addis Ababa, Ethiopia"

The format of the correspondence was also thoroughly

researched, as I wanted the protocol to be letter-perfect:


> "May it please your Majesty:
> I have only recently heard of the death of your second son and I wish to extend my deepest sympathy.
> We have never met but this does not alter my sincere feelings over your personal loss.
> I remain, Sir, with the greatest respect, your Majesty's most obedient servant,
>
> Marty Roland"


Although, I believe, I received some type of standardized formal acknowledgment for my condolences, there was no other communication from that country.

There was another source of news developing much closer to home, which received my full attention.

I consequently made several serious attempts to become embroiled in the action.

Fidel Castro was staging a revolt in the Sierra Maestra Mountains in the Oriente Province of Cuba, and was becoming daily news.

His successes were apparently mounting.

Although I was living in Florida, the vast majority of Floridians, at that early stage of the revolt, knew little or nothing of Castro, only the fact that he was a rebel.

In a continuing attempt to become personally involved in what was happening 90 miles off our shore, I sent a cablegram, my third, to: General Ramon Batista, the dictator in Havana, Cuba.

It carried the same general message as the others:

> "Can obtain favorable public opinion of you through commercial publications as a free lance writer covering your present conflict. Available immediately."

At the time of my transmission to Batista, I also knew little or nothing of his dictatorial regime. Had I known of his despotic rulership, I would not have sought his assistance.

Fortunately, I never received a reply, and when I mentioned it to a Cuban acquaintance who owned the local camera shop, he told me to consider myself lucky, as it would not have been a healthy arrangement.

"OK," I said. "How about getting word to some of your Cuban buddies that I want to be parachuted into the Sierra Maestra's to fight my way out with Castro."

He looked at me in surprise and said, "If that's what you want, I'll try."

When I saw him a few days later, I asked him if he had passed the word along. He nodded, and in a low voice added a cautionary warning, "Let's hope that none of Castro's friends find out that you've tried to contact Batista first."

"Why?" I asked, without thinking of the consequences of the answer.

"Because if they do, they might come looking for you."

In the days that followed nothing happened. I was never approached by anyone as to my recent offer to help Castro. There was, however, continuous coverage in the media about the fighting in Cuba, and it goaded me further.

On June 5, 1957, I sent the following letter to: Ralph Rennick, News Director, WTVJ in Miami:

"Dear Mr. Rennick:

I am a Free-Lance writer and am offering my services as a correspondent to Fidel Castro and his 'Freedom Fighters.'

Since your recent telecast of Castro, which incidentally was a terrific job, I felt this query to you would be quite in order.

As to my past experience, I've chosen solitary ventures into the jungles of Central and South America, as well as those of the South Pacific during the war, and am therefore well equipped to handle any emergencies that arise in guerrilla tactics.

I have not only been fortunate to have some of my pieces appear in our men's adventure magazines, but I also have an agent in Switzerland who is currently handling additional stories of mine and is in the market for more.

He has contacts with French, Italian and German newspapers and syndicates, and the opportunity to have Castro obtain European publicity through my writings, is a very strong possibility.

If you can direct this letter to the proper channels, I would not only be very grateful, but I am sure that Castro and his cause would benefit greatly by my coverage. My telephone numbers is JA4-5200, should you or any of the leaders wish to contact me."

On that same date, in an effort to leave no stone unturned, I also wrote a similar letter to columnist Herb Rau of the *Miami Daily News.*

In that letter, I offered him exclusive copy of all my writings about the revolt for his *"Dateline Miami"* column, "if some of the leaders of Castro's forces — can make use of my services."

Whether I was considered some type of kook, or whether my own involvement would compromise their own journalistic efforts, I never knew.

I was never contacted by either source.

Although rejections were fast becoming a way of life for me in my chosen life style, I never gave up trying.

To further bolster my efforts in the foreign field, I received an official-looking letter covered in large green and pink stamps from Saigon. Before I opened it, I knew undoubtedly that it was in response to my own earlier query to President Ngo-Dinh-Diem of Vietnam.

When I opened the mail, the cover letter was addressed to "*Ong* Marty Roland," and the salutation was to "*Thua Ong*," followed by a half-page letter written in Vietnamese.

As impressive as their correspondence was to me in their native language, I wondered what it meant and where I could get it translated. My bewilderment quickly disappeared when I noted an English translation that was stapled to the tissue copy of the letter, dated "19 *Thang* 7 *Nam* 1957:"

"Dear Sir,

President NGO-DINH-DIEM has received your letter of May 8, 1957 by which you kindly offered your services to Vietnam.

The President has charged me to thank you on his behalf and request you to let us know the conditions required for your cooperation, which would consist in writing articles about Vietnam for the MEN'S MAGAZINES, newspaper Syndicates and Television programs as proposed in your letter.

In the meanwhile, we are sending you, in a separate packet, a few booklets about Vietnam, and will also send you regularly our other publications as well as the English weekly *TIMES OF VIETNAM.*

With best regards,
Yours truly
TRAN-CHANH-THANH
Secretary of State for
Information and Youth"

The content of that letter was one of the few encouraging replies I had received and I immediately drafted a response:

"July 25, 1957
Tran-Chanh-Tranh

Secretary of State for Information & Youth
Saigon-Cholon
National State of Vietnam

Dear Sir:

I wish to extend my sincere appreciation to the President for his kind response to my offer and also to yourself for your gracious letter on his behalf.

In answer to the President's request for my conditions, I ask only for one thing. That stipulation is for travel arrangements to and from your country, plus the cooperation of your government in enabling me to obtain the necessary material.

The time that I will be able to spend in Vietnam, on the various phases that I have outlined in my first letter, will be unlimited.

Although I am a Free-Lancer, I ask no fee of my services to your country. However, when the time comes that Vietnam has substantially benefited through my achievements, — then and only then — will I gratefully accept any form of compensation. At such time, I will leave the matter entirely to the President's discretion in determining my worth and value to Vietnam.

> I remain,
> Sincerely,
> Marty Roland"

After I wrote the letter, I reread it to see if what I asked was too much. I decided that my request was reasonable since I was leaving my return to the states open-ended — and since I would have to take an extended leave of absence from my job. Of course, I hoped that if my offer was accepted, my journalistic abilities would finally gain me some long-awaited recognition — and more importantly, my postal career could finally be terminated.

How seriously my conditions to President Ngo-Dinh-Diem were considered, I was unaware since any further correspondence from them apparently ended.

I realized the summer of 1957 was also rapidly coming to an end, and I had to decide — and decide fast — when and where I was headed.

Fortunately, earlier in the summer, I had entertained a new thought as to my next plan of action, if all foreign letters were to fail.

That thought was to complete a book that I had started earlier in the year. It was to be tentatively titled, "The Adventurer," and was to be a fiction piece loosely based on the Cuban situation and my own prior experiences in Central America during the summer of '54. I had even given thought to where I would go to finish the book. Because I had heard Mexico was inexpensive to live, and because I had been there previously, I chose that country as my new destination.

Little did I realize that my decision would encompass far more than completing a book, and turn out to be just as challenging and fruitful as my South American trip.

# 23

On Thursday, August 1, 1957, staff writer, Duane Jones, of the *Miami Herald* did another inspiring piece on my upcoming trip to Mexico. He also was the first reporter to do a story of my British Guiana venture two years earlier and was eager to do a follow-up of my latest exploit.

This time, the intriguing headline on the article was:

## "DIAMOND HUNTER CHUCKS JOB POINTS FOR A MILLION DOLLARS"

Below the story was a smiling confident photo of me at my cluttered desk at home working on my new book. Consistent with the heading of the story, and indicative of an industrious writer, was a second pencil stuck behind my ear. In the foreground of the picture, resting on my desk, was my sheathed hunting knife.

The caption on the photo said:

> **"Marty Roland is Poised for Another Hunting Trip — off to the wilds of Mexico this time."**

Above the busy photo appeared the informative article:

> **"FORT LAUDERDALE** — Marty Roland, the postal clerk who hunts wild animals and diamond mines in his spare time, will start on

another junket Monday.

This time he's going to Mexico, where he plans to "hunt whatever there is to hunt there."

And in Vera Cruz he plans to finish writing a book that he hopes will net him a million dollars.

"I'm shooting the works this time," Roland said in announcing that he's quitting the post office job he's held five years.

"I'm relying on my book," he explained. "If it doesn't sell, I don't know what I'll do. I'll be broke and will have to start all over again."

Roland hopes his luck will be better than it has been the past couple of years.

In 1955 he went to British Guiana in search of diamond mines. He didn't find any, but came home with a small diamond given him by a sympathetic native. Roland figured it was worth about $500.

Then last year his wild animal expedition to the jungles of South Africa had to be canceled because of the Suez crisis. So Roland stayed home.

But he's spent considerable time in Latin American countries and his new book concerns revolutions he's seen and read about.

Roland has completed five chapters and expects to finish the book in a month or six weeks. It's to be titled "The Adventurer" and is to include approximately 60,000 words.

"It's a big gamble, but I'm willing to risk it," he said. "I'm hocking everything I own to finance the venture, including my car, a 1952 convertible, and several suits of clothing, size 36."

"I'm going for broke this time, and some of my friends say that's exactly how I'll end up — broke."

Of course, my family knew of my intentions before the publicity appeared in the *Miami Herald,* and needless to say, there was concern.

"Why do you have to go to Mexico to finish your book? Why couldn't you do it here?" they asked.

And the most recurring question I heard was "Why did you have to quit your job?"

Obviously, my responses, as meaningful and as important as they were to me, were unsatisfactory.

Co-workers, friends and acquaintances were more understanding, and even jealous to some extent.

"I don't blame you, you're single," or, "I wish I were you," or, "I wish I could afford to go with you," and even a few who added, "If I'd have known sooner, I'd have helped you."

These latter comments I had heard many times before, and took them all with a grain of salt. To my jealous buddies, I had a stock reply, "If you didn't get married so young, you could do the same thing."

Although the announcement of my sudden departure — and especially quitting the Post Office after six years — seemed impetuous to many, it was a course of action I had long considered.

As much as I hoped — and even expected — one of my distant foreign trips to materialize, I had to have an alternative plan, just in case. Hunting in Mexico seemed a good choice and was almost as important to me as completing my book. To be prepared, weeks earlier I purchased a new shotgun. I traded in the old double-barreled one that I used in South America. I still didn't want to rely on it again, although it seemed fully functional. My new one was a more expensive model, an over-and-under 16 gauge that was in high demand by hunters because of its unique design.

That new shotgun would prove to be a good investment, especially in the interior of Mexico. However, I didn't realize the problem it would cause me before my return to the states.

I had all my other equipment, so I didn't need to purchase anything else. The only item that I couldn't take with me was my .357 pistol because handguns were not permitted. I figured that if I really needed one on a hunting trip, I could probably borrow one from a local. That assumption was correct. When I began my hunt, I was able to get one from my guide.

On August 5, I was en route from Miami to Mexico City on a Mexicana airline. It was a long and slightly turbulent flight, especially when we entered the mountainous airspace near Mexico City, the mile-high city.

Once on the ground, I had to go through customs to declare my shotgun. It caused no problems since I was entering their country to hunt, and a notation was made somewhere that I possessed a shotgun.

Rather than stay in Mexico City for a day or so, having been in that capital city before, I elected to catch the next flight to Vera Cruz, my destination.

There was no particular reason I chose that city other than the fact it was a sleepy port city on the Gulf of Mexico, and travel agents had told me that accommodations there were very reasonable.

I knew that my primary reason in choosing Mexico was to finish my book. Then, time permitting, I would do a little hunting.

Somehow, I got sidetracked.

My impressions of a quiet seaport were borne out when, after checking into a small hotel near the waterfront, I wandered around the section near the docks. As quaint and restful as the section was, neither it nor the hotel was conducive to writing.

One of the first things I did was to locate a U.S. Consulate Office to let them know of my presence in the country. It was a practice I had never thought of on previous trips, but the rationale made sense after it was explained to me.

"How will anyone ever know of your whereabouts if anything ever happens to you," other foreign travelers reminded me.

The young clerk in the Consulate made a brief notation about my presence in that city and about where I was staying. When I advised the American representative that my stay at the hotel was only temporary, she shrugged her shoulders as if to say what good is that information to the Consulate then?

I reluctantly agreed to the apparent uselessness of that information to the American authorities, but added that at least interested parties would know that I had successfully reached the city of Vera Cruz and would probably be somewhere in the State of Vera Cruz, as well.

With our meeting of the minds on that subject, I asked if the clerk knew of any boarding houses or small hotels in the general vicinity that might suit my needs. Fortunately, she was most helpful on that subject and supplied me with several other sources of information that might direct me to appropriate places.

For the next several hours, I combed the immediate area but could not locate housing that was both reasonable and suitable for work. The next morning I resumed my search, which took me even further into the countryside.

On my last contact, I managed to find a private residence that had a clean spare room to rent. The price was right, food was available by the *madre* of the dwelling and the setting was almost idyllic in a lightly treed section with barnyard fowl clucking gently below my window. However, there was no place to write — my main reason for being in Mexico. Besides the bed, all the small room had were a chair, a narrow dresser and an equally narrow nightstand.

It was my final address on the list of places supplied me, and I was almost tempted to choose it. However, writing on the corner of a nightstand or a dresser was not what I had in mind to complete a book.

I returned to my hotel, found a nearby local cantina, where I had a cold *cerveza*, and pondered what to do next. During the course of my musing, the bartender, who was as fluent in broken English as I was in limited Spanish, was in a talkative mood. Where was I from? Where was I going? Etc. , etc. . . Since I was equally talkative, I asked him about the area and if he knew of any suitable places. He knew of none. During the extended conversation, I mentioned that I also came to Mexico to hunt.

"Oh, *señor*," he continued, "the State of Vera Cruz is good for hunting — especially *en las montañas*."

"*Qué animales?*" I asked him.

He rattled off a string of names of game in the area, and when he came to "*tigres*" I stopped him.

"*Donde?*" I wanted to know.

"I have *un amigo bueno* who likes to hunt," he continued.

"*Donde vive?*" I pressed.

"*En* San Andrés Tuxtla," he said.

I made circular movements in the air with my hands questioning where San Andrés Tuxtla was, and asked him how far it was from Vera Cruz.

"About *ochenta milos desde aquí*," he answered in Spanish and then corrected himself in case I didn't understand, "eighty miles, *señor*."

"*Qué direcion?*" I wanted to know.

"*Sud*," he said quickly, and then followed up with "south on the *Golfo de Mexico*."

"*Qué nombre*, and how do I find him?" I asked slowly.

He gave me a full name quickly that I couldn't follow.

"Manuel?" I said repeating what I thought he said.

"I write," he said as he scribbled a name and address on a piece of paper.

"*Gracias, muchas gracias*."

"I will call him for you, *señor*," he offered, as he held his hand up to his ear with an imaginary phone. "*Cuando* — when will you go?"

"*Mañana*, or the day after *mañana*."

He nodded his head in agreement, and I wrote my name down for him.

"*Bueno, señor.* I will call him *esta tarde* — this afternoon. You will see me later, yes?"

"I'll be back," I said, leaving to return to my hotel.

At the desk, I inquired of San Andréas Tuxtla, and if buses went there.

"*Sí, señor,*" the clerk answered brightly and then pointed down the block to a nearby bus station.

I found out the bus schedule, learned the days of the week that the bus departed and returned to the cantina later that afternoon.

The bartender gave me a wide smile when he saw me. "It is all arranged, *señor,* for him to meet you."

"Did you tell him when?"

"Only what you told me, *señor. Mañana,* or the day after."

He gestured expressively with his hands.

"*Graçias, otra vez,*" I said.

"*Por nada, señor.* It is my great pleasure."

We shook hands and he grasped my arm. "*Buena suerte, señor, con los tigres.*"

I nodded acknowledgment and left.

That night sleep didn't come easily. I was anticipating a new hunt.

# 24

Early the next morning, I waited at the bus station before an old bus pulled up to the entrance. Fortunately, I was early enough to be at the head of the compressed line of travelers that formed at the curb: women with their small children and peasants with every imaginable type of baggage and supplies.

As I squeezed aboard the bus with my gear and shotgun, I asked the driver when we would arrive in San Andréas.

"*Dos horas – mas or menos,*" he said. It was a typical response.

I found an empty seat behind the driver so I could ask him where to get off. I didn't want to miss the unloading point, as it was not like riding a bus in the states.

The packed interior of the bus was an accumulation of every imaginable odor possible: sweat mixed with cooked food and the constant exhalations of fifty-plus passengers. The bumpy road added to the atmosphere.

At the end of the trip, which was more "*mas*" than "*menos,*" the bus rumbled into a bustling marketplace in the town and most of the occupants disembarked.

"San Andréas Tuxtla," the driver announced proudly, and I gladly climbed out with my gear and cased shotgun.

Nobody paid attention to the *norteamericano* who wandered through the streets looking for a taxi. With my dark hair and tanned skin, I blended in with the masses.

When I located a cab, I handed the driver the address. He looked at it and nodded.

"*Sí, señor, pronto.*"

I leaned back in the seat and took in the changing colorful sights of people, vendors and smaller wooden houses on the outskirts of the town.

He stopped in front of a large shack that was not quite as ramshackle as the others in the area.

"*Aquí está, señor.*"

I grunted acknowledgment, looked at the house and paid the driver in pesos.

I had no sooner alighted from the taxi and walked up the narrow dirt path to the front door, when a middle-aged Mexican greeted me warmly.

We exchanged names as he led me inside and introduced me to his wife and the several children who crowded around a table in the kitchen.

His English was broken, but understandable. Apparently he understood me, as well, since I tried to interject more Spanish in the conversation than English.

I gathered that he would take me on a three- or four-day hunt "for *tigres,*" if that was my wish. He gave me the price of what it would cost.

I asked him to repeat it because he spoke fast, and I wasn't sure I had heard correctly.

"*Cuatro cientos y ochenta pesos,*" he said in a low voice that was almost apologetic.

The peso, at that time, was roughly eight pesos to our dollar, and I quickly calculated the total cost to be about $60 U.S.

I repeated the amount in English to make sure there was no misunderstanding.

"You mean 480 pesos?" I asked incredulously.

Apparently, he sensed my amazement at the figure, and quickly added, "*un caballo, tambien.*"

"A horse?"

I raised my voice slightly as I said it, not really questioning him but wondering why there was only one horse.

"*Sí señor, para usted. Es necessario.*"

"*Por qué, para me only?*" I wanted to know.

"It is many miles," he said simply.

"*Es todo?*" I asked again referring to the total cost.

"*Es todo par mi,*" he emphasized as he tapped himself on the chest, "*y el caballo.*"

"*No mas?*" I wanted to know figuring that the total cost was pretty cheap for a three- to four-day hunt.

"Food," he said in English, "a *leedle* more."

"*Cuanto mas?*"

He thought about it a moment.

"*Dos cientos pesos — no mas,*" he added quickly.

That was about $25 U.S. I decided that was very reasonable for the number of days we would be out. I readily agreed, and we shook hands on the agreement.

"*Bueno,*" I said enthusiastically. "*Cuando?*"

"*De la mañana,*" he answered.

Because I was so satisfied with the cost of a guide, I initially neglected to ask him where we were going.

Then I thought about it. "*Donde va?*" I asked.

"*Trienta o cuarenta milos,*" he said, gesturing in the distance.

I took out a detailed topographical map I had of Mexico and spread it out before him.

"*Donde va?*" I asked again.

He studied it carefully and then traced a gnarled finger over a small body of water inland and then back to the coast.

"*Aquí está,*" he said as his finger circled a small area near the Gulf of Mexico that looked desolate and uninhabited.

The closest landmark I could discern was the name, Punta Zapotitlan, a piece of land that jutted into the water. I also noted that just above the town of San Andréas Tuxtla was the Volcano de San Martin, which I presumed was inactive. Just below the area where he indicated we would hunt was the notation that it was some type of reservation in the Sierra de San Martin.

It, too, looked deserted. I was pleased.

"Is it about thirty or forty miles from here?" I asked in English.

"*Sí, señor. Y tigres son allí.*"

I liked the answer about the *tigres*.

"*Grande?*" I asked hopefully.

"*Mas or menos,*" he answered, nodding his head.

It was the typical Spanish response, and I nodded my own head in understanding.

With our transaction completed, I asked him to recommend a place where I could sleep overnight.

"There is one nearby, *señor,*" he said, escorting me outside to an old pickup truck parked at the side of the house.

He drove me to a nearby small hotel, that was clean, and I checked in with my gear. He set a time for the next morning and left.

As promised, he arrived early the following day with one of his older sons, who served as our driver.

My guide, Manuel, had already thrown his gear in the back of the truck and motioned for me to do the same.

"*Son listo, señor?*"

"*Sí,* I'm ready."

The truck rumbled north through narrow streets and dirt roads toward the small village of La Palma. We stopped near a large inland body of water, the Laguna de Sontecomapan, which I learned emptied into the Gulf. It was so large, you couldn't see the far side.

At the edge of the *laguna*, Manuel got out of the truck near some small boats pulled up on the bank. He approached one of the older men, spoke to him briefly and then returned.

"It is arranged," he said, extracting his gear from the rear of the truck. I did the same, as Manuel rapidly spoke to his son in Spanish. The son nodded his head and drove off.

"He will return for us, when we return," he noted.

"*Ahora, el hombre* will take us across *la laguna,*" he said, indicating the wide expanse of water.

He hadn't mentioned a boat, but he was my guide, and I relied on his arrangements.

It was a short, flat-bottomed boat with an outboard motor. There was barely enough space for the three of us, plus our gear. The owner efficiently made room, and the motor kicked over nosily, quickly moving us away from the shore. The boat slapped the top of the small waves as we bounced over the water toward the opposite shore. We were the only craft I could see, but the closer we approached the forested shore, the more small boats I spied. Some small shacks were nestled in the trees.

The owner guided the boat expertly toward a small cove. As we glided toward land, he cut the motor.

"*Somos, aquí señor,*" my guide announced, waving his hand toward the heavy jumble of trees.

He paid the owner a few pesos, thanked him, slung his own shotgun over his shoulder and hoisted his gear. He motioned me ahead as he walked up a short embankment to some shacks we had spotted in the distance. I followed.

Some native boys ran to meet us at the top of the hill, and he greeted them and said something I did not understand. They immediately took off toward one of the buildings. A few minutes later, two young Mexicans emerged and walked toward us. Both looked to be in their twenties and knew my guide. He introduced me as *El señor* and they acknowledged me with an "*Hola, señor.*" They led the way toward one of the shacks.

They were to be our guides on the hunt. Since neither of them spoke English, Manuel would be the translator.

My guide and I waited outside while they entered their small wooden building. After a few minutes, they stepped outside again. One of the two, who appeared younger, I'll call José, only had a single-barreled rust-colored shotgun, similar to those the natives carried in British Guiana. The other, I'll call Pablo, had a newer shotgun and a long-barreled pistol tucked in his belt. Both carried the ever-present machetes. When he saw me eyeing the pistol, he offered to let me see it. It was a dull blued .38 caliber revolver, but it looked functional. I asked Manuel if there was one I could use. He asked the Mexicans.

Pablo smiled a gap-toothed grin at the request.

"*Sí, señor,*" he answered, disappearing into a nearby shack.

He reappeared with a four-inch, .38 caliber pistol in about the same condition as his own.

"*Aquí, señor,*" he said, holding it out for me to inspect. It also appeared to be operable.

"*Gracias.*"

"*Por nada, señor,*" he said, seeming pleased that I liked it. He also reached into his pants pocket and took out six .38 caliber shells and offered them to me.

I thanked him again.

They closely followed my actions with the pistol, undoubtedly expecting me to slip it into my own belt. Instead, I reached into the bottom of my bag and took out my old gun belt. The three of them watched appreciatively as I loaded the gun and slipped the short revolver into my holster. I then strapped the gun belt around my waist. It was looser than it should have been. The last time I used it, it held my six-inch .357 magnum, a longer and wider revolver.

They all smiled at the sight and said in unison, "*Bueno, señor.*"

Satisfied with my good luck, I looked around for the first time. It was a small settlement with sparsely distributed shacks. Towering trees loomed above us, but not as large as those in South America. It was tropical, but it was not the thick impenetrable jungle of the Guianas.

The young Mexicans said something to Manuel that I didn't quite hear, and they moved out ahead of us. We followed.

"We go to get horse," Manuel offered in English, while we walked.

"*Donde?*"

"No far," he said. "Perhaps *un milo o dos milos* to village."

Although we walked on a dense forest trail, I could smell salt air and mentioned it to Manuel.

"*Sí, señor, el Golfo,*" he said, gesturing to our left.

I couldn't see the Gulf of Mexico but knew it had to be nearby.

After an hour or more of trudging on the trail, we saw some shacks ahead and were greeted by the yelping of dogs in the distance.

We stopped at a nearby open shack with no door or windows. The two young Mexicans entered the small building while Manuel and I waited nearby. Within a few minutes they reappeared and beckoned us over.

"*Señor,*" Manuel stepped aside waiting for me to precede him.

Once inside we were cordially greeted by two older Mexican peasants, husband and wife, who rattled off the names of the small children surrounding them.

"We will eat here," Manuel volunteered as the wife cleared off the crude table.

From Manuel's own knapsack, he pulled out a bag of dried beans and a bag of flour that he gave the woman. She thanked him and busied herself around some type of earthenware stove.

While we waited for the food to be prepared, the husband motioned us outside and walked to what can best be described as a corral. It was not like any corral I had ever seen before. There weren't any horizontal railings or solid gate of any kind. Instead, there were several layers of tree branches pushed together to form a barrier. The crude gate formed part of the haphazard side of the corral and was merely pushed into place and lashed shut with vines.

Inside this cramped stockade, two horses milled about. Manuel nudged me, "*Su caballo, señor.*"

"*Sí,*" I said, eyeing them warily. I was not a horseman and had not ridden one since I was a kid.

Manuel noticed me apprehensively looking at the two small horses. They appeared malnourished.

"They are..." he said, hesitating as he searched for the English word to describe them. "...quiet."

I assumed he meant to say "gentle," but I still didn't look forward to riding for miles on bony animals that I couldn't control.

"*Graçias,*" I said half-heartedly, trying to appear appreciative.

"Which you like?"

I shrugged my shoulders. I truthfully didn't like either. Manuel and the husband waited for a reply.

I chose the one nearest to me, a nondescript brownish horse with a cropped mane that looked more like a large colt than a horse.

"*Bueno, señor,*" Manuel spoke, nodding the choice to the owner. He acknowledged the selection.

Manuel paid the man, who seemed satisfied with the transaction, and then said aloud to the three of us, "*Comemos.*"

"We eat, *señor,*" Manuel said, guiding me back toward the shack.

As hungry as I was, the strange food didn't taste half-bad, despite the barnyard surroundings.

With the open windows and the lack of a door, chickens strutted or flew in and a fat pig wandered around the dirt floor snapping up scraps. Continually trying to jump up on the table were the household cats, which the observant husband quickly knocked off.

After we ate, Manuel suggested we all rest a bit before setting off again. I grabbed my bag and headed outside to find a good place to lie down.

"No, *señor,*" Manuel insisted. "You sleep here." He pointed to a solitary cot on the side of the room.

I looked at him, then around the room. I saw no other beds or cots in the small space.

"Whose bed?" I asked him.

"It is the bed of *el esposo y la esposa,*" he answered without hesitation.

I looked at them, as they nodded their heads.

"No, Manuel," I protested, "I can't. It is their bed." I stressed what I said.

He held up his hand. "You must, *señor*," he said, pointing to the bed again. "If you do not, it is an insult," he emphasized.

I looked back at the couple, and they vigorously nodded their heads in agreement.

I thought about it a moment and then sat down on the cot, stretched out and closed my eyes. Before I dozed off, I had a recollection of the chickens clucking nearby and the pig approaching the cot to check me out.

I was awakened a couple of hours later by Manuel.

"We go now, *señor*. All is ready."

Outside, the two young Mexicans were waiting with the horse, which had been saddled with a hard leather mount. Manuel held the animal steady, handed me the reins and indicated that I should mount.

It was as Manuel had said earlier, a "quiet" animal, and it moved slowly as the four of us headed out of the small settlement. I rode uneasily in my uncomfortable perch.

Before long, we were out of the forested area and were approaching the wide blue-green expanse of the Gulf of Mexico. Between the distant horizon and us was an unbroken line of gently rolling waves lapping on the sandy beach.

Manuel guided the horse until it clomped heavily in the moistened sand where water met beach. The two Mexicans walked ahead with Manuel nearby. Before us and behind us stretched miles of endless shoreline. Not a boat or person could be seen anywhere. The sand bore no human footprints or animal tracks of any kind. It was as if we were on some barren planet. Far to our right was unbroken foliage that masked the thick jungle behind it. Behind that, large trees clung to the hillsides that formed the base of the mountainous terrain.

Manuel saw me eyeing our surroundings and made a large sweeping motion with his outstretched hand.

"*Tigres* live *en las montañas, señor.*"

"*Bueno,*" I acknowledged but wondered how far we still had to travel. My discomfort on the stiff leather saddle was beginning to increase.

Our small procession continued for what seemed like interminable hours over the packed sandy surface. The constant jarring motion of the horse's hooves as it lifted them and slapped them down again began to chafe my buttocks where it met the board-like leather.

Finally, I had had enough, and I rose up in the saddle and reined the horse to a halt.

"I'll walk," I told Manuel as I rubbed the cheeks of both buttocks.

He smiled as I dismounted.

"You ride," I told him.

He shook his head and called to one of the Mexicans to take my place. Pablo, the older one, readily accepted.

The trek continued for another hour or more, until we reached what seemed to be the end of the beach. Checking my map, however, it probably was Punta Zapotitlan. Beyond that point the shoreline dipped sharply to the south, which made it appear as though we were at the end of the beach when really we weren't. It extended for miles around the bend.

As if on cue, the others stopped simultaneously.

"We stop here," Manuel called out the obvious to me, motioning for José and Pablo to move out. We sat on the sand and watched the young men as they headed south on the beach to disappear into the thick brush that bordered the Gulf.

After awhile Pablo galloped toward us on the weary horse and announced to Manuel that they had located a good camping site. We followed to a secluded area about a half-mile from the beach. Dense foliage and large trees protected it. José had already started a fire. The sun was beginning to set, and it was getting cooler.

The horse was tethered, watered and fed while Manuel prepared our evening meal. I took a look around.

Although we were on the flats, around us rose low jungle foothills. It reminded me of British Guiana. I unslung my shotgun and indicated to Manuel that I wanted to explore our immediate area. He nodded and told Pablo to accompany me. We covered about a quarter mile around the campsite, keeping the fire in view, and searched for jaguar tracks. We saw none and returned.

We ate, and the three of them stretched out by the fire.

"We rest *ahora*," Manuel said. "We hunt *anoche* — at night," he added.

I nodded. I knew that all animals hunted at night and wanted another jaguar while they were on the prowl for food.


It had been dark for several hours when Manuel got up. José and Pablo rose easily and were stirring the dying fire when I finally pushed myself to my feet. We all rolled our thin blankets and placed them near our packs. The blankets had covered the sandy scrub undergrowth and offered some minor comfort for sleeping on the ground — but not much. As soon as the sun set, our meager cover was little protection from the mosquitoes that rose from the foliage and descended on us.

The night was moonless, but the blackened shapes of trees that loomed nearby jutted into the darkened sky and intensified the bleakness around us. The fire's dancing embers dully illuminated our small group as we inspected our shotguns to make sure they were ready to fire.

Manuel handed me a battery-operated headlamp that I strapped to my forehead and switched on. The others did the same, and we all stepped away from the fire. Manuel indicated that we would take the low ground, while José and Pablo would take the higher ground to our left. The hunt began with the four of us moving as silently as possible. Four beams of light stabbed the darkness and bobbed up and down. The farther in we hiked, the more spread out we became, until we could neither see their beams nor hear their movements. Crashes in the jungle made us stop to listen and then go forward again. It was reminiscent of my Guiana hunt. Occasionally our beams of light focused on luminous eyes reflecting back at us, but they were set too close together and too low on the ground to be jaguar.

After what seemed like a couple of hours, we saw José's and Pablo's lights far ahead of us at a higher elevation. Manuel gestured that we should climb the gentle slope and head toward them. Their beams remained stationary until we reached their position. Pablo held his finger to his lips indicating that we should be quiet while he and José's eyes searched the jungle above them. Then, Pablo shook his head and spoke in a low voice to Manuel. I heard the word "*tigre*" and saw him give a wide sweep of his arm at a section he had just left.

Manuel confirmed to me what he whispered and said they both thought they had heard one in the distance. The heavy sounds of movement through the brush ceased, however, and they believed it had eluded them.

Manuel held his hand up and motioned for José and Pablo to take the lower section back to the campsite while we held to the higher ground.

Two more hours passed as we combed the mountainous jungle for what we believed was the elusive jaguar. We heard and saw nothing. What we did encounter, though, were droves of mosquitoes that kept us moving faster onward. Finally, we arrived at a point above the campfire where we saw José and Pablo outlined against the rising flame.

Our descent was noisy in the crackling undergrowth, and if there were any jaguar in the area, they were long gone. The Mexicans were as disappointed as we were and apologized for not raising a *tigre*. It was their intention to drive one toward us. Regrettably, the jaguar was not in on the plan.

There were only a couple of hours of darkness left, and after the horse was seen to, a bottle of tequila was passed around. Rotation of the bottle among the four of us, with heavy swills of the firewater, contributed to complete relaxation before the fire, and then sleep.

With the rising of the sun, we were all awake simultaneously. José assisted Manuel with the food preparation, while Pablo saw to the horse. I waited and wondered what the plan would be for the day. After we ate, Manuel conferred with the Mexicans as to where we would all search during the day for tracks. They agreed to go back up into the foothills while Manuel and I concentrated on the low stretch of land south of our campsite and around the sloping bend. We separated, and Manuel set a time when we would all return.

We probed the thick foliage, searching the ground for tracks and checking nearby trees for signs of resting jaguars. We saw none and heard no rustling in the undergrowth as we moved farther from our site. By midmorning, we had covered two or three miles and had seen only a few old jaguar tracks. If José and Pablo had spotted any, we wouldn't know until we returned to camp.

As the sun rose higher in the morning, it got hotter and more humid. We were nowhere near the Gulf. We were moving further inland and stirring up more mosquitoes. Manuel, who had been warding them off as much as I, finally held his hand up.

"We return to camp, *señor*," he said, pointing in the direction we should head.

With the sun directly overhead, we arrived back at the site. José and Pablo already were there and were exercising the horse.

When they saw us approach, they smiled broadly.

Pablo was the first to speak.

"*Tigre, señor*," he said, gesturing excitedly into the foothills.

"*El animale?*" Manuel wanted to know.

"No," he answered, giving a word for track that I had

never heard before. José pointed to the ground.

"*Grande?*" I asked.

They both gestured as if to say maybe so and maybe not.

"Perhaps, *señor,*" Manuel interpreted. "We must return before dark."

"*Bueno!*" I said enthusiastically.

"*Ahora.* We eat and then rest," Manuel continued.

After the brief meal was prepared and eaten, the Mexicans left to search for firewood for the night.

When they returned with enough dead wood for the evening, we all took a little siesta in whatever shade we could find.


It was late afternoon when the four of us set out to find the jaguar tracks again. The climb was steady, and we tried to be as quiet as possible in the tangled undergrowth. It was after six o'clock when we reached the spot. Although the sun was still out, the high trees had partially eclipsed the daylight. The Mexicans knew where to look.

Manuel nodded as they pointed out the jaguar pads.

"No *grande, señor,*" he said, hesitating. "No *pequeño,* either."

As I looked at the tracks, I was satisfied that at least a jaguar was in the vicinity.

We all checked the trees near the markings in the ground, but saw nothing.

"Any carcass nearby?" I asked Manuel, remembering my Guiana hunt.

"Carcass?" Manuel repeated not understanding the term.

"*Sí,* carcass — dead *animale para el tigre,*" I explained.

Manuel brightened, nodding his head. "*Entiendo, señor.*" He motioned for José and Pablo to begin a search of the area.

Finally, after careful examination, Pablo called to us excitedly.

"*Aquí, está. Aquí, está.*" He pointed to the edge of a clearing where we saw a pile of leaves near a fallen tree.

Below the leaves and vegetation was the partially eaten remains of what appeared to be a wild pig.

They all smiled, and Manuel carefully covered up the gory discovery.

"We must remain nearby after dark," he said. "But it is still light now." He pointed up at the fading twilight.

I knew that the jaguar would return when it was hungry.

"For now, we search for other *tigre*," he said, gesturing to the two Mexicans. The four of us studied the area that sloped away from the jaguar kill.

We had been gone less than an hour when the sun finally set. Suddenly, the heavy crackling of branches broke the stillness of the jungle from the area we had just left.

We looked at each other and mouthed the word "*tigre*." We all gripped our shotguns and ran uphill toward the area. The ground around the burial of the pig was disturbed and the carcass was gone.

"*Tigre come, señor*, and take food," Manuel said simply.

José, who had been standing at the far edge of the small clearing, called out to us. He pointed to the ground again and spoke to Manuel animatedly in Spanish.

"What did he say?" I wanted to know.

"Another *tigre, señor*."

My disappointment disappeared at the unexpected news.

"José says he thinks it is *tigre* trail and that more come this way."

I couldn't believe my luck

"We need *animale* to bring *tigre* back," Manuel said.

"Dead *animale*?"

"Or live," he answered.

"Unfortunately," I said, "we have no live *animales*. No pigs, no goats, *nada*."

"*Solamente, nosotros*," he said dejectedly as he lapsed back into Spanish and pointed to the both of us.

"Suppose..." I said, hesitating for a heartbeat. "...suppose we are the *animales*?"

He started to smile, but when he saw I was serious, he stopped.

I continued, "Why can't we be the decoys?"

He repeated the word and asked what it meant, although he probably understood more than he let on.

"If we sit here in the dark between the tracks of the second *tigre* and where the carcass was, we will be on their path," I explained.

He looked at me silently a moment, and then at my new over-and-under shotgun that I grasped. He nodded slowly.

"I think — *yo penso* — it will work," I said confidently.

"Perhaps," he said slowly. "If that is what you wish."

I shook my head.

"Then I must tell Pablo and José of your plan," he said turning to leave.

I called out to him. "If they hear them, maybe they can drive them to us."

I didn't try to inject my Spanish into the request, but I'm sure he understood what I said.

While Manuel was gone, I mentally calculated our vantage positions for the night. There was an eliptical partial clearing set among high trees. From the end where the tracks were found to the side where the carcass was buried, it was approximately forty to fifty feet. From one side to the other was about thirty to forty feet, maybe less. The path or trail, if José was correct, ran directly through the egg-shaped clearing. I located a low fallen tree at one side where we could perch while we watched opposite ends of the clearing. At the most, we were no more than twenty-five feet from the trail. We can't miss, I thought, at this distance.

It was, of course, a risk. But so was the hunt itself. These jaguars were apparently smaller than those in Guiana, so I wasn't overly concerned about the danger.

Manuel returned. "It is all arranged," he said.

I briefed him on my plan, and if he was worried about sitting in the dark as a decoy, he didn't show it. We checked our headlamps to make sure they were fully operable. I had already checked my shotgun and made sure that the safety was off. We waited as it grew darker. The mosquitoes droned around us, and I could hear Manuel brushing them off. I'm sure he heard my actions. The evening turned into night. My eyes became accustomed to the darkness, but they strained as I searched the far end of the clearing that I had chosen to watch. There was little movement in the jungle around us, and other distant sounds were muffled. I wondered how José and Pablo were faring in their own positions. I couldn't hear them at all.

Manuel stirred noiselessly beside me on the other side of the fallen tree. I adjusted my awkward position as quietly as possible and waited. The night moved forward very slowly. I tried to see the time on my watch but couldn't.

After several hours of perching on the hard tree, I rose slowly to stretch and reposition myself. That's when I heard heavy crackling in the undergrowth near us and then shouts. The shouts were then followed by two shotgun blasts.

Manuel and I jumped to our feet and flicked on our lamps. We couldn't discern where the shots came from, but Manuel determined it was from near where the jaguar tracks were sighted.

We ran to the area illuminated by José and Pablo and saw them standing over a dead jaguar.

As we approached they both started apologizing for making the kill.

"*Por qué muchachos?*" Manuel demanded of them.

They gestured wildly at the jungle, their headlamps bouncing up and down, as they replied excitedly.

"What'd they say?" I wanted to know.

"They say..." he explained slowly, "...it was necessary. *El tigre* was moving behind us."

# 25

The Mexicans found some strong vines, bound the front and hind paws together and slipped a sturdy branch through the lashed legs. It was a small jaguar, about six feet long. It probably weighed in at less than 200 pounds. They hoisted the dead animal to their shoulders and carried it back to the campsite.

The fire had burned down, and when they lowered it to the ground beside the embers, the horse sensed it and spooked. After he was quieted down, we all returned to the big cat and examined it more closely. Both shotgun blasts had caught it squarely in the chest and side, and it went down instantly and never moved. It appeared that they were at different angles when they fired, but their aims were accurate and deadly.

Manuel and I congratulated them again on their marksmanship, although I would have preferred to be the one that brought it down.

"*Mañana*, I skin it for you," Manuel offered. "*Pero ahora*, it is late and we sleep."

The Mexicans built the fire up for the remaining hours before daylight, and the four of us curled up in our blankets.

The next morning we were all up at sunrise, taking one last look at the animal in daylight before Manuel brought his knife out. He turned the dead jaguar on its back and expertly cut through the hide without damaging the pelt itself or the flesh beneath it. He started below the jaw and cut slowly down to its rump and peeled back the spotted hide. He then sliced along each leg and the underside of the tail and peeled back those intact sections. When he finished, he spread it out on the ground and asked the Mexicans for some salt. They retrieved a bag from their gear. Manuel opened it and dumped the salt on the underside of the pelt. He rubbed it in thoroughly and then rolled the entire hide into a ball. He then handed it to me.

"For you, *señor*," he said with a flourish. "When you return home, you do again."

I didn't feel it belonged to me since I wasn't in on the kill. I offered it to Pablo and José.

"No, *señor*," they both objected, pushing it back to me.

Manuel, who was standing nearby, interjected.

"They want you to have it, *señor*. Accept, *por favor*."

I looked at them again and saw that they were very sincere.

"OK! *Graçias*," I said and shoved the skin into my gear. They all smiled at my acceptance.

"Before we go, *señor*, we swim?" Manuel asked, pointing to the gulf in the distance.

"*Bueno*," I answered quickly. I was eager to wash some of the dirt off me. It had been a few days, and I needed to get wet, even if it was in salt water. Besides, the antiseptic effect of the salt would heal the innumerable mosquito bites and relieve their itching.

"We leave *el caballo aquí*," Manuel said aloud gesturing toward the horse. "We return when we are finished to swim."

José and Pablo readily agreed and bolted toward the water a half-mile away.

At the edge of the gently lapping surf, we all stripped and plunged gratefully into the warm water. It was just like the Florida beaches with water temperatures between eighty-five and ninety degrees Fahrenheit. It was what I was used to, and it felt great. The only difference was that the four of us were solitary figures on that immense beach. As we swam and drifted lazily in the slow incoming waves, I happened to glance up in the blue skies. There, at 20,000 to 30,000 feet, was an airliner. That unusual sight of a twentieth century symbol in our desolate surroundings was completely incongruous with the idyllic scene that engulfed us.

We splashed in the surf for about a half-hour, quickly dried off on the beach and returned to our campsite.

We broke camp, saddled the horse and began the long trek back to the settlement.

Manuel held his hands toward the horse indicating that I should mount up. I glanced at the poor animal and remembered the long plodding ride to our location. I slowly shook my head.

"No, *graçias*, Manuel. I'll walk."

I motioned for either Pablo or José to take the horse. They looked at each other briefly, and Pablo decided to ride.

Although the long hike back was hot and sweaty in the rising sun, the two or three hours passed quickly. Before long, we moved away from the beach and headed inland. The yapping dogs in the distance alerted the older Mexican of our return. He greeted us on the path and asked of our hunt as he grasped the reins of the horse.

"*Bueno*," Manuel answered, having me show off the bundled jaguar skin.

The old Mexican touched it gingerly. "*Muy bueno, señor.*"

He asked if we wanted something to drink while he guided the horse to a trough filled with water.

"*Aqua, tambien, solamente.*" Manuel, the Mexicans and I nodded in agreement. He offered us rainwater that he had collected near his shack.

We all thanked him for his hospitality and returned on the same tangled jungle trail that we had trod a few days earlier. The trek back to the Mexicans' village also didn't seem as long as it had on the way in because I was now aware of my surroundings.

Once we arrived at their settlement, I thanked both Pablo and José individually.

"*Es nada, señor,*" they chorused.

I unbuckled my gun belt and pulled out the revolver that Pablo had loaned me before the hunt. I regretted that I had been unable to use it and shook my head slightly as I handed it to him. He smiled and indicated that he, too, was sorry that I was unable to use it.

Manuel and I headed toward the water's edge of the Laguna de Sontecomapan and found another small boat owner willing to take us back to the other side.

As we bounced over the waves of the large lagoon toward the opposite shore, I wondered what to do next. Although the jaguar hunt was successful, it was not completely to my satisfaction. I briefly thought about trying again elsewhere, but dismissed it. I didn't have the time, and I wasn't sure how much more it would cost. I realized I had to find a suitable location to get back to my book. It was, after all, my main reason for choosing Mexico.

Fortunately, we didn't have to wait too long for Manuel's son. When he arrived in the pickup truck, Manuel slowly related the story with emphasis on us sitting in the darkened jungle as decoys. The boy was enthralled by the description and made him retell it. When he finished his tale, he had me show the boy the rolled-up *tigre* skin. He, too, had to touch it, but not as gingerly as the old Mexican had done.

The bumpy trip back to San Andrés Tuxtla was done in silence. When we arrived at Manuel's house, he thanked me profusely. He then drove me to the same small hotel I had stayed in a few days earlier, and the next morning I was en route back to Vera Cruz on another old crowded bus.

There was still a vacancy at the place I had stayed in before, and as soon as I checked in, I immediately headed back to the local cantina for a cold *cerveza*.

"*Señor*," the same bartender greeted me warmly. "How was your hunt?"

I briefly described what had happened, and he was quick to add how sorry he was that it was not me who shot el *tigre*. He also inquired if I was satisfied with Manuel, as my guide, since it was he who recommended him.

I assured him that I was most satisfied and that Manuel never questioned me when we both sat alone waiting for *el tigre*.

"*Bueno*," he said. "*Manuel es mi amigo, y es un hombre bueno.*"

"However," he added, you are both most *afortunado*, that the other two killed *el tigre* before it got to you."

I really hadn't considered the possibility, but grudgingly conceded he could be right.

"*Donde va?*" he asked me my next destination.

I told him I really didn't know, and asked if he had any suggestions where I could write in peace.

He thought about it briefly and then left momentarily to get a drink for another patron who had just walked in. When he returned, he held his forefinger up to his temple. "I know, *señor*," he beamed.

"*Donde?*"

"Fortin," he said.

"Fortin," I repeated.

"*Sí.*"

"Where is it?" I asked in English.

"Not as far as San Andréas," he said. "Maybe *ciento kilómetros.*"

"*Ciento kilómeters*," I said aloud, doing the conversion math in my head. "That's about sixty miles." I repeated it in Spanish. "*Sesenta milos.*"

He nodded his head. "*No mas, señor*," he said, adding, "*es muy hermosa.*"

I liked what I heard and asked him if the bus went there.

"*Sí, señor*," and also added that it was near "*montañas alta.*"

"How high?" I asked.

He shrugged his shoulders.

"You will like it, *señor*," he insisted.

I had another *cerveza* and we made small talk about Mexico. I thanked him for his information and left. The bus left midmorning the next day.


It was a slightly larger and newer bus and was not as packed as the other two had been. Perhaps, I thought, it's because we're going up into the mountains and there's not as much traffic as on the coast. There were fewer small children I noticed, and also less agricultural products being carried by the passengers, who seemed to be better dressed.

The road was in pretty good condition, and the ride wasn't as uncomfortable as the trip to and from San Andréas Tuxtla. There were only a couple of small towns, more like villages, on the first half of the trip and the stops were very brief. As we drove higher toward the mountains, there were three or four other villages set close together near the road. The next sizable town, perhaps it could be considered a small city, was Cordoba. It loomed ahead of us, and the driver called out the destination before we arrived. A number of people got off the bus, and the driver stretched his legs for a minute.

"How far to Fortin?" I asked him.

"*Qué*?" he responded, apparently not understanding what I said.

I hesitated and searched for correct words in Spanish. "*Cómo...cómo...distante a Fortin?*"

I wasn't sure if that was the correct phraseology but he must've partially understood my question.

"No far," he answered simply and slid behind the wheel again.

He was right. Within a short time, we passed a small sign beside the road that read Fortin.

"*Señor*," the driver called out. "Fortin."

I thanked him and looked out the window as the small village came into view. It was clean and neat, and as Mexican villages go, it was quite quaint. The bartender was right again, I thought. I had no idea where I was going to stay or who to ask for information. As the bus slowed down to make a sharp turn, we passed a stone fence beside the road and what appeared to be some type of resort within its compound. Over a narrow entrance was a sign, *Fortin de las flores.*

"Fortin of the flowers," I said half aloud. I was impressed with what I saw.

The bus stopped in the town square, and I briefly asked the driver about the place.

"*Es un hotel,*" he answered. "*Muy fino.*" With that, I stepped to the ground and he put the bus in gear.

I wondered how fine it was, and more importantly, how expensive it was.

I looked around the square and saw only small houses, some stone and others of wood. They all looked to be in better condition than those up and down the coast and in San Andréas. I also noticed a small church on a nearby hill. There were no commercial establishments where I could ask someone about housing arrangements. It didn't look promising. I headed toward the church to ask the local priest for lodging advice, figuring if anybody would know, he would. Still lugging my gear and my sheathed shotgun, I did look a little out of place in a town that appeared to be more of a resort than a commercial town.

As I turned a corner to walk up the short incline to the church, I saw a taxi. *Cab drivers and bartenders know everything,* I said to myself. I hailed him and asked him the same question I was going to ask the priest.

My Spanish was choppy but he understood what I was seeking.

"*Nada aquí,*" he said, gesturing around the area. "Maybe *distante,*" he said, motioning farther away toward the outskirts.

I was a little frustrated. I liked what I saw of the area.

"What about *Fortin de las flores*?"

"*Fortin de las flores*," he said aloud. "*Es muy elegante, señor. Es un recurso.*"

At the time, I did not know what the word *recurso* meant, but found out later that indeed it was a resort, a resort for well-to-do Mexicans.

Not to be put off by its exclusive outward appearance, I asked the taxi driver what he thought the cost might be to stay there.

"*Es caro, señor,*" he answered, raising his bushy eyebrows.

"*Cuánto costa?*"

He mentioned an approximate amount. It was as he said, "*caro,*" but I didn't feel like wandering around aimlessly as I had done in Vera Cruz. I knew I couldn't afford it for a prolonged period of two or three weeks, but figured I could handle it for a short while.

"Take me to it," I said impatiently.

"*Qué?*"

I rephrased it as simply as I could in English.

"*Al hotel,*" I stated firmly and pointed in the direction of Fortin de las flores.

He smiled broadly and opened the door of his vehicle.

It was as I had imagined and others had described it. It had class. A long drive lined in flowered bushes led to a main entrance that resembled a large hacienda with a restaurant. Beyond the entrance were individual rooms or cottages on a tiled walkway, with a small patio in front of the rooms.

Stepping inside the lobby I noticed sliding glass doors that adjoined a small swimming pool. Around the pool were chairs, tables and reclining lounges. As I looked beyond the pool, I saw what appeared to be mountains in the distance half-obscured by low-lying cloud cover.

*This is it,* I said to myself.

"*Señor,*" the desk clerk interrupted my thoughts,

"May I help you?" he asked in Spanish.

"*Sí,*" I responded. Remembering the word for vacancy, I asked him if there was "*una vacante.*"

Recognizing my stilted Spanish as a *norteamericano*, he replied affirmatively in English with a noticeable accent.

When I asked the cost, his answer was about what the taxi driver had cited. It was *caro*, as I anticipated from the surroundings, but told him that I would like it for "*dos semanas maybe mas.*"

He appeared pleased at my continued attempt to carry on the conversation in Spanish.

"*No problema, señor.*"

After I checked in, he motioned to one of the bellboys to escort me to my room. The Mexican bellhop knew little or no English, but was eager to carry my shotgun as well as my duffel bag.

The room was fairly small but was attractively furnished and even had a small table by the window that fronted on the walkway. Fortunately, my room/cottage was an end unit so I had no pedestrian traffic past my door to disturb my writing. Weather permitting, I could even go outside to write on a small round table on my private patio.

My routine was fairly structured once I became acclimated to my new environment. I swam in the morning, had a light breakfast and then worked on my book the majority of the day. On rare occasions, I even worked into the evening hours. I naturally had my *cerveza* late in the afternoon by the heavily scented pool, which always had gardenias thrown in it in the morning. I imagine that's where the name came from, Fortin de las flores.

During the first week to ten days of my stay, I was the only American at the hotel. It was off the beaten track for tourists from the states or from other countries. Consequently, I was more or less forced to speak only Spanish to the employees, since most spoke no English. The constant daily conversations, however brief, were a boon to learning the language quickly. I would think the word or expression in Spanish rather than in English. That procedure seemed to shorten the speaking process.

On one particular afternoon, I sat beside two elderly American women who were having an animated conversation about the State of Vera Cruz. In the midst of their talking, my waiter who had been the bellhop when I first arrived, brought me my usual *cerveza* and we engaged in a brief question and answer session of our own, in Spanish.

One of the women suddenly turned to me and asked me for confirmation about her position on their discussion. Her Spanish was poorly constructed, but she wanted to know about the City of Vera Cruz and its surroundings. Having recently learned the answer to her question and wishing to put her at ease, I answered her quickly. However, my reply was in perfect English.

Before I had an opportunity to tell her that I was also an American, she paid me a pleasant — but undeserved — compliment.

"For a Mexican, you speak perfect English."

I didn't have the heart to disillusion or embarrass her and tell her the truth, so I let it go at that. For the next couple of days whenever I saw them, I maintained their impression.


The days passed quickly and although my writing appeared to be going well, and I found the hotel quite pleasing, I was getting restless. I knew I would have to make plans to leave within the week and return to the states, but I wasn't satisfied that I had accomplished everything that I wanted to do.

Breaking my usual routine of going back to my room to work, I sat around the pool having coffee earlier than usual. It was a bright clear morning with a light wind blowing. As I looked at the mountains far in the distance, I saw for the first time a magnificent sight that I had not known existed. The cloud cover that had always obscured the mountain was gone. Instead, there was a gigantic snow-capped peak that sparkled in the sun.

I singled out my waiter/bellhop and asked him about the mountain.

"*Es Pico de Orizaba,*" he answered.

I wondered to myself how I could fail to notice a mountain that big and that beautiful. I asked my waiter the same question, as though he could explain my lack of observation.

He motioned with his hands that the clouds always covered it during the day. "*Temprano de la mañana,*" (early in the morning) the mountain was usually visible, he explained.

I nodded my head in understanding. In the two weeks that I had been there, I had neither gotten up that early nor sat by the pool facing the mountain.

I couldn't take my eyes off its majestic beauty.

"*Cómo alto?*" I asked again.

"*Es dieciocho mil y siete ciento pies,*" he stated unequivocally.

"You mean 18,700 feet," I said in astonishment, forgetting for the moment that he couldn't understand me.

He smiled at my enthusiasm.

"*Sí, señor,*" he said automatically.

For a moment my mind was blank as I continued staring at its glistening peak. I had no interest in mountains before I went to Mexico, but the more I gazed at it, the more I realized that it was a challenge I could not resist.

I decided, at that instant, I would climb Pico de Orizaba, Mexico's highest mountain and the third highest in the Western Hemisphere.

# 26

I began to scramble for any information, that was available about Pico de Orizaba and mountain climbing. All I cared was, as they say, "it was there," and that was reason enough for me to climb it.

As for the latter, the mountain-climbing aspect, I knew absolutely nothing about scaling a mountain. I had never climbed one in my life. The closest I ever came to climbing anything was a hill of about 500 feet in elevation when I was a kid in the Catskill Mountains in upstate New York. Even that was only done during the summers, and I doubt if I did it more than two or three times.

Subsequent to my adolescent and teenage years, I always lived at sea level. It was either in New York City or in the Pacific during my Navy days, or eventually in south Florida. Consequently, I was never exposed for any length of time, to any of the rarefied atmospheres of high elevations. Although I did have a very brief encounter with the effects of the lack of oxygen on the brain, it was fortunately only for a few seconds.

During flight training for Navy aircrew, a group of us were placed in a depressurized chamber that simulated a 40,000-foot altitude. We were instructed to remove our oxygen masks for those few seconds and observe the reactions of our buddies, who also were without oxygen. We all acted giddy and behaved like we were drunk. That's what happens at high altitudes without a mask, we were warned.

It was an unsettling experience and was a sensation that I would soon undergo on the mountain.

When I first thought about climbing Pico de Orizaba, that vivid recollection never entered my mind. I knew that I was in good physical condition and possessed, what I thought, was better-than-average strength and stamina. However, I also knew that I needed a certain amount of basic mountain-climbing gear, and undoubtedly would need a guide. Inasmuch, as the waiter/bellhop was of little help to me in that regard, I sought the assistance of the desk clerk, who spoke English.

His immediate response was, "It is very difficult, *señor.*"

When I agreed that it probably was, he asked me point blank, if I was a climber.

When I admitted that I was not, he looked at me steadily for a moment.

"Then you must have a professional guide, *señor.*"

I thought about the wisdom of that comment, and agreed wholeheartedly with him.

"Do you know of any?" I wanted to know.

"*Si, señor,* I know of one."

"How soon can you contact him?"

He looked at the clock on the wall in the lobby.

"He is at work now, but when he returns home, I will call him," he said.

Pleased at my good fortune in being able to locate a guide, I returned to my room. As the hours passed, however, I became concerned that he might not be able to get everything arranged before it would be time for me to leave. For the rest of the afternoon, I couldn't concentrate on the book and could only think of the mountain. I returned to the pool area to view the snow-capped peak once more. Just like before, clouds obscured the mountain. I waited in an area where the desk clerk could see me. It was late in the afternoon, and I believed that the guide's workday would soon be over. My impatience was finally rewarded after five o'clock when I noticed the desk clerk on the phone.

As I watched him intently, carefully monitoring his conversation, he suddenly held up his hand and motioned for me to come to the phone. I almost knocked over a table in my exuberance to get to the lobby and front desk.

The clerk held the phone in his hand and directed me to a nearby extension.

"This is Octavio de la Llave, the guide I spoke of," he said quickly, "he will speak with you."

The guide's English was excellent and I didn't have to think through all my questions so I could rephrase them in Spanish.

Yes, he was interested in being my guide. However, as his friend had already explained to me, it would be a difficult climb. Did I have any experience at all in climbing?

When I admitted that I had none, there was a brief silence.

"Are you sure that this is what you want to do?" he asked.

When I assured him that it was and that I also was in excellent physical condition, he relented.

It would only be the two of us on the mountain, he continued. I said I understood.

He assumed that I had no equipment of any kind, and I confirmed that as well.

What of cold weather clothing, he asked? Again, I told him I had none.

More silence.

"You will have to buy some clothing in Cordoba," he continued again.

"When can we go?" I asked.

"I will stop at the hotel tomorrow about this time, and we will go into Cordoba to find you something to wear."

I then asked a question that I almost felt foolish in putting to him, but of course, it was necessary.

"*Cuánto costa?*" I said automatically in Spanish, and then corrected myself quickly, "How much?"

There was no hesitation on the phone, as he answered me.

"You will only have to pay for the two days that I would be off work, plus other minor expenses to get us to Pico de Orizaba," he said.

I couldn't believe that would be the only expense, but didn't belabor it on the phone.

"We will discuss all the details tomorrow," he said.

I tried to contain my excitement at the news.

"OK," I answered.

"*Hasta mañana*," he said pleasantly and then hung up.

The desk clerk, who had been following the conversation, knew that we had an agreement.

"He is my friend," he offered. "You can trust him."

I thanked the desk clerk for his assistance.

"Octavio is a member of the Legion de Orizaba, a professional mountain climbing society," he said proudly. "He knows *el* Pico well."

I felt good after the conversations and eagerly looked forward to the following day.


As promised, Octavio arrived just as he said he would. I was waiting by the pool when I saw a stocky, light-skinned Mexican approach the desk clerk. He pointed me out to the visitor, and as soon as he passed through the glass doors, we introduced ourselves.

"I am Octavio," he said.

"I am Marty," I answered.

"I will call you *Marteen*," he responded.

His handshake was firm and strong. I was impressed by his neat appearance, although he apologized for coming in his work clothes. I learned that he worked in a factory in Cordoba, the nearby large town that I passed through on the bus to Fortin. He looked to be in his early- to mid-thirties. His accent was very slight, and he spoke with knowledge and authority as to what would be needed for the mountain and on the climb.

"I have the rope, crampons for your boots, ice pitons, carabiners and an extra ice axe, " he offered.

I nodded knowingly, although I was barely aware of all the items that he mentioned. "However," he continued, "you will need a *balaclava*, goggles, and of course mittens, heavy socks and warmer clothing." He stopped briefly. "What kind of boots do you have?"

Again, I demurred to the question.

He hesitated again. "It does not matter," he continued. "Although this time of year is not a good time to climb, we should find all we need in the sporting shops in Cordoba."

His assurances as to the availability of gear for me proved regrettably to be incorrect. We combed through three or four shops in the town and could only find a portion of what I needed. Goggles and a *balaclava*, the head covering, were in abundance and I had no trouble selecting those two items. As to the "warmer clothing," there was very little to be found, anywhere, because it was still summertime.

The only pair of mittens I found were lightweight and didn't seem to be acceptable for the frigid temperatures that we would encounter. Even Octavio appeared a little concerned about their thickness. I considered getting a larger pair to slip over the first for warmth, but decided against it because their bulkiness would render me unable to close my hands over any equipment I would use. As to locating heavy socks, again there were none available. The only choice I had was to purchase two or three thin socks. I elected to buy three pair. The warmer clothing also proved to be a problem. There was none anywhere to be found. When Octavio inquired, he was reminded that it was *verano* (summer) and that it was *también temprano* (too early). He shrugged and apologized to me because of their scarcity at that time of year.

"That's OK," I said, "I'll just wear several layers."

I already had a short sleeve skivvy shirt I would wear as my first layer. I then bought a medium-weight sweat-shirt to wear over that as my second layer. As to my third layer of clothing, I picked out a thin flannel-type baseball jacket. A heavier baseball jacket would not fit under my fourth piece of clothing. The final layer that I brought with me into Mexico was an old *Ike*-style jacket, rayon in composition.

Octavio seemed to agree with me that the several layers of clothing would probably be OK. He had not yet seen my Ike jacket but my description of it with its water-resistant qualities satisfied him. When I got back to the hotel and I tried on all of my items of clothing, I felt bulky and looked like a tightly wrapped cocoon. I was also very warm.

"You will need it all, Marteen," Octavio assured me, "it is very cold on the mountain."

"How cold?"

"At the top it will be about  twenty degrees below zero, Fahrenheit," he said.

"In the summer?" I asked in amazement.

He nodded. "Maybe more."

After the purchase of the warm clothing, Octavio reminded me that we had to look for boots.

Our survey of the shoe stores in the area proved to be as unfruitful as the shopping trip for the clothing. There were absolutely no climbing boots to be found. The only boots that we located were high Mexican hunting boots made of very stiff leather.

"It will be very uncomfortable on the climb," Octavio commented, emphasizing his words.

"Where else can we go to find any?" I asked.

"If there are none in Cordoba at this time, there is nowhere else to go," he shrugged.

"Will the crampons fit on the soles of the boots?" I wanted to know.

He examined the boots." They will fit," he said slowly, "but..."

I interrupted him before he could repeat his admonition about their unsuitability.

"I have no choice," I told him. "If there's nothing else

available in town, I'll have to get these."

I was not happy about the high stiff boots, nor was Octavio from the look on his face.

I cursed myself for failing to bring my well broken-in GI combat boots that I had worn in Guiana. They were heavy and bulky for packing and I didn't think that I would need them, since my main reason for the Mexican trip was the book. Although I knew I undoubtedly would hunt jaguar again, time-permitting, I decided that my low-cut shoes would do. However, it was too late to worry over spilled milk. I told myself that I had managed before in tough situations, and I had no doubt that I could handle the discomfort of the Mexican boots.

I would find out soon enough the after-effects of wearing those boots.

Once back at the hotel, all my gear was laid out to Octavio's satisfaction. The question about the boots rose again, and the warmth of the socks. I tried on the two thin pair in the slightly oversized boots, and there was still room to move my toes.

Octavio hoped that the two lightweight socks would provide enough warmth for my feet since we would be climbing in snow and on ice.

"I'll bring the third pair, just in case," I assured him.

The time for departure was set for two days later. Octavio laid out the plans. We would take a train from Cordoba to the town of Orizaba, a distance of about ten kilometers. The town was at the base of the mountain. A guide with mules would meet us at the Orizaba station. We would then ride the mules another ten kilometers to the mountain. After that it was just the two of us.

Everything was arranged, and I had little to be concerned about. The only thing was the mountain.

The next morning, I was up early to view my new target. It sparkled majestically in the sun, and I visualized our presence on it. We would be but specks on its massive sloping side as we made our way up to the top. It occupied my thoughts all day. I was neither worried, nor overly concerned about the climb. I was just excited.

The morning of our departure, Octavio was at the hotel early enough for coffee. We sat and stared at the mountain, while the hotel employees sprinkled sweet-smelling gardenias in the pool.

"It is beautiful," he said, referring to the snow-capped peak in the distance.

It was more an off-hand statement rather than one of admiration. I had to agree with him.

"*Listo, Marteen?*" he said in a low voice as he lapsed into Spanish and rose from his chair.

"I'm ready," I said, grabbing my knapsack with the assorted pieces of clothing. I wasn't wearing any of my new gear because it was still warm at our elevation. Octavio advised me that we would dress more warmly as we approached the mountain.

We were both preoccupied with our own thoughts, so the ride from Fortin to the train station at Cordoba was made in silence.

It was an open-windowed train with far fewer passengers than one usually found on the buses. As we neared the mountains, a cool breeze blew through the cars. It was a short ride, and we experienced a series of sharp, jerky movements before we pulled into the old station and the train came to a screeching halt. At the end of the long dusty platform, we found our guide with three mules. I did not look forward to straddling a mule, remembering my very uncomfortable ride on the almost emaciated-looking horse along the Gulf of Mexico.

Octavio introduced me to the old guide. He knew no English and responded with a simple nod of his head. He offered me one of the squat mules, which looked well fed, and assisted me in mounting it. There didn't appear to be much life in the animal until the guide on the lead mule moved slowly ahead. I was in the middle with Octavio behind me. Although the other mules responded to their being prodded forward, mine didn't. Apparently, it sensed that there was an amateur rider on its back and would only move slowly and reluctantly after I pounded its flanks.

The dusty road out of town soon turned into a narrow rocky winding trail that spiraled upward. The mules moved ahead even more slowly, or so it seemed. Mine in particular needed goading just to maintain the steady pace that the guide set on the leading mule. Although Octavio had mentioned that the ride would be about ten kilometers, he didn't mention that a sizable portion of the ride was uphill. It was a tortuous ascent on the top of an unyielding animal that seemed to take no pleasure in going forward. My hands throbbed from continually pounding the mule, and my throat was dry from yelling encouragement to it to move out. Both the guide and Octavio had similar problems, but not to the extent I had.

After what seemed to be about a two- or three-hour ride, we were engulfed in the misty clouds that I had noticed from the hotel. I could barely see the base of the mountain and the valley below. All I could see were brief glimpses of the trail ahead that disappeared into low-lying clouds.

Finally, after another two hours, perhaps more, we were on rocky level ground that had numerous large crevices in the side of the mountain.

The guide yelled something and directed his mule toward one of the larger crevices.

Octavio pulled his own mule ahead and called to me.

"This is our cave for tonight," he announced. "We will sleep here until our ascent tomorrow morning."

I nodded my head in acknowledgment as I guided my own mule toward the cave. We dismounted, and the guide led the animals into the cave. It was large enough for them and for us to lay our sleeping bags on the ground at the rear of the entrance.

The guide took care of the mules while Octavio and I prepared for the night and following day. It was late afternoon, and the weather had turned much cooler.

"How high are we?" I asked Octavio.

"About 11,000 feet," he answered. "How do you feel?" he wanted to know.

"OK," I said. "But I'm starting to get a little headache."

"It is the altitude," he said. "You must rest a little, for it can get much worse."

The guide approached Octavio after tending to the animals and spoke to him rapidly.

"He must leave now, but he will return for us tomorrow," Octavio said.

"Isn't there enough room?" I said as I gestured around the fairly large cavern.

"It will be too cold tonight for the mules."

"How cold?" I asked inquisitively, not really having an idea of the temperature drop.

"About zero," he said matter-of-factly. "It would be well to dress warmly now."

The guide roped the animals together and led them out of the cave entrance.

"*Hasta mañana*," he called back to us.

"We must eat a little and then rest a while," Octavio said, reaching into his knapsack. He took out some chocolates and dates and offered them to me.

I was not particularly hungry.

"You must eat some," he insisted. "It will give you energy."

He lit a small lantern while he took out some warmer clothing. He laid his outer jacket near his sleeping bag, and indicated that I do the same. He also gave me a set of crampons for my boots and an ice axe. He flicked on two flashlights, and satisfied that both worked properly, gave one to me.

"We will need these in the morning," he reminded me.

"When do we start the climb?" I asked excitedly.

"At two," he responded quickly.

"Two," I repeated.

He must have noticed the tone in my voice. I wasn't

concerned about the time and told him so. I was merely surprised. An hour was never mentioned, only the fact that it would be early.

We spoke for about an hour as he went over what to expect on the climb and the equipment he had. We would take the easier of the two routes to the peak, he said. We would take the avalanche route. It would be safe this time of year because there wasn't much snow yet. We would not need the crampons until we hit the ice pack. He also held up the rope that would bind us together on the ice pack, and the carabiners, the links to which the rope would be attached.

He repeatedly commented that he was worried about the unsuitability of my hunting boots for climbing. They were very stiff and would cause me difficulty on the steeper grades, he feared. I tried to reassure him by explaining that I had worked oil into the instep of the boots to make them more flexible. He was even more concerned about their thinness and worried about the danger of frozen feet. He didn't think the two pairs of light socks were sufficient to keep my feet warm. I reminded him of the extra set of light socks I had. That would give me three pairs of socks inside my boots. He hoped it would suffice, he said, as he fingered his own heavy socks in his thick mountain-climbing boots.

It was starting to darken outside the cave. The mist closed in around us. The inside of the cave had grown dark, and the meager light from the small kerosene lamp gave an eerie glow to its interior.

Octavio crawled into his sleeping bag and motioned for me to do the same.

"Tomorrow will be a long day," he said. "We will be on the mountain until the afternoon and will need a good night's sleep."

I grunted acknowledgment. I knew it would be many hours of climbing before we would reach the top.

At that time, I had no real concept of what lay ahead, what the next few hours would entail.

Octavio put out the lantern. "I will wake you at two," he said.

It was not quite dark enough in the cave to sleep. The anticipation of an unknown adventure coupled with a persistent headache kept me awake for awhile. To take my mind off the dull pain in my head, I focused on the challenge of the climb and reaching the pinnacle of the mountain.

I finally drifted off to sleep, and the next thing I knew I was being shaken into consciousness.

"It is two, Marteen," Octavio said in the darkness. "We must get ready to go."

He lit the lantern, and the inside of the blackened cave suddenly reminded me of the night jaguar hunts. It was cold — bitter cold — and that snapped me back to the reality of where I was.

I dressed quickly and put on all the layers of clothing that I had. Although bulky, I was warm and felt satisfied with my forced choice of clothing. I then concentrated on putting on my boots. When I slipped my feet, wearing the two pair of light socks, into my boots they felt cold. I thought about the snow and ice that faced us on the mountain and decided to put on the third pair of socks. The slightly larger boots accommodated the extra pair of socks, and my feet felt a little warmer. However, my toes were cramped. I thought nothing of the discomfort, only the fact that my feet felt better. I said nothing to Octavio.

It was a decision, on both counts, that I would later regret.

Octavio slipped the rope over his neck and shoulder and handed me my ice axe. After he turned down the kerosene lamp, he flicked on his flashlight. I did the same, and we stepped out of our hole in the side of the mountain. A blast of frigid air hit my face, and I pulled the *balaclava* down to cover it. It was minus-fifteen, and would get colder the higher we climbed. I rested my goggles on my forehead until the sun rose. With only our flashlights to guide our pitch-black path, we started the climb over ice and rocks. My legs soon began to tire, and my throat burned from the dry air. My cramped toes also began to get numb from the cold, and I tried to wiggle them for movement and circulation. Octavio picked his way carefully forward and occasionally glanced back to see if I was keeping pace with him. I could see nothing ahead of us, only what the waving beams of light illuminated.

In the beginning, we rested every hundred feet or so; then the distance between stops increased. I thought of nothing but the climb itself, of putting one foot in front of the other and just plodding forward and upward. It was cold, very cold. My eyes watered from the unrelenting wind and my eyelids partially froze shut until I rubbed them gently. I tried not to think of the outside temperature, only of moving and keeping warm. My fingers started to tingle from constantly grasping the ice axe. Because my mittens were fairly large, I was able to curl my fingers inward and press them into the palms of my hands for some semblance of warmth.

As the hours dragged on, however, I inwardly cursed each rock that blocked me from my destination. On some of the larger obstacles, Octavio hesitated momentarily to see how I fared. I just nodded dumbly and waved him forward again, my solitary beam of light dancing crazily on the rocky shapes ahead.

By the time the sun appeared on the snow-encrusted side of the mountain, I saw for the first time, a steep ice pack that stretched out before us. It looked to be at least a forty-five-degree incline and glistened like a sheet of glass under the sun's rays.

Octavio stopped and indicated that we were to put on our crampons. He easily clamped his onto his own boots. I, however, had a little difficulty doing my own. When he noticed my clumsiness, he offered to help. Within minutes, I was ready. He then uncoiled the rope from his shoulder and quickly adjusted one end to the carabiner around his waist. He hooked the other end to one that dangled from my own waist.

"OK, Marteen?" he asked in a voice that was almost lost in the low howling of the wind.

I looked ahead at the immense stretch of ice that lay before us. I tried not to think about it. I just nodded my head.

"We will move slowly," he said aloud again, as he adjusted his goggles. I shifted my own downward over my eyes and gave him a thumbs up.

We started out carefully with approximately thirty feet of rope between us. Octavio reached the ice pack first and dug in with his ice axe and then his crampons as he climbed upward. When I reached the edge of the ice pack, I did the same. It wasn't quite as slippery as I had anticipated, as the edged sharpness of both the ice axe and the crampons penetrated the surface of the ice. With my firm grasp of the axe, I was able to propel myself upward while the crampons gripped for stability. Movement was slow and tiring, as I was unused to climbing. Moreover, the continued exertion — and the altitude — made the constant throbbing pain in my head more severe. I hadn't really taken much notice of it for the first couple of hours, as I told myself that it was only a headache that would pass.

However, it did not pass. The higher we climbed, the worse it became. Even the light touch of the goggles on my forehead was too much. I couldn't tell whether the pressure on both sides of my temples was more intense than the pain in my forehead. It all seemed to blend together. Sensations of cold became secondary. Only the pain remained.

When we reached 15,000 or 16,000 feet, we were on the avalanche route. (If Octavio ever told me specific elevations, I have no recollection. In fact, details of the balance of my climb are very foggy.) I do recall looking down at the top of our ice pack and saw the results of past avalanches. Below us were thousands of boulders that had rolled downward, crushing and carrying everything in their path. In my haze, I also vaguely remember that it was an awe-inspiring sight. A vivid recollection when we stopped our upward scale, and one I cannot forget, was the extreme pain in my head. It felt as though a spike was being driven into my forehead. That sensation was followed by nausea. It was a condition that was precipitated by the high altitude and the decreased oxygen. Octavio would later refer to it as *mal de la montaña,* or "mountain sickness."

When I stopped retching, the pain subsided slightly but I was dizzy and felt all my strength drained from my body.

"You must rest a bit," Octavio noted. "Do you want to continue?"

*I don't want to continue,* I told myself, *but I have to!*

I nodded my head slowly. I inhaled deeply and tried to catch my breath.

"I'll go on," I said. "I'll just rest a minute," as I leaned on my ice axe for support.

I saw Octavio eyeing me warily, and I wearily pushed myself to my feet.

"How far?" I asked.

"Perhaps 3,000 feet more," he answered. "Are you sure?"

"I'm ready," I replied in a weak voice that I tried to make sound firm.

He stepped out slowly, still attached to me by the rope. We were beyond the ice but still faced craggy formations and snow.

As I moved and climbed awkwardly up the rocks, feelings of apathy began to sweep over me. *Why am I here?* I wondered. *I am not a mountain climber and don't particularly care about mountains.*

However, I pushed those thoughts aside and kept climbing toward the peak. Octavio stopped more often to let me rest briefly. I remember leaning on my ice axe and groaning, a sound I tried to muffle so Octavio wouldn't hear me.

In time we began to see the mountain's top. It looked close, but it wasn't. Distance is deceiving over snow and ice, and it was disheartening to know I was progressing so slowly.

The final 1,000 feet were the worst. A rapidly developing blizzard suddenly engulfed us. It was hard to see Octavio as the heavy flurries partially obscured him. I had to constantly wipe my goggles to see ahead. Were it not for the slight tension on the rope, I wouldn't have known he was still there. The closer we got to the mountaintop, the more exhausted I became. I just wanted to lay down in the snow and sleep. I remember calling out to Octavio and telling him to "just talk to me," to keep me from drifting off. My last recollection in that blinding blizzard is of crawling on my hands and knees to finally reach my goal.

Reaching the pinnacle of Pico de Orizaba was rewarding...very rewarding. Although I was physically drained from the exertion and experienced an overpowering wave of relief, I felt still more. I was overtaken by a rush of elation that overshadowed the other sensations.

Octavio slapped me on the back and raised my arm in a victory salute. However, the celebration was short-lived as the snow was coming down heavier at our elevation. We rested a few minutes, but knew we had to leave shortly. He guided me to a crude metal flagpole that protruded over a yawning crevice at our feet. Orizaba was an inactive volcano. From my knapsack, he extracted a banner given to us by the Fortin town officials. He then had me tie it in place.

"It is your honor, Marteen," he yelled above the wind.

He admired it briefly then tapped my arm. "We must go now."

The climb back down the mountain was made in a fraction of the time that it took us to reach the top. Where it was possible, Octavio showed me how to ride the ice axe down like a sled. I placed both feet on the blade that rested on the hard-packed snow or ice beneath us. The handle of the ice axe extended between my legs at an angle to the slope. I gripped the handle firmly and held tight as it moved quickly forward. Whenever the speed became too great, I used the cleats on my crampons to slow me down or brake.

Back at our 11,000-foot camp, the guide and mules were waiting. The snow at the upper elevations had turned to an icy rain. We made our four-hour ride back down the trail. My clothes were wet, and from the waist down, my body was nearly frozen.

It was almost evening when we arrived in the town of Orizaba again.

Octavio asked how I was when he saw me shivering from the cold.

"OK," I chattered through clenched teeth, "but my feet are a little numb."

On the mule ride back down the mountain I had noticed that there was very little feeling in my toes. I didn't dwell on it, though, thinking the circulation in them would return once I dismounted.

Unfortunately, that never happened. I still had no sensation in my toes.

Octavio appeared worried when I described how they felt, especially after I told him I had worn three pair of socks instead of the two pair I had initially planned to wear.

"Your toes were cramped," he noted. "You had no circulation in them. That was not good."

I did not realize the danger, but it was too late to undo what I had done.

"You must remove your boots and socks as soon as you return to the hotel and keep your feet warm and dry," he said.


The train was not long in coming, and the ride back to Fortin went quickly.

Octavio dropped me off at Fortin de las flores and reminded me of his advice.

"You did well, Marteen," he called out to me. "I will

see you after work. *Hasta mañana.*"

Back in my room, I removed my wet clothing, boots and socks. I felt all my toes. They were still cold to the touch. I thought a warm bath would resolve the problem. But it didn't. I was growing more concerned and called the desk to see if there was a local doctor. I was told that no one would be available until the next morning. Perhaps a hot drink, I thought. I went to the bar to get something and saw my friend, the bellhop/waiter. I briefly described the climb and its aftermath. He offered to massage my feet for me to get the circulation back in the extremities. I readily agreed, as I could not adequately reach them to do a thorough job.

I didn't know that I had literally frozen my feet, especially my toes. I also didn't know that the rubbing of frozen tissue would cause the cells in the extremities to rupture.

The bellhop/waiter did what we both considered a good job. However, because there was an uncomfortable tingling in the toes, I terminated our session. I noticed afterward — and for many days thereafter — that if I tapped my feet or my shoes against a wall I still had no feeling in my toes.

The next morning I visited a nearby doctor, told him of the mountain climbing episode and explained my symptoms.

"When are you returning to *los Estados Unidos, señor?*" he asked.

"Within the week," I answered.

"I would not wait that long," he said seriously.

"Why?"

"Because, *señor*, you have frozen your toes, and the sooner your own doctor sees them and treats you the better."

# 27

Although I had originally intended to stay a few more days in Fortin, the doctor's somber diagnosis changed those plans. I knew that I had to get home as soon as possible and spent the following morning preparing for the long trip.

The English-speaking desk clerk was very helpful in making all the necessary contacts. There was the bus trip back to Vera Cruz, which didn't present any problems because it operated on a daily schedule. However, all plane reservations from Vera Cruz to Mexico City were booked and I was delayed for a few days. Fortunately, the clerk did get me on a flight at the end of the week. All that remained to be done was reservations on the Mexicana flight back to Miami and even that worked out with a couple of calls.

"It is all arranged, *señor*," he said proudly. "I have even called Octavio, as you requested, to let him know of your departure."

I didn't want to miss seeing Octavio before I left and half-expected to be able to leave sooner. I was a little concerned about my feet, but was not worried. I thought if I immersed myself in the warm water of the pool as much as possible I would help the circulation and speed the healing process.

I thanked the clerk and returned to my room to gather my gear. Although I wasn't scheduled to leave for another three days, I didn't want to leave things until the last night. As I organized my baggage, double checked my tickets, and counted my money, I realized that I didn't have as much cash left as I thought I had. In fact, with the various connections, and other unexpected expenditures, I was going to be short on pesos. My only solution — and I didn't relish the prospect — was to sell my new shotgun to make up the anticipated shortage. Again, my very knowledgeable desk clerk was my first thought, and again his assistance proved invaluable. Yes, he definitely knew someone who might be interested, as I had a most unusual over-and-under model. He admitted that he had never seen one like it before and felt that his friend, a hunter and collector, would want to see it. He would call him and try to get him over that evening.

A short while later he contacted me again and told me his friend would be over before he ate dinner. The clerk volunteered to stay beyond his normal working hours to help translate since the man was not that fluent in English.

As promised, late in the afternoon the desk clerk brought over a middle-aged Mexican who wanted to see the unusual shotgun. He didn't have to be convinced to buy it. As soon as he viewed it, he had to have it. I even made a slight profit on the transaction. Because of the desk clerk's extraordinary efforts for me, I made it worthwhile monetarily for him.

That evening, Octavio stopped by to see me. He was aware that I would be leaving soon and my reason for having to do so. His concern was genuine when he saw me.

"How are your feet, Marteen?" he wanted to know.

"You mean my toes?" I corrected him. "There's no feeling in them," I said, kicking the wall to emphasize my point. I gave him a half-smile.

"I'm very sorry, Marteen, I didn't realize."

I cut him off. "It's not your fault," I stressed.

"The local doctor said it would be OK once I saw my own doctor in the states," I lied.

He seemed relieved.

"I have something for you, Marteen. You deserve it." He reached into his pocket and took out a small lapel pin. It was an oval-shaped pin with a small blue and gold pennant on its face. On the left side of the pennant was an ice axe. Above and below the pennant were the words, "Legion," and "Orizaba."

"I spoke to other members of the club," he continued, "and they wanted you to have it as you are the only non-professional climber to ever reach the top."

He paused a moment before he spoke again. "You are now an honorary member of the 'Legion de Orizaba.'" He pumped my hand for emphasis.

I was completely taken by surprise and was flattered by the honor to be recognized by professional mountain climbers.

I momentarily forgot about my feet and just stared at the lapel pin in my hand. Its presentation to me, and what it represented, made the rigors of the climb seem worthwhile.

Octavio wished me a safe journey and hoped that my frozen toes would return to normal very soon.

The following morning the desk clerk greeted me with a smile and handed me the daily paper.

"You are famous, *señor*," he said. "See here," and he pointed out a small piece in the Excelsior newspaper, known as *El Periodico de la vida nacional* (the newspaper of the national life).

The short article, dated *Agosto* 26 (August 26) from Cordoba Ver, mentioned that "*El montanista estadunidense Marty Roland*" (the mountain climber from the United States) intended to climb Pico de Orizaba.

It appeared on *Martes* 27 *de Agosto de* 1957 (Tuesday, August 27) in Mexico City's paper — the day after I climbed it. It failed to mention Octavio's name, and it bothered me that he was not given credit, as well.

The morning of my departure, I took one final look at the magnificence of Pico de Orizaba shimmering in the early light of the sun and remembered the climb.

The bus ride to Vera Cruz and a short taxi ride to the airport were very timely. I checked the time when I arrived at the airport and noted that if the connecting flight to Mexico's capital — a distance of only 200 miles — was not delayed, I would have plenty of time.

The arrival at Mexico City's airport went smoothly, and with over two hours before I boarded my Miami flight, I knew I had time to wander around. I checked my bags into a storage unit and did a little shopping, buying gifts for the family and friends, and a few souvenirs for me.

By the time I spent most of my remaining pesos, I returned to the storage unit and retrieved my baggage. I had about an hour left. I checked into the ticket counter and was directed to Customs before my boarding was authorized. I expected to be waved through since I had nothing of value or questionable. Instead, the custom's official looked puzzled as he went through my luggage.

"*Donde está su escopeta?*" he wanted to know.

"My shotgun?" I said in amazement.

"*Si, señor.*"

"Oh, I sold it," I said in English automatically, without thinking what I had said.

"You did what, *señor?*" he said in quick response, staring at me briefly.

As soon as I saw his reaction I knew I had said the wrong thing. I immediately corrected myself.

"I'm sorry, I meant to say I lost it," I said.

He shook his head at my announcement.

"I'm sorry, *señor.*" he said firmly. "Then you must pay duty."

"Duty?" I echoed, not believing what I heard.

He cited some exorbitant figure that was almost as much as the shotgun was worth.

"*No lo tiene,*" I said in Spanish. I wasn't sure my usage was correct so I added in English, "I don't have it."

He repeated himself. "*No escopeta,* you must pay duty."

"I have to leave," I insisted.

He was just as adamant as he pushed my baggage back toward me.

I had to think of some valid excuse why it wasn't my fault for losing it and could only think of the boat ride after my jaguar hunt. I then went into an animated description of how my shotgun slipped off the small boat into the Laguna de Sontecomapan, and even added the word "ploop" to emphasize my vivid word picture of the event.

He was not amused at my description and would not relent.

"*No escopota,* no duty, no leave. I'm sorry, *señor.*"

"Who do I have to see to get permission?" I demanded.

"Only the Minister of the Interior can permit you to leave," he announced grandly.

Exasperated I said, "Where can I find him?"

"*En Distrito Federal,*" he reverted to Spanish.

I knew he referred to Mexico City and looked at my watch. It was only a few miles from the airport. I had less than an hour remaining before my plane took off. I told him I would be back. To my surprise, he said he would hold my bags until the flight left. He also told me the address and gave me an official form the Minister would have to sign for approval. I grabbed it and ran out of the terminal to a nearby waiting taxi. I had less than a hundred pesos remaining and found out from the driver that the ride would cost about twenty-five to thirty pesos. I told him to speed it up.

He pulled up in front of an official government building, and I dashed to the information desk in the lobby. I hurriedly asked where I could find the Minister of the Interior and was directed to a particular office on one of the upper floors. I located the room number and entered. A secretary greeted me in the spacious room and asked my business.

Half out of breath from running, I told her that I was a *"norteamericano"* and that it was *"muy importante"* that I see the Minister *"pronto."* My rapid description of my problem must have caught her by surprise because her reaction was immediate. She unhesitatingly pointed to a closed door. I understood her to say that he was "in-conference." I glanced at my watch and saw that the time was fleeting. As I stood in front of the huge closed doors, I heard muffled voices within. I rapped softly at first and waited briefly. Nobody came and no one called out from within. I looked at my watch again and saw that a few more minutes had passed. Impatiently, I opened the door quietly and quickly scanned the room and the "conference-in-session." There appeared to be about twenty people all standing around and having animated discussions within small groups. I tapped a nearby official on the shoulder and asked where I could find the Minister of the Interior. Without even a questioning glance he pointed out a large swarthy man in an almost white suit speaking to two other officials. Without hesitation, I approached him and breathlessly announced again, that I was a *"norteamericano"* anxious to return home and was stymied by customs because I had lost my *"escopeta"* in the Laguna de Sontecomapan and was forced to pay a duty. I explained that it was not my fault that the shotgun fell in the lagoon. Also, I mentioned that I had spent all my remaining pesos before I went to the ticket counter, not realizing that I was required to pay duty. In my hand, I held the official form the customs official had given me.

He looked at me inquisitively for a minute and then at the paper in my outstretched hand. Either my harried expression or the importance of his discussion with the two officials prompted his immediate reaction.

He extracted a pen from his jacket pocket and asked me where he had to sign. I pointed out the block, and he signed it with a flourish.

I glanced down at it quickly to assure myself that it was done, and then thanked him profusely.

"*Gracias, muchas gracias,*" I said with sincerity, as I turned to leave.

He waved me out and continued his discussion.

Once outside the building, I found a nearby taxi. I couldn't think of the word "fast," but remembered "*rapidamente*" as I waved pesos at the driver and shouted for him to take me to the "*aeropuerto.*"

"*Si señor, pronto,*" he acknowledged, and took off like he had been on a launching pad.

I nervously glanced at my watch again and saw that I had about 20 minutes remaining to board the aircraft.

At the airport, I almost threw the extra pesos at the driver, jumped out of the taxi and raced to Customs waving the official form in my hand. The same official was on duty and motioned me forward to the head of the short line. He looked at the signature in the space provided and nodded his head.

"*Muy rapido, señor,*" he yelled to me as he removed my bags from beneath his stand and personally escorted me to the passengers boarding the flight.

I looked down at my watch for the last time. I had made the flight with ten minutes to spare.

# 28

As the plane circled Miami International Airport, I wasn't sure who would meet the flight. I had telegramed my family and new girlfriend of my arrival plans. It was the latter who greeted me when I stepped off the plane. Both she and my family were worried about my frostbitten toes, having first learned of the condition of my feet through the newspapers.

The first article shown to me when I arrived home was one that appeared in the *Miami Herald* on Friday, August 30, 1957. It was Associated Press coverage from Mexico City, apparently written the day before. The same serious, unsmiling photo taken of me when I disembarked from the British Guiana flight two years earlier was at the top of the short article. Below the picture were the words:

## "MARTY ROLAND
## ... THE TOUGHEST THING"

Beneath the somber picture was a short piece:

### "LOFTY PEAK IS SCALED BY WRITER

MEXICO CITY — (AP) — Marty Roland of Fort Lauderdale, said Thursday he and a guide scaled Mexico's highest peak early this week and "it was the toughest thing I ever did."

It was the first mountain climb for Roland, a free lance writer.

The peak was 18,700-foot Citaltepl, or Orizaba, third highest in North America. The extinct volcano is near the town of Orizaba in the state of Vera Cruz.

Roland said he suffered some mountain sickness, dizziness from lack of oxygen; and that the toes of both feet are still slightly numb from frostbite. His nose, which stuck out of a mask, is badly sunburned. He returned to Mexico City from Orizaba today."

"Why didn't you tell us?" they all wanted to know, "especially about your feet."

"I'll be fine," I tried to reassure them, although I didn't really know at that stage. "I'll see the doctor first thing Monday morning, OK?" I hoped that would satisfy everyone.

"What about your nose?" my concerned mother wanted to know.

"Oh, it got a little sunburned," I joked as I gingerly touched the scab that had formed after the climb four days earlier.

"How can you get a sunburn at the top of a mountain that's almost four miles high?" my younger sister persisted.

The questions kept coming and the concern about how I fared continued.

"The reporters wanted to know all about you while you were gone," my mother said. "This story just came out this morning."

She handed me a long article that appeared in the *Fort Lauderdale Daily News*. It also was dated Friday, August 30, 1957.

The *Daily News* staff reporter Ann Fries did a very comprehensive piece that expanded on the original Associated Press coverage in Mexico.

## "POSTAL CLERK TELLS OF CLIMBING PEAK AND TIGER SHOOT

Marty Roland, a 28-year-old Ft. Lauderdale postal clerk will fly into Miami tonight with a tiger skin from a Mexican jungle hunt and the reputation of having scaled Mexico's highest mountain, the third largest in North America.

His mother Mrs. Irma Roland, 916 SW Eighth Ave., said her son has always been adventurous, and she hoped his recent expedition has cured him.

After making the 18,700-foot climb up Mount Orizaba, this week, Roland was reported as saying, "it was the toughest thing I ever did."

He said he suffered some mountain sickness, dizziness from insufficient oxygen, and that his toes were frostbitten.

Three days before the climb, the dark-haired adventurer wrote his mother that, 'I am now trying to get a guide who will take me all the way up to the top of Orizaba. Think anybody envies me? Just happens to be 18,000 feet.'

"Very few people have made the top and there is one good reason why I will not only try, but I will do it. How's that for positive thinking?"

The excitement-loving man also told his mother he was bringing her back a tiger skin from a hunt he was on earlier that week.

"It was a rough hunt," he wrote. "Hunting at night with a headlamp strapped to my head in not only a jungle, but a mountainous jungle."

"My guide and I sat on the jungle floor with lights off, acting as decoys while two other Mexicans arched around to draw the tigers."

"So what happens? We do the tough part, and they see the tiger first and kill it."

## SKEETERS ARE BUSY

He said the worse thing that happened to him was deep scratches from the bushes and being "eaten raw by the mosquitoes."

On one expedition Roland said he and his guide contacted two Mexicans who had never seen an American before. Later, he said, they were stranded and were forced to sleep in a shack "with chickens on one side of a room, three cats, a pig and six people."

On the night before the climb Roland wrote that he and his guide planned to attack the mountain early in the morning.

"By Sunday night [August 25] we'll be at 10,000 feet or better and will be sleeping in sleeping bags on the ground. We'll begin our final assault at 2 or 3 a.m. Monday and by noon we'll have reached the peak, over 18,000 feet."

He added that he would be glad when it was all over and that it would be a pleasure to get home.

Mrs. Roland said her son has been on other adventure trips, but she never worried like she did this time. In 1955 he went diamond mining in British Guiana.

She said Roland originally went to Mexico to finish an adventure novel he is writing, but somehow got sidetracked on the tiger hunt and mountain climbing expedition.

"He wants to be a writer," she said. "He thinks he has to experience things before he writes about them. I just wish he would lose his wanderlust and settle down and write."

When I finished reading the extensive article, I looked up at the group surrounding me.

"She's covered everything," I said in admiration.

"That's not all," my mother continued, "a photographer wants to come out tomorrow to take a picture of your tiger skin."

The next morning, the photographer called and was soon there, snapping away.

A short photo piece appeared in the *Fort Lauderdale Sunday News* on Sunday, September 1, 1957.

It showed a smiling photo of me handing over an outstretched pelt of the jaguar to my mother, who was equally pleased.

The abbreviated wording noted:

"ADVENTURER — Marty Roland who scaled the 18,700-foot Mount Orizaba in Mexico this week, brings his mother a leopard skin from his expedition —"

I was grateful for the additional publicity, but I'm sure there were knowledgeable readers who questioned the use of the term "leopard," since there were no leopards in Mexico. They are only found in Africa. However, in defense of the description of the spotted hide, it did resemble a leopard.

I was able to get a doctor's appointment on short notice when I called his office Monday morning.

"Let's have a look at those feet," the doctor said when I told him of the climb and described their present condition.

His touch was gentle as he probed the entire foot first and then the toes.

"Do you feel this?" he queried. "Do you feel that?" he continued.

To my negative responses, he lightly massaged the base of the toes on both feet.

"How about that?" he finally asked.

"Somewhat," I replied.

"OK. You can put your socks and shoes back on."

He looked serious as he started scribbling on a prescription pad.

"You definitely did freeze your toes," he said.

"I know."

"What you don't know, however, is that they could have turned black on you on the mountain, and dropped off."

I looked at him for a moment, not expecting that kind of response.

"Even now," he continued, "there's still danger of gangrene setting in."

I was stunned by what he said.

"What's the prognosis?" I asked him slowly.

"Well, first of all, if you smoke, I'd stop immediately."

By the manner in which he said it, I didn't even question the reason why. Apparently he also sensed I was a smoker, as were most people in that era.

"The nicotine in cigarettes constricts the capillaries in your extremities," he added, "especially in your toes."

He handed me a prescription for pills. "The dosage is on the bottle," he said. "I want you to continue taking these until you see definite improvement."

I nodded in agreement. "What do they do?" I wanted to know.

"They'll increase your circulation," he noted.

"Is that it?" I queried him. "How does it look doc?" I had to know the answer.

"Well," he responded, "you're young and healthy, and if you do what I said, you should be OK."

"Great!"

"There's no guarantee, son," he said, observing my reaction. "You did a lot of damage to your toes."

I nodded again knowingly.

"There's no reason to see me again unless there's a downward trend in your condition."

He wished me luck and left.

I threw away my partially opened pack of Luckies, and didn't even think about lighting up again for the next two to three months.


Interest in my latest adventure ran high in Fort Lauderdale, and I began to think about ways to capitalize on what I had done. I had quit my job at the Post Office and had no desire to return. I began to think more and more of going to New York to "make my fortune in the big city," as they used to say. Out of the blue, I received a query from the *Miami Herald*. Would I like to write a feature story of my climb for their Sunday edition. I jumped at the opportunity. How long, I wanted to know? About 1,000 words, they responded. No problem, I answered.


On Sunday, September 15, 1957, the very long article appeared. Across the top of the page in bold print was the heading:


## "HE SCALED THE HIGHEST MOUNTAIN IN MEXICO"

Above the caption in smaller heavy wording:

# "GLAMOROUS?  NO, IT WAS JUST HARD WORK"

On the far right hand side of the story was a photo of me. Below it was the caption:

**"Mountain-Climber Marty Roland . . .be glad you only read about it."**

The editorial note at the top of my article noted:

"Marty Roland, 916 SW Eighth Ave., Fort Lauderdale, back from scaling Mexico's highest mountain, says he wouldn't do it again. This is his story."

Below my byline was the opening lead:

"On Aug. 26, 1957, a bearded American, his face covered with a mask to protect it against the elements, stood swaying on the snow-capped summit of the highest mountain in Mexico.

From his knapsack, he pulled out a green and white banner, and as it fluttered in the high wind, he tied it triumphantly to a metal rack that perched over the yawning crevice of the huge crater.

Sounds exciting, doesn't it?  Like something many of you wish you could do. Be glad that you only read about it.

There is nothing exciting or glamorous about doing something tough. It is only a self-imposed assignment that is grueling, monotonous and dangerous.

I know what I'm saying. I was the bearded American."

The balance of the episode was the highlights of the climb with the details I saw and rigors I endured. It was still very fresh in my mind, having made the climb just two weeks earlier. Writing about it and then reading it was more like a vivid dream come to life.

Because the theme of the piece was downplaying the glamour of the experience, I closed it out with:

"Today my toes are still numb and doctors tell me there's a chance that gangrene will set in.

Being an adventurer isn't what it's cracked up to be. I've been hailed as a celebrity and patted on the back. Some people say I've made a 'name' for myself.

But when I walk in a restaurant and order a cup of coffee the 'name' doesn't cut any ice with the waiter.

Coffee, they tell me, is the same price to all customers — even mountain climbers."

It was the last newspaper coverage I would receive from the *Miami Herald* or from the *Fort Lauderdale Daily News* of my foreign exploits.

My Mexican trip was also my final attempt at foreign adventure.

Two weeks later, I impulsively married in Fort Lauderdale, and was en route to New York City on the following day to pursue a "name" that I believe I had worked hard to attain — and had not achieved.

The future, however, had other adventures in store for me that would prove to be just as threatening as those I experienced on foreign soils.

# Epilogue

For all that I had done — and tried to do — in my brief but intense pursuit as an adventurer, I did not stir up any waves in New York. For that matter, I didn't even create any minor ripples. It's not as though I didn't try.

In October or November 1957, I was picked to be a contestant on three separate music quiz shows. My selection was not only a result of my fortunate in-depth knowledge of song lyrics and melodies, but because I deliberately entered "Free-Lance Writer-Adventurer-Explorer" as my occupation on their background cards. They were, I believe: "Tic Tac Dough," "Do Re Me," and "Stop the Music."

However, the week before my scheduled appearances on all three shows, the big scandal of rigged answers on the popular "$64,000 Question" show hit the media. All quiz shows were immediately canceled — mine included.

It was to be my "big break," I thought. Not only was I confident in winning the money involved in each of the shows, but I was sure the publicity would be unlimited. It never happened. Neither did my attempt to appear as an unusual guest on Jack Paar's "Tonight Show."

The responsibilities of married life and raising a family then became paramount. I concentrated on the more stable aspects of normal life and put my aspirations on a back burner. I did not, however, forget or abandon them.

In early 1963, while living in Central California, I renewed my attempt for recognition of my past endeavors. Groucho Marx was the host of another quiz show broadcasting from Hollywood — "You Bet Your Life."

I composed what I considered an offbeat and intriguing letter that might garner me a spot on his show.

On February 20, 1963, I sent him the following letter.

"Dear Groucho,

I am a Federal employee by necessity, a freelance writer by profession and an adventurer-explorer by nature.

However, six years ago, at the ripe old age of 28, I retired from my foreign roaming and curbed my wild brainstorms. Reason: it is not practical to drag a wife and children into the jungle or to the top of a mountain. The extent of my travels since then has been from state to state in various job capacities. The latest of which is in the Management Field with the Air Force at Vandenberg Air Force Base. The extent of my "wild" ideas has been the power of positive thinking; the study, in an amateurish way, of the mind over matter, which for a short while included self-hypnosis and for the past year or two have become a "health faddist." To myself, these ideas and actions are normal but to others they've considered them and me a "little" unusual.

However, the people I know now did not know me six years ago and if they consider me slightly unusual now they would have had me committed then. In that period of my background, which also lasted for about six years, I considered myself a composite of Hemingway and Jack London with a smattering of Tarzan and a good-sized chunk of "Jungle Jim" thrown in. I traveled the Islands of the Caribbean and penetrated the Interiors of the countries of Central and South America. I lived among native and Indian tribes, diamond prospected in steaming jungles, killed everything from boa-constrictors to jaguars, discovered a huge waterfall (three times the height of Niagara Falls) and climbed a 4-mile-high frozen mountain.

I've taken guns into Latin American countries that were in the throes of conflict, been detained in some and booted out of others. I've offered my services to everybody from Generalissimo Chiang Kai-shek to President Ngo-Dinh-Diem (Vietnam) to Mahendra Bir Bikram of Nepal. I've even offered to kill a lion with a spear with the Masai natives in Kenya, cross the Sahara by camel, climb Mt. Kilimanjaro just because I liked its name, and countless other things that I can't even recall now. All for publicity — a "name" and the all-important $$ bill.

The result other than a few published pieces — I'm in hock and have been ever since my self-imposed exiles or attempts at same. I have had malaria, dysentery and parasites in my intestines and almost lost my frozen toes through gangrene. All of which, I'm not kicking about and would gladly do the same again. The only gripe is the "name" which constantly eluded me and which I felt I rightly should have attained. If you or your sponsors see fit to include me on your program as one of your contestants I am sure that you and your viewers will not be disappointed, and I might be one step closer to my goal — not to mention the "dough" involved on the show itself.

Yours truly,
Marty Roland"

It didn't work. There was no interest or response from the program.

I gave up my illusions of discovery and focused on family life, working and pursuing an education.

In 1968, while living in Northern California, I had my name legally changed from "Martin Roland" back to my birth name, "Nicholas John Mangieri," a name that had been changed to "Martin Roland" (Martin being my confirmation name) when my mother remarried.

By 1970, I had attained a certain modicum of success. I was a mid-level civil servant with a growing family, had obtained my bachelor's degree, had attended graduate school and was pursuing a law degree. In spite of those mundane accomplishments, I yearned for more adventuresome fulfillment.

I became a deputy sheriff in California, and then eventually relocated to Alaska to become a police chief in a small town. The move, while personally rewarding, was fraught with danger because of municipal corruption. That experience prompted a nonfiction exposé book, *"Frozen Shield: Alaska Cover-up."*

Disillusioned and frustrated with local politics, I relocated to Washington, D.C., in the late seventies and became a federal agent. That four-year stint, delving into fraudulent activities in our nation's capital, proved worse than my Alaskan exposure. The corruption I viewed first-hand, and the cover-ups I experienced during my investigations, prompted still another nonfiction exposé book, *"Broken Badge: The Silencing of a Federal Agent."*

After my federal retirement, writing and publishing became my new avocation, a calling I could control.

Looking back on this present book, which was a prequel to the first two books, I realized it was the most gratifying experience I have ever had. The exceptional perils of a jungle or of a frozen mountain presented far less danger than the unanticipated ramifications of doing one's job investigating dirty politicians.

*Nick Mangieri*

# About the Author

Nick Mangieri, a native-born New Yorker and Navy veteran, has served as Chief of Police in Alaska, Deputy Sheriff in California and Private Detective in New York. He was a Federal Agent with the Department of Labor attached to the Inspector General's Fraud Division, assigned to South Florida and Washington, D.C. His background and interests are wide and varied and include work as an analyst for federal and state governments and as a free lance writer for men's adventure magazines. As such, his self-imposed junkets took him into the interiors of Central and South America, where he diamond prospected in the jungles, hunted jaguar and mountain climbed. He graduated from the University of the Pacific and obtained his graduate degree from Virginia Commonwealth University. He's also attended law school and done post graduate work, including  doctoral studies. He's an avid outdoorsman, jogs regularly, works out at a gym daily and has even been a rodeo rider. Married and the father of four, he is a licensed Private Investigator.

## To Order:

### Postal Orders:

### Valor Press Ltd.
Nick Mangieri
P.O. Box 369, Lightfoot, VA 23090

### Fax Orders:
(757) 565-0827

### Payment:
by check or money order

**Amount:**
Passport to Danger............................$17.95
Frozen Shield....................................$19.50
Broken Badge ...................................$19.50

**Shipping:**
$3.95 for the first book ..................... _____
$1.84 for each additional book......... _____
Priority Mail:$4.50 per book ............. _____

**Sales Tax:**
Add 4.5% for books
shipped to Virginia addresses .......... _____


**TOTAL:**.............................................. _____

# Addendum 1
# Photos

**Right:** This shot of me was taken near a mountainous jungle river in Cartagos, Costa Rica, in 1954, shortly before my encounter with the boa constrictor.
**Below:** The table-like plateau of Watabaru Mountain, 200 miles from nowhere, keeps a silent watch over the diamonds.

**Left:** An artists depiction of an incident in 1955 during my night jaguar hunt in the British Guiana jungle.

**Above:** Our only connection to the outside world and civilization was a river boat that came up the Kurupung River with supples and mail twice a month.
**Left:** An Akawaio Indian boy I met during my jungle treks. He didn❑t trust me enough to come down from his perch.

**Right:** Ready to board a previously chartered Grumman Amphib to fly me back to civilization after a monthlong solo diamond prospecting expedition.

My guide, Shanks cools off with his son, Dudley, in the sluggish Tacouba Creek, which would rise six to eight feet during the rainy season.

**Above:** Two *pork-knockers* on a crew of six work a large pit near a shallow creek.
**Right:** A typical native prospector □ *pork-knocker* — dressed in tattered clothes, stands by his pit.

**Left:** My 70-year-old Indian guide, Shanks and his 10-year-old son, Dudley, carry our mining implements as we walk to our pit. a sieve is draped over Dudley□s head.

**Left:** A *pork-knocker* stands in knee deep water in my my pit and works the seive. He s just dumped gravel from the box on his left into it for sifting.

**Right:** My first pit, which took five days to dig. In the center is a lode  gravel that s pushed  up from beneath the jungle floor. In it we found  indi-cations, black carbon compositions that are forerunners of dia-monds.

**Left:** My *pork-knocker* helper pulls gravel with a hoe down across the *tom box* and through the *tom iron*.

**Above:** Somewhere near the top of the 18,700-foot Pico de Orizaba in Mexico, that country's highest mountain.

**Right:** Me as I looked when I began my adventurous expeditions in South America, Central America and Mexico.

# Addendum 2
# Maps

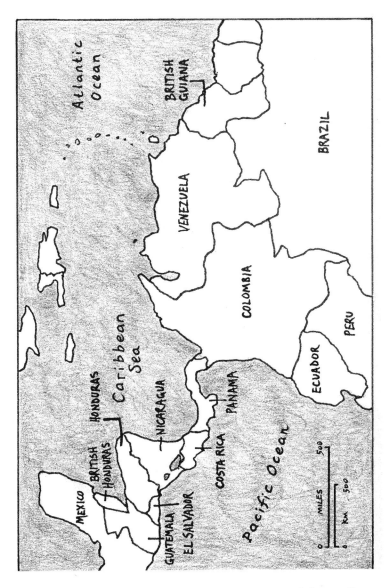

Map showing part of Mexico, Central America and the northern part of South America, the region where my adventures took place.

Map of British Guiana as it looked when I went there in 1955 to prospect for diamonds.

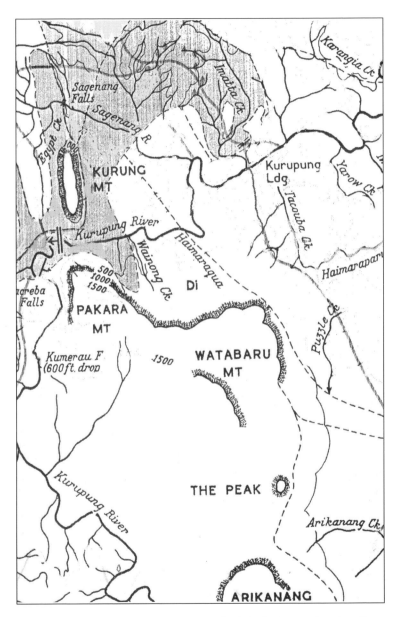

1955 map of the Mazaruni District, British Guiana, showing the area explored, hunted and prospected.

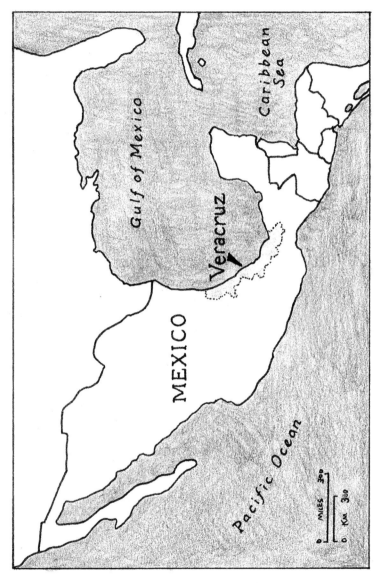

Veracruz is located on the eastern shore of Mexico along the Gulf of Mexico.

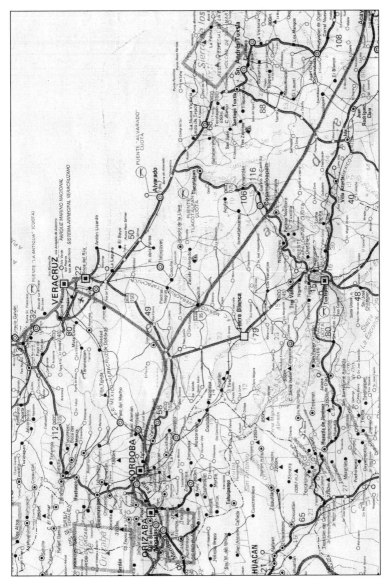

A detail of the state of Veracruz showing the 18,000-foot mountain, Pico de Orizaba (rectangle on left) and San. Andres Tuxtla (rectangle on right). In between are Veracruz and Cordoba.